For Whom the Bell Tolls

JONATHAN MANTLE

For Whom the Bell Tolls

The Lesson of Lloyd's of London

SINCLAIR-STEVENSON

First published in Great Britain
by Sinclair-Stevenson
7/8 Kendrick Mews
London sw7 3hg England

Copyright © 1992 by Jonathan Mantle

British Library Cataloguing in Publication Data
A CIP catalogue record for this book
is available from the British Library.

isbn 1 85619 152 4

Typeset by Falcon Graphic Art Ltd.
Printed and bound in Great Britain
by Clays Ltd, St Ives plc

To Olivia

CONTENTS

ACKNOWLEDGEMENTS

The author is grateful to the following for their help in his researches for this book. Some of the names have been changed at the request of those concerned to protect themselves and their families:

IN AMERICA: John Badham; Zoe Bennett; Dr Geoffrey Francis; Dale Jenkins; Dr John Mathias; George Meller; George Nordhaus; Proskauer Rose Goetz and Mendelsohn; Richard Rosenblatt; The Securities and Exchange Commission; The Senate Permanent Subcommittee on Investigations.
IN AUSTRALIA: Dr Gavan Griffith.
IN THE BAHAMAS: Michael and Maire Oakes; Edward St George.
IN BERMUDA: Robert Zildjian.
IN CANADA: Ken Lavery; Alan Lenczner; Jacki Levin; Dr George Pakozdi; Glenn Smith.
IN GREAT BRITAIN: Earl Alexander of Tunis; Betty Atkins; Enid Bemrose; Tom Benyon; Roger Bradley; Hugh Bourn; Oliver Carruthers and the *Digest of Lloyd's News*; John Clementson; David Coleridge; Michael Colvin MP; Ed Cowen; Giles Curtis; David D'Ambrumenil; Damon de Laszlo; Martin de Laszlo; Lady Delves Broughton; Paul Dixey; Nick Doak; Alfred Doll-Steinberg; Paul Finan; Clive Francis; Xenia Francklin; Jennifer Grossman; Rupert Hambro; James Hanning; Sylvia Hatton; John Hinchliffe; Christopher Hitchings; Cassandra Jardine; Lord Kimball; Robin Kingsley; Denise Knights; Eddie Kulukundis; Sir John Langford-Holt; Sean McGee; Paul Marland MP;

Richard Micklethwait; Lady Middleton; Edward
Molesworth; Christopher Moran; Janis Nash; Peter
Nutting; Dominique Osborne; Ian Posgate; John Redwood
MP; Geoffrey Rickman; Angus Runciman; Charles St
George; Nicky Samengo-Turner; Lord Savile; Christopher
Sinclair-Stevenson; Tony South; Charles Sturge; Edda
Tasiemka; Christopher Thomas-Everard; B.A. Timbs;
Marjorie Walsh; Robin Warrender.
IN IRELAND: Desmond O'Neill.
IN ITALY: Stephen Garland.
IN MALTA: John Pearson.
IN NEW ZEALAND: Elizabeth Harker.
IN SPAIN: Wilfred Sherman.
IN SWITZERLAND: Ricardo Cerdan; Andrew Grossman.

The author also wishes to acknowledge the following
publications:
Ian Hay Davison: *A View of the Room* (Weidenfeld 1987)
Godfrey Hodgson: *Lloyd's of London* (Allen Lane 1984)
Ed Punchard: *Piper Alpha: A Survivor's Story* (Star 1989)
– and acknowledges the help and advice of the many
working and external members of Lloyd's who wish to
remain anonymous until sunshine drives away the mist.

The author also acknowledges the following for
permission to reproduce photographs:
Times Newspapers Ltd: 1, 3, 7, 14, 15; Richard Watt: 2;
Nassau *Tribune*: 4; *Daily Mail*: 5, 6; *Guardian*: 8, 10;
Financial Times: 9, 13; Rex Features: 11, 16; Press
Association: 12.

PROLOGUE

On the one hand, Lloyd's of London is an insurance institution.

A client in search of insurance cover goes to a broker. The broker takes the risk onto the floor of 'The Room' at Lloyd's. The broker goes round The Room with a form called 'a slip' until he has found enough 'active underwriters' to underwrite the policy.

If it is a small policy he might only need one active underwriter to supply the cover. If it is a large risk he might need fifty or more. But the procedure is the same in both cases. The broker collects enough underwriters to supply 100% of the insurance cover and then goes back to his client. The broker takes his commission. The client is insured at Lloyd's.

If the client claims on the policy the active underwriters have to pay their agreed percentage of the loss. If the client does not claim on the policy the active underwriters have made a profit. The active underwriters have to calculate their risk exposure and hope to be in profit at the end of a year; but they will not know for sure until three years have passed. This is how long it takes at Lloyd's to close an underwriting year's accounts.

On the other hand, Lloyd's of London is an insurance institution unlike any other.

The active underwriters do not accept risks from the brokers on the basis of assets from their shareholders, as they would in a normal insurance company. They do so as the front men and women for syndicates of members who generally have little or nothing to do with the insurance business. These external members supply most of the market's operating capital. In return they expect – and in the past have received – handsome profits which the taxman has treated leniently in recognition of Lloyd's contribution to Britain's invisible earnings.

The members or 'Names' at Lloyd's commit themselves to underwriting a certain sum of business each year: say £500,000. This £500,000 is divided into smaller sums or 'lines' of £10,000 or £20,000 on a spread of thirty or forty syndicates. Members have to deposit one-third of that £500,000 with Lloyd's but, although they must also show minimum assets of £250,000, they do not have to put up all of the cash and may meet these requirements in a number of ways including bank guarantees on their property.

The more members there are on a syndicate, the bigger that syndicate's 'capacity' or underwriting power. There are syndicates with thousands of members and capacities of hundreds of millions of pounds and syndicates with less than a hundred members. The active underwriters of the biggest syndicates are rich and powerful figures whose syndicates often 'lead' or take the first chunk of big and profitable risks broked on the floor of The Room. But a smaller specialist syndicate may in relative terms be just as profitable.

The members share syndicates' profits according to the size of their 'lines' and the success of the active underwriters. Members cannot place themselves on syndicates but rely on their members agents to do this for them in the hope that their members agents know what they are doing. A good members agent hears and interprets the gossip of the market. A bad members agent may not. The difference between a good and bad members agent is as crucial to members as the ability of the active underwriter is.

A further factor unique to Lloyd's is that if the claims flood in and a syndicate makes an overall loss on a year, there is no limit to the liability of that syndicate's members to meet those losses. Traditionally big losses at Lloyd's have been few and far between. Why else would members have clamoured to join?

By the early 1990s, members were beginning to ask themselves this very question.

THE CONVERSATION

'There's something I want to talk to you about.
It's only a possibility, you understand.
But it might just be the answer to your problems.
It's strictly between ourselves, of course.
Are you interested?'

ONE

AN EMPIRE
WITHIN ITSELF

This is the story of how a world-famous financial institution tried to maintain a semblance of dignity while its morals, some said, descended to below those of a Lebanese casino. It is the story of how an exclusive club threw open its doors to new members for whom greed and gullibility were the sole entry qualifications. Above all, it is the story of a man-made disaster that need never have happened; for, once upon a time, Lloyd's of London was not only a Great British institution, but a uniquely easy way to make money. Only when it became too easy for a small number of people to make it in very large amounts, did a large number of people start having to lose.

By the summer of 1992 Lloyd's was in crisis. Losses and calls for cash for the most recent completed underwriting year, 1989, were heading towards £2 billion, the worst in its 300-year history. Thousands of members around the world were resigning or trying to resign, unable to meet solvency requirements and yet trapped in an accounting system from which even death was no escape. There were suicides and breakdowns and divorces and a blizzard of lawsuits. In New York a group of members were attempting to bring a suit against Lloyd's under the RICO Act ('Racketeer Influenced Corrupt Organisation'), normally reserved for money launderers and cocaine traffickers. The Rowland Task Force Report, commissioned by Lloyd's to find a route forward into the competitive 1990s, had for all its sagacity been overshadowed by inquiries into allegations of negligence and insider dealing. There were questions in Parliament. The Prime Minister was worried. The Queen was concerned. There were rumours of a Government bale-out. The solvency – and future – of Lloyd's itself was in doubt.

Yet until recently what was known about Lloyd's outside 1, Lime Street was a PR man's dream. Lloyd's was a blue-chip institution whose new buildings were opened by the Queen and whose chairmen were frequently knighted. Lloyd's was an exclusive club – at its height it had only around 34,000 members – yet the assets of those members enabled it to be a player in the international insurance markets. Lloyd's did over half its business overseas and was a major contributor to Britain's invisible earnings. Because of this Lloyd's wrote its own rules and in 1982 effectively passed its own Act of Parliament. Lloyd's lived a charmed life – and planned to go on living that way.

But now the good years were over for Lloyd's and their like would not come this way again. Massive losses caused by a series of natural catastrophes compounded by lack of regulation and doubtful market practices had brought Lloyd's to its knees; and revealed a house of cards that for some years had been dangerously close to collapsing. But what was Lloyd's? What did it *think* it was? What did its members think it was? In the many misconceptions on the part of the latter lay the answers to the first questions.

Lloyd's was an insurance institution. But it was not like any other insurance institution. It did not have shareholders or a board or a managing director. You could not buy or sell shares in Lloyd's. Lloyd's had a chairman, but not in the conventional sense. He was not one of the great and the good brought in to keep an eye on things in the twilight of his career, but often a major player in the market. But then Lloyd's always said it was a market and not a business.

Instead of shareholders, Lloyd's had members. Once upon a time, until the 1960s, these members came from the wealthiest levels of British society. But by the mid-1960s there were not enough of these members left who were willing or able to underwrite international insurance business. First foreigners were allowed in, then women (the order of events was no accident).

But although the new members of Lloyd's were not all Viscounts or Earls with stately homes and vast acreages of grouse moor they were still told that Lloyd's was an exclusive club to which they were privileged to belong. No matter that they were the capital providers without whom Lloyd's could not have remained in business – membership of Lloyd's was promoted as membership of a unique and powerful club and the British liked to feel they belonged. Membership of Lloyd's appealed to the snobbery of the emergent British professional classes who aspired to the old values or simply suffered from the uniquely British hang-up about money; if you were *nouveau riche* you wanted to disguise it.

And being a member of Lloyd's was such a good way to make money, more money than you could have made anywhere else in the same way. In fact, there was nowhere else you could make so much money in the same way. For a start you could leave your money where it was already and earn a return twice, three times over in a good year. As long as you pledged your assets to Lloyd's in case there was a loss, you only needed to cover your deposit (a bank guarantee did this nicely – the bank made a charge and Lloyd's did not want or need to know the nature of the security) and to pay the salary of your members agent.

There were good years and bad years, but there were more good than bad, and after a while you felt it was a bad year if you made not a loss but a smaller profit. The active underwriters of your syndicates underwrote the risks, and when they did not turn into claims, you received a share of the profits. If the risk turned into a claim, you paid a share of the loss. It was as simple as that.

There were handsome tax breaks for offsetting losses against regular income. Of course you were reminded before you were elected that you had 'unlimited liability' down to your last set of cufflinks; but no one, particularly your members agent who looked after your interests, ever seemed to know anyone who had been forced to hand over the cufflinks in question.

But slowly, imperceptibly, and fatally, the profits became smaller and so did the tax breaks and the criteria and composition changed of Lloyd's membership. In 1960 membership was mainly the preserve of a few thousand rich people who could show minimum assets of £75,000 in liquid or near-liquid form – that was £¾ million in 1992. By the 1980s however there were 30,000 members and the minimum assets were only £250,000. One member was elected on the strength of a bank guarantee obtained on a Ferrari. The double horror of Lloyd's in 1992 was that an unprecedented influx of relatively recent members were faced with a series of natural catastrophes magnified by market practices for which they were financially ill-equipped to pay.

This is the story of an English gentlemen's club which won the right to be accepted as a modern international financial institution and in the process of doing so lost its way. It asks the question, could Lloyd's of London, once synonymous with 300 years of utmost good faith and honourable dealing, change fast enough to avoid the one catastrophe against which it had failed to insure – its own self-destruction?

As the pressure mounted on all parties the traditional barriers of secrecy began to break down – a book such as this would have been unthinkable even five years ago. Yet the men and women who ran Lloyd's still seemed unable to let go the glorious past and grasp the problems of the present, let alone the future. In Lloyd's year of reckoning, that glorious past still beckoned ever more seductively.

It is tempting to see the rise and fall of Lloyd's in parallel with that of Britain as a world maritime power. Whether or not marine insurance took place when Edward Lloyd, formerly a journeyman framework stocking knitter, established his Tower Street coffee house in 1688, which became the meeting place of the forerunners of underwriters and brokers, has never been established. Early examples of insurance known to have been offered there are 'Assurance from Lying', 'Rum Assurance' and 'Assurance of Female Chastity.' This was six years before the foundation of the Bank of England in 1694. In later years Lloyd's liked to describe itself as 'older than the Bank of England.'

The marine business that did eventually take place at Lloyd's coffee house, if not in 1688, then shortly afterwards, was both a world apart and frighteningly similar to the business done 300 years later. Gossip was the name of the game and inside information was the hardest currency. The Captain's Room at Lloyd's was a centre for marine intelligence extracted over coffee from returning seafarers. Who had been sighted, who had docked safely and who was overdue? Before and during a voyage insurance cover may not have been taken out at all. The key thing for a merchant with a stake in an overdue ship was to find someone to insure it who did not know it was overdue.

300 years later, Lloyd's brokers would still arrange to reinsure overdue ships and their non-maritime equivalents. The difference was that both insurer and reinsurer knew (or thought they knew) the latest gossip (or 'intelligence' as it was now known).

By the 1720s Lloyd's had a newspaper (*Lloyd's News*, subsequently *Lloyd's List*), a Committee, premises in the Royal Exchange opposite the Bank of England and a Chairman, John Julius Angerstein.

Angerstein was an epic figure. He could single-handedly persuade the Prime Minister to issue a government loan, boast that he did not even know the names of 80% of his underwriters and left a collection of paintings important enough to form the foundation of the National Gallery. Under Angerstein's implacably haughty chairmanship Lloyd's established the Patriotic Fund during the Napoleonic Wars for brave naval officers, and prospered mightily as Britain became the world's greatest naval power.

The fire that destroyed the Royal Exchange in 1838 drove

Lloyd's back to the London Tavern and the Jerusalem coffee house nearby – but by 1844 it was back at the Royal Exchange. By 1857 it had also acquired the bell of the British frigate HMS *Lutine*, one of the worst Napoleonic War losses Lloyd's had suffered. The wreck was exposed by freak storms in 1857; the bell and various other items were transported to Lloyd's. There the bell would toll for many years, once to signify disaster and twice to signify safe arrival of a vessel. The tradition would cease, perhaps prematurely, in the 1980s.

The Angerstein era was succeeded by that of Cuthbert Eden Heath, an admiral's son who began in 1880 as a marine underwriter but developed the Lloyd's non-marine insurance market; his first policy covered jewellery for theft and other loss. Angerstein was the spirit of Lloyd's buccaneering ascent; Heath was the sober 'father of Lloyd's' in its modern form. He pushed through reforms as unglamorous and effective as his jewellery policies.

Heath was a man in marked contrast to the Secretary of Lloyd's at the turn of this century, Colonel Henry Hozier. Hozier was a man in the Angerstein mould and more – an explosive, imaginative autocrat and technocrat, he had studied medicine in Paris, served with the Royal Artillery in the China War, covered the Franco-Prussian War as a correspondent and accompanied Lord Napier's expedition to Abyssinia. After witnessing the Siege of Paris and serving in the Intelligence Department of the War Office he became Secretary of Lloyd's in 1874.

Hozier's great achievement was to predict the importance of merchant naval intelligence in the early 20th century and to set up a string of signal stations from the Lizard to the Suez Canal, all linked to Lloyd's in London. To this end he travelled the world, running up vast expenses, setting up his signal stations and a network of local Lloyd's agents. By 1906 he had seen his signal stations superseded by those of Marconi, challenged the British Postmaster-General to a duel and tried to obstruct the marriage of his daughter Clementine to the young

Winston Churchill. He was forced to resign and died in Panama, a disappointed man. But the network of Lloyd's agents would be an enduring and underestimated legacy.

Cuthbert Heath outlived Hozier by 30 years and saw the organisation of Lloyd's evolve as a corporation established by an 1871 Act of Parliament. He also pioneered the practice of gentlemanly self-regulation of the market in which he was a player.

In 1906, when the San Francisco earthquake struck and did $300 million of damage to cargo ($100 million at Lloyd's), Heath's was a leading syndicate involved. Other insurance companies collapsed or repudiated their obligations. But Heath cabled his San Francisco agent with the words that were to establish the reputation of Lloyd's in the United States of America: 'Pay all our policy-holders in full irrespective of the terms of their policies.'

The growing size of risks accepted had led by then to the creation of the syndicate system, whereby the working underwriter no longer wrote part or all of a risk by himself, but on behalf of a syndicate of 'Names' or members. In 1908, after an underwriter bankrupted several of his Names, Heath initiated the first underwriters' solvency test. In 1912 the spirit of Heath was again present when the Lutine bell rang once and Farrant, formerly a porter at Clapham Junction station and now Lloyd's 'Caller', climbed onto the rostrum. 'Gentlemen,' he intoned, 'the *Titanic* now lies at the bottom of the Atlantic.'

Two weeks later Lloyd's underwriters had paid off all claims (the hull alone was insured for £1 million) and still managed to make a profit on the year. Legend would even have it that the *Titanic* was reinsured on a handshake *after* the terrible news had come through.

The years between the First and Second World Wars saw Lloyd's grow and take on new areas of business. An early aviation 'slip' or underwriting policy document insured a pilot on a flight from Newfoundland 'to final destination in England' for £1,000 – 'two attempts allowed.' In 1928 Lloyd's occupied the first building of its own opened by King George V in Leadenhall Street.

Like the buildings which followed in 1958 and 1986, these were not the headquarters of an international insurance company. They were market places, owned and to a minimal degree managed, by the Committee and Corporation of Lloyd's (the powerful governing body and the permanent administrative staff), where individuals did international insurance business.

This uniquely British gentlemanly free-for-all meant that occasionally the morals of the market place had to be given as much attention as its manners. As the saying went: 'Individually we are underwriters; collectively we are Lloyd's.'

In 1923 'Harrison's folly' led to £200,000 being levied among underwriters, so that compensation might be made for the ineptness and corruption of one of their number. They were under no obligation to contribute and Chairman Arthur Lloyd Sturge was under no obligation to make them do so. He did say however that, if Harrison's liabilities were not mutualised in some way, then 'the name of Lloyd's will be seriously injured and will never recover in our lifetime.'

The biggest syndicate put up £10,000 and the smallest 8d, and the commitments were honoured to Harrison's policy holders. 'There was no pause, no hold-up,' one eye-witness recalled, 'even amongst those associated with the business. It was as if an officer in a regiment had fallen, and his place instantly been filled.'

In the medium and long term this was also a shrewd investment which secured goodwill and even more lucrative business – a lesson to be forgotten by those who embraced the principle but not the price of self-regulation in the 1980s.

They might have recalled the words of Cuthbert Heath in a 1931 issue of *Syren & Shipping*:

'. . . there is one thing which is still with us and shines as brightly as ever. It is the honourable feeling that, privileged as we are among traders in that our contracts are those of *'uberimae fidei'*, our good faith must also be the supreme law of our existence. I feel quite certain that underwriters generally are still as determined as ever to do what is fair rather than insist on legal rights.'

Even in its rare moments of publicity Lloyd's would not refer to events such as the Harrison affair, and it would be many years before anyone outside Leadenhall Street knew much about what went on there. Lloyd's was the archetypal example of the British theory of 'need to know' – but it knew enough about publicity to damp down public inquisitiveness with a few 'boy's own adventures' from time to time. 'For me . . . the old gateway to Lloyd's in the Royal Exchange building was the gateway to romance, travel and adventure . . .'

Thus wrote the Lloyd's marine broker R.W. Thompson in 1950; none of his recollections dealt with events more recent than the 1930s.

When the loss of the French passenger liner *L'Atlantique* in 1933 saw Lloyd's resist the claim on the grounds of arson, it caused an international sensation. The French government (having subsidised the building of the ship) cried *'Perfide Albion'* and the French courts eventually ruled in the policyholders' favour.

The whole business was hushed up and only deemed suitable for popular consumption over 30 years later; at a time when Lloyd's was again under scrutiny and sensitive enough about publicity to prove it could make some sort of disclosure about its affairs.

It is easy to examine those days under the artificial light of today's press, and to forget that Lloyd's was rarely under the light because in those days it had nothing much to hide. By the late 1930s Lloyd's had become the exclusive, secretive, dynastic club whose values would endure in some quarters to the bitter showdown of the 1990s.

Occasionally an outsider, informally vetted by friends who were members, made the opening moves in an assault.

'I have never been so baffled in my life,' wrote Charles Graves in *The Sphere* in the late 1930s. 'I drank cocktails at the Savoy bar with four members of Lloyd's, lunched with another and played squash racquets with a sixth. Each of them threw up a smoke cloud . . . Members of Lloyd's, I discovered, dislike and even resent any publicity about their financial affairs. It makes one suppose that they are doing better than it is desirable for the public to presume . . .'

Eventually he managed to cross the portals in Leadenhall Street. Here he encountered a potent blend of heritage, charm and apparently complex business practices. 'Our member is most anxious that we do not produce notebooks or shew any sign of intelligent layman interest in our surroundings. It is therefore not until we leave The Room that we are able to ask pertinent questions . . .'

Even then the interloper was left little the wiser. But in this case he was not to be deterred. 'Since writing the above,' he declared, 'I have spoken to yet another member of Lloyd's. He was much more helpful.'

Graves's friend told him that there were 349 syndicates and 1,700 'Names' or members underwriting predominantly marine and non-marine business, the latter reflecting the growing element of aviation insurance (including $280,000 for Adolf Hitler's personal Junkers aeroplane) and a smattering of insurance for motor vehicles. Accounts were left open for three years in order to assess the exact claims; but thereafter they were always closed:

'The biggest underwriters are Messrs. Drysdale and
Heath, followed by Messrs. Poland, Aubrey, Glenvill,
Pulbrook and Cleland. The biggest brokers, I gather,
are Leslie and Godwin, C.T. Bowring, C.E. Heath (again),
Sedgwick, Collins, Willis Faber, and Bevington, Vaizey and
Foster. He told me that every Name can expect to make at
least a thousand a year, though this fact was afterwards hotly
contested by yet another member of Lloyd's.'

If this figure was right, it meant that a profit of nearly £1,175,000 was taken out of insurance by the members each year in the late 1930s.

The working underwriters dominated Lloyd's in those days; they led the business and they and their syndicates provided the capital base for the market. The brokers brought in business, but not new members – the existing underwriters could cope with Lloyd's small but hugely influential share of the world's insurance market.

Like the tribe that hid from the world, the underwriters recruited their juniors and members of their syndicates from among their families and closest friends, and the great names at Lloyd's were dynastic. Paul Dixey, a future Chairman of Lloyd's, joined in the late 1930s as the grandson of a broker and the son of an underwriter and Chairman.

The world was on the brink of war, and Cuthbert Heath was dead. But at Lloyd's it was business as usual, at least as far as it concerned the *Picture Post*:

'Here is Mr G.H. Valentine, father of the Kent and England cricketer, a leading underwriter on gold ... "The Deputy Chairman at lunch in the Captain's Room, with his son ..." The Chairman of Lloyd's and guardian of its great tradition of good faith, built up over 200 years of honest dealing ...'

World War Two brought an understandable boom in marine and aviation business. When the Germans overran Norway in 1940 the entire Norwegian fleet – £100 million worth of ships – was quietly insured at Lloyd's. Without this, no Norwegian owner or captain anywhere in the world would have taken his vessel out of port. The whole deal was done in less than an hour 'leaving terms to be arranged later on.'

In 1941 the Lutine Bell tolled twice at Lloyd's for good news:

the German battleship *Bismarck* had been sunk. The following year underwriters paid up when a man disappeared with £780,000 in banknotes; eighteen years later, when he began to spend them, Lloyd's investigators traced him, chased him around the world and recovered most of the money.

In 1943 an aeroplane carrying 16 ferry pilots and industrial diamonds and emeralds insured for £73,000 by a syndicate at Lloyd's crashed in the Sudanese desert a few miles from Khartoum. The ferry pilots were killed and the gems disappeared into the sands. William Crocker, a London lawyer, was dispatched to investigate.

On his way his ship was torpedoed and Crocker spent several hours on a raft, still clutching his briefcase. From Cairo he flew to Khartoum where he hired a car and drove into the desert. Here he calculated the aeroplane's speed on impact and the cargo's momentum from the wreck, and unearthed an eight-carat emerald in the exact spot indicated by his figures. Crocker eventually located most of the remaining jewels and returned to London, where he ended up as President of the Law Society.

There was no such happy ending after the 1943 storms in Texas. They cost 'The Room' £1,125,000; but Lloyd's always paid up. Lloyd's syndicates also underwrote the insurance of the San Francisco-Oakland Bay Bridge, at £10 million the largest policy slip to date. There were heavy merchant shipping losses from U-Boat sinkings in the Atlantic, but other syndicates made a fortune during the V1 and V2 raids on London out of 'buzz-bomb' insurance – selling policies at £1 a month per £1,000 of cover against death or loss of limb ('death and spare parts' as it was known).

The Chairman in 1946 was Sir Philip D'Ambrumenil; his son David joined as a broker in 1951. In 1946 Peter Cameron-Webb joined the firm of Janson Green as a junior underwriter on Toby Green's box, followed in 1947 by Toby Green's son Peter Green and in 1954 by Peter Dixon.

Over thirty years later an extraordinary drama would engulf those four scions of the Lloyd's establishment, D'Ambrumenil, Green, Dixon and Cameron-Webb, when Dixon and Cameron-Webb perpetrated and got away with the biggest fraud in Lloyd's history.

But the Lloyd's of the postwar years proved that it could and would discipline its miscreants. Alec Wilcox was caught in 1954 filing false accounts for his marine, non-marine and motor syndicates. Lloyd's took out a private criminal prosecution and Wilcox went to prison, as did his accomplices.

Furthermore the Committee of Lloyd's, in the spirit of Cuthbert Heath, took the view that compensation should be paid to the 'Names' or members who had supported Wilcox's syndicates and been ruined as a result of his folly. This was based on the view that theirs were not fair business losses, but the consequence of the Committee of Lloyd's own failure to uphold the rules of the club; a decision that gave relief to the Names at the time, and false hope to their far more numerous and distressed successors in the 1980s and 1990s.

The risks assured in the austere postwar years could be every bit as exotic in their way as those assured in Edward Lloyd's coffee house. In 1949 Washington shopkeepers took out $200,000 worth of cover in case Harry Truman did not turn up for his presidential inauguration. In 1952 a US TV network took out insurance against the Republican or Democratic conventions not finishing on time. The Democrats were carried away by their own exuberance and overran by a day. Lloyd's paid up.

1954 was a bad year. Hurricane Carol devastated the west coast of the United States and taxed the system of spreading the risk insured between syndicates, costing Lloyd's £37,500,000 – one syndicate of fifteen men lost £1,000,000 alone. But, in a piece of forensic work worthy of Crocker of Khartoum, investigators for the lead aviation underwriter Robert Gordon travelled to the scene of the BOAC air crash at Prestwick on Christmas Day, 1954. Included in the cargo was £1 million worth of diamonds.

The disaster area was sealed off and the ground crisscrossed with numbered squares. The top soil was then removed to a hangar and sifted. Over £600,000 worth of diamonds was recovered.

But unless the underwriter had had a particularly long and liquid lunch, and the broker knew it, the risks were not underwritten on the basis of anything other than a sober assessment. A broker may have had a month to assess a particular risk before he took it onto the floor of The Room – an underwriter had 60 seconds – perhaps less.

Roy Merrett, who like Paul Dixey had joined during the interwar years, was the acknowledged king of underwriters. Merrett had begun underwriting at the time of the Spanish Civil War, writing risks on Republican ships going into Bilbao. By the mid-1950s he had 303 names on his marine syndicate and his non-marine syndicate had 85. His underwriting power or 'stamp capacity' was formidable and he never wasted an opportunity. His political instincts were legendary and it seemed there was nothing he could or would not do. But, while he made his reputation work for himself to fabulous effect, Merrett was a quick thinker who did not believe in magic: 'I would automatically turn down,' he said, 'insurance on stockings and clothing to some South American countries where there is often delay in port warehouses and customs – and a shortage of such commodities among the wives and sweethearts of customs and warehouse officials.'

Merrett and Dixey tended to see broking as a career that could give a good grounding to a potential underwriter. Brokers to them were merely 'useful' beings whose existence was otherwise of little interest. Robin Warrender, who came to a small Lloyd's broker from Eton and Trinity, Oxford in the early 1950s, would represent the new generation and an entirely different approach.

But in these postwar years Lloyd's of London appeared to all intents and purposes to be a club that had survived with its pre-war values intact; this included its policy towards its members, of whom there were around 3,000 by this time. If they were 'working members' with jobs in the market, they were expected to abide by the same codes of behaviour laid down by their regiments and public schools. If they stepped out of line, which was rarely, like Wilcox, they would be dealt with smartly to discourage other would-be offenders. A welcome was extended to the sons and nephews of working members, in the knowledge that their fathers and uncles and elder brothers would keep an eye on them.

If new members were permitted to join as 'external Names' – whose combined underwriting power, grouped in syndicates, by this time made them the majority of members – they were still joining from specific areas of British society. Lord Savile, elected in 1950, was an Etonian Grenadier Guards officer with 18,000 acres of Yorkshire. Sir Marcus Kimball, elected in 1953, was a Cambridge undergraduate. The sole question at his Lloyd's interview was: 'What are you going to do with all the money, boy?'

'I'm going to take a pack of hounds,' replied Kimball.

'That's a very good thing' replied the Committee member, 'but I hope you realise the danger of Welsh blood . . .' and Kimball's introduction to Lloyd's consisted of a lecture on hound breeding.

Clive Bemrose, elected in 1952, was employed in his family's Derbyshire printing business. He had been left money by his father and was a close friend of an agent for the Lloyd's broker, J.H. Minet. He told few people he had joined Lloyd's apart from his wife, who trusted his judgement in the financial affairs which he always managed so punctiliously.

Bemrose wrote in his private diary:

'If Lloyd's does bring in several thousand pounds per annum in a few years, I shall feel very tempted to give up business and devote myself to home, scouting, magistrates, gardening and music. There seems little reason if all goes well, in working for what at present brings in £1000 after tax, which should be replaced by Lloyd's . . .'

What mattered in all these cases was that the new member could show sufficient underwriting power in the form of money. Lloyd's would accept as security neither property, nor land, not least because both were worth a fraction of what they are today. Nor would Lloyd's accept anything other than gilt-edged government stocks. In order to pass the Lloyd's solvency test, and do so annually, a member had to be able to show £75,000 effectively in liquid funds – around £750,000 today.

In return for doing so, and for posting a deposit, the member would enjoy an annual return on his investment from Lloyd's without actually having to put up much of the money. This was as long as it was available to meet any losses – in theory to the extent of unlimited liability. Every new member was reminded that he could be liable for losses incurred by the syndicates on which he was underwriting 'down to the last cufflink' – a scenario, he was also reminded, that had rarely if ever happened.

For the first three years, because it took this long for claims to be settled, new members were required to plough back their annual cheques from Lloyd's into their reserves. The more cautious-minded among them continued to do so. Either way, they were laughing all the way to the bank.

By the mid-1950s Lloyd's unique asset base and expertise meant it enjoyed an influence out of all proportion to its share of the world insurance market. The dollar trust fund set up to meet North American claims in New York City in 1939 now received nearly half of Lloyd's annual premium income. $500 million worth of Lloyd's business a year came from America.

'Its agents,' noted *Esquire*, 'are stationed in the four corners of the globe, from Zanzibar to Zululand. There are few calamities on this planet, ranging from a sudden shower on an English tea party to a catastrophic fire in a Burmese teak factory, that do not concern the policy underwriters in London.'

'Lloyd's,' *Esquire* concluded, 'is very nearly an empire within itself.'

But, by the mid-1950s, empires were beginning to go out of fashion.

TWO

A1 AT LLOYD'S

In 1957, after the launch of *Sputnik 1*, the first satellite, the Scottish Tailoring Mercery Company of Sydney, Australia, was reported to have taken out an insurance policy against 'death caused by accident' through the satellite falling on their heads. The policy was for AUS $ 22,400 and the premium was AUS $ 70. The insurer was Lloyd's of London.

In the event *Sputnik 1* disintegrated harmlessly after completing 1,367 circuits of the Earth and travelling 43 million miles. By that time the Australian policyholder should have been reassured that the British underwriter had such confidence in the Soviet space scientists that he thought the chance of the satellite falling on their heads was only one in three hundred or 0.3%.

Lloyd's liked to be seen to keep up with the times. In the same year *Sputnik 1* was launched the Queen Mother opened the new Lloyd's building in Lime Street, London. The 1958 building, as it was known, had a 45,000-square-foot underwriting room and boasted one of the largest air-conditioning plants in Europe. Lloyd's was growing in every direction. The membership was over 4,000 and the annual premium income was approaching £200 million.

But an arcane and proven gentility still ruled. The great and the good – and the working members – still wined and dined in 'The Captain's Room.' Below the Lloyd's shield, supported by two sea-lions, the figure of a naked young man knelt on the world and held aloft an unsheathed sword. A room was devoted exclusively to relics of Lord Nelson. The Committee Room was furnished with pillars and plasterwork taken from an eighteenth-century mansion designed by Robert Adam. The Committee was served by red-and-black-liveried attendants who harked back to the coffee house days and still answered to the cry of 'Waiter!'

Downstairs, business was done as it had long been done; by brokers crisscrossing the floor of 'The Room' with a policy which they had accepted on behalf of a client, and for which they were now seeking cover. They found this in the shape of the underwriters at their boxes. The brokers collected underwriters' stamps on their policy slips for 100% of the policy and moved onto the next piece of business. The underwriters and their assistants entered the business in their syndicate books.

In time the policy would be renewed, or a claim made, and higher premium charged, or a reserve made against a claim happening. In three years' time the 1958 underwriting year would be 'closed' and reinsurance obtained against any further claims. Figures would be released to the members for the syndicate's losses or profits on that year. It was virtually unknown for an under-writing year to be left unfinished or 'open.'

The broker, the underwriter and the members of the syndi-cate would all take their cut. The bigger the syndicate, the more powerful was the underwriter and the bigger the business for the broker. The profit from an underwriting year was like the light from a distant star – it took three years to reach the naked eye, but when it arrived it lit up the heavens.

Lloyd's also took with it to Lime Street the tradition of sorting out its own problems. In 1958 when the Roylance syndicate got into what was politely termed 'a spot of bother' it was agreed at a 'lively' meeting of 500 members to use the Central Fund to bail it out.

This was the £6,000,000 'lifeboat' fund reserved to help pay claims in the short term, and not for the purpose of aiding distressed members. The objections were on two main grounds: it was dangerous to set a precedent that might be exploited by cynical and unscrupulous underwriters, and in any case the incompetent should enjoy punishment and not reward.

Or, as the objectors muttered to each other while shouting out the former: 'Why should I pay for some other bugger's mistakes?'

The problem was that the bugger in question was none other than Lieutenant-Colonel Robert Roylance, a former Chairman of Lloyd's with 111 syndicate members including several members of parliament and peers of the realm. Roylance had retired having made inadequate provision for American tornado claims, a common enough mistake at Lloyd's, but one made by him for many years and on an epic scale. His deputy had inherited a problem estimated to be up to £2 million. His 111 influential members stood to lose an average of £18,000 each (over £180,000 today).

Eventually a loan was made to the Roylance syndicate enabling it to go on trading. The reasoning on the part of the Committee was that the loan would be shortly paid back by tax rebates on claims the syndicate had against the Inland Revenue.

The Committee's judgement proved to be correct, but so did the fears of those who had voted against the Roylance bail out. Henceforth, they said, there was even less to stop underwriters who might not have been born greedy but were easily made so, from exceeding their premium limits and 'writing on the back of the Central Fund.'

But the Roylance affair was dwarfed by the disaster Lloyd's faced in the same year, 1958, when the Indonesian government seized 40 ships belonging to a large Dutch company, worth over £11 million. A clause in the policies stated that, if the vessels were held for over four months, the owners could claim a total loss. One Lloyd's syndicate alone was liable for £500,000.

In these circumstances Roy Merrett and Paul Dixey undertook

to travel to Djakarta in an attempt to persuade the Indonesian government to release the ships.

The omens were not promising. Merrett had once been invited to visit Indonesia and was now hoping his hosts would prove affable when it came to the present difficulty. Dixey had once met the Indonesian Foreign Minister at an Essex garden party. Armed with these contacts and various letters of introduction, the Lloyd's men set off for Djakarta.

In Karachi Merrett succumbed to amoebic dysentery and was nursed by his pregnant hostess (Merrett later became the child's godfather). In Singapore they were advised not to travel further because of infighting among the Indonesian military. They proceeded nonetheless to Djakarta, where they spent several weeks waiting for the Indonesian government to make the next move and trying not to appear desperate as the four-month deadline came nearer and nearer.

Eventually Dixey was about to return to London when he tried one last throw. He telephoned the wife of the Foreign Minister whom he had last seen at the Essex garden party.

The wife answered. 'He hasn't seen you?' she said. 'But he wants to see you, I know he does. I'm going to arrange it,' and she rang off, leaving Dixey to go on packing.

A few hours later the telephone rang again. This time it was the Indonesian Foreign Minister, inviting the Englishmen to tea. 'Why are you going back to London?' he asked.

'We've got to produce the original policy,' Dixey replied. Inwardly he was in anguish. He knew that, by the time they had done so, the deadline would be up and many members of Lloyd's would have suffered heavy losses.

'Mr Dixey,' the Foreign Minister addressed him with an innocent gaze, 'you did know we were always going to give you those ships back . . . didn't you?'

Merrett and Dixey were rewarded for their efforts with a presentation at Lime Street.

Younger and more junior players in the market continued

to be rewarded for five years' service with working membership. This entitled them to belong to syndicates as 'working members' or 'working Names' on a reduced show of assets of between £7,000 and £15,000. They wrote reduced premiums on those syndicates, but if they and their syndicates did well, and their assets increased, the sky was the limit.

A number of people entered the arena at this time who would become successful and in some cases notorious players in the following decades. David Coleridge, an old Etonian and descendant of the poet Samuel Taylor Coleridge, joined R.W. Sturge & Co. in 1957 having been elected a member of Lloyd's two years earlier.

Ian Posgate was a deputy underwriter who was elected a working member in 1957. Posgate was a Cambridge mathematics graduate with a brilliant head for figures and a ruthless talent to surmount the obstacles he perceived it was the job of the Committee and Chairman of Lloyd's to place in his way.

Posgate would come to admire Merrett and dislike Dixey with equal vigour. Two decades later he would become the highest-paid man in Britain, before a head-on conflict with the authorities found him innocent of criminal intent but brought him down at the height of his underwriting career, highlighting for many the hypocrisy at the heart of Lloyd's in the 1980s.

The newly-elected working Names were not necessarily active underwriters. Peter Miller, elected in 1958, came into Thomas R. Miller, the family broking firm. Michael Church followed his father into Lloyd's as a broker for the marine department of C.E. (Cuthbert) Heath, the founding father of the modern Lloyd's whose principles he venerated.

Robin Kingsley, elected in 1959, was the son of a stockbroker and had worked for five years as a junior on R.L. Glover's underwriting box for marine syndicate 162. Syndicate 162 had 12 Names, mostly Scottish landowners. With such a small capacity the syndicate never led any risk, and the closest the young Kingsley came to underwriting was stamping renewals when the active underwriter had gone home early or the deputy could not get his car out of his rural garage in the morning because of the snow.

After seven years on the Glover box Kingsley was still only third in line. Full of enterprising ideas for the future, he joined a brokers as a first step towards putting them into practice; in this way he would meet a wider section of the market.

Charles St George was elected a working member in the same year, but would have a more colourful career than many of his contemporaries. Born Charles Barbaro Saint Giorgio in Malta, he came from a rich family of impeccably exotic credentials. His family had moved during the war to Ireland where the young Charles found himself living near the Kerr family in the Curragh. Bertie Kerr was thought the best judge of horseflesh in Ireland and took the young man racing. By the time Charles was showing his own unique eye for a horse, Bertie Kerr had still only taught him a fraction of what he knew.

The St Georges cemented their bloodstock connection through Kerr and the family of William Hill, whose daughter married Charles St George's brother Edward. William Hill had the most successful chain of bookmakers in Britain. Charles St George came to Lloyd's via the Guards and a retired General Gascoigne as a 'half commission man' with no fixed job but a toehold in the market. When the Lloyd's broker and members agent Oakeley Vaughan came up for sale, St George leapt at the chance.

The role of the members agent was to look after the affairs of the members he had introduced to Lloyd's. This meant keeping their accounts, dealing with their accountants, paying their annual cheque (or requesting it, in the event of a loss) and above all placing them on a good selection of syndicates so as to minimise the chances of the latter eventuality.

For these services the members agent took a share, with the managing agents who ran the syndicates, of the member's annual 'salary' or fee he paid for underwriting, and of the member's underwriting profits. In 1960 for a member underwriting £100,000 of business these profits could be up to £8,000 a year: at the time this was the salary of a High Court judge.

A members agent with a high number of successful underwriting names was making a lot of money in salaries and profit commissions. While he was expected to back the same syndicates as the members he represented, he was not liable down to the last cufflink for any of their losses; only his own. A good underwriting year for his Names meant a hefty commission for him to use as a hedge against a bad year in which as a working Name he might also suffer losses. A members agent's overheads were low: an office near Lloyd's, in, say, Fenchurch Street or Houndsditch; secretarial help; and an entertainment budget to wine and dine his members individually at that all-important annual lunch.

There were other ways in which the members agent could benefit from his proximity to the market. If he needed syndicates on which to place his Names, the syndicates in turn needed his members to increase their capacity. Whenever there was an upturn in business, new members were literally at a premium. Agents would lunch their friends in the accounting and legal and banking professions and remind them of this, ever so gently, over the brandy.

Nobody would be so vulgar as to mention money. Lloyd's was not a place to be talked of in terms of trade or tradesmen. An agent did not have to coach his lunch guest as to how to make the pitch. 'There's something I want to talk to you about. It's only a possibility, you understand. But it might just be the answer to your problems. It's strictly between ourselves, of course. Are you interested?'

If anything it was like salmon fishing. You had to have patience and choose the right stretch of the river. The right fly. The right moment. The right fish generally landed themselves, anyway.

And, for the vulgar who were interested in figures, the fisherman could expect a bounty of at least £1,000 for each new member who joined.

By the early 1960s the growth in membership meant a correspond-ing growth in members agencies. Some like Sir Francis Dashwood or R.F. Kershaw were independently owned and operated. Others like Oakeley Vaughan were brokers and members agents. Many of the smaller but still highly profitable concerns were owned outright by the big brokers.

The brokers had come a long way since the early 1950s when they were regarded as 'merely useful' sources of business. Their growing ownership of members agencies meant they had greater power over the managing agencies who actually ran the syndi-cates. They could offer new members to hard-pressed syndicates wanting to underwrite bigger premiums; and they could offer them business. Soon the brokers would build up wholly-owned managing agencies and employ underwriters of their own.

An underwriter confined to his box in The Room could not have bypassed a broker to underwrite *Sputnik 1* or any other risk for that matter. In an age of satellite technology, even the most successful underwriters at Lloyd's were beginning to look trapped in gilded cages on the floor. 'Underwriters are reluctant to change,' Robin Warrender told the *Sunday Times* in 1963. 'It's the broker who provides the new business.' These brokers were growing rapidly, offering innovative insurance programmes to international industrial companies, many of which had hitherto only dealt directly with insurers. At the same time they were dramatically extending their involvement in North America, and benefiting from inflationary increases in insured values and the pace of economic growth since World War Two.

Warrender and others like Reggie Cheeseman of Bland Welch, Charles Hughesden of Stewart Smith, and Hugh Stenhouse, saw that insurance broking had a huge earnings potential, largely unrecognised at the time by the investment community in London.

Before 1961 there was only one insurance broker listed on the Stock Exchange, a small player called Scott North, owned by Cockshoots Holdings, and then acquired by Hugh Stenhouse to form the nucleus of his Group. Warrender linked his broking company Tudor & Co. with Samson Menzies, run by the brother of the legendary spymaster and head of MI6, Sir Stewart Menzies, to form Fenchurch Holdings. One by one over the next few years the leading Lloyd's brokers obtained listings for their shares on the Stock Exchange, creating a new breed of Lloyd's millionaires, or the 'Broker Barons' as they came to be known.

The *Sunday Times* American writer, Joseph Wechsberg, created the most detailed and vivid picture of Lloyd's to date; a considerable achievement bearing in mind that the first ever picture of the Committee of Lloyd's had only been published three years earlier:

> 'To work for Lloyd's is a passion rather than a profession. Young men grow up in the very special atmosphere of The Room, learning the traditions, unwritten rules, Lloyd's esprit de corps and code of decency. They like the sense of freedom, the relaxed schoolboy atmosphere, the anonymity . . .'

Wechsberg also encountered that heady blend of business complexity, heritage and charm: 'No man at Lloyd's (as in any well run, discreet organisation) knows exactly what the other fellow is doing, and no one in its marble-filled headquarters in Lime Street knows everything about the entire operation . . .

'Everything depends upon one's underwriter. They are an interesting bunch of men . . . Many come from old City dynasties, others are second, third and fourth generation Lloyd's men . . .'

Wechsberg met Roy Merrett, whose son Stephen would shortly become a working member, and who told him, 'I have spent the happiest hours of my life in The Room.'

He met Paul Dixey, who told him about their mission to Djakarta. He met the Chairman John Ridgers, 'a grey-haired man of quiet dignity and considerable charm', and was shown the Chairman's chair, made of wood from the *Lutine*'s rudder:

'We must show ourselves to the world,' the Chairman told him. 'After all, we have nothing to hide.'

He met the active underwriters. 'Longer contracts are rarely made,' he wrote, 'because future syndicate members might inherit too many risks they don't like . . .', a reference to the 'long tail' policies in fact underwritten by many at Lloyd's at the time.

He heard all about the old days, and the doubtful deals. '"It couldn't happen today," a prominent Lloyd's man said to me. "There is an unwritten code of decency here . . ."'

But behind the marble façade some young working members were privately voicing misgivings. What Lloyd's presented as a desirable form of continuity seemed to them a collective inertia at odds with the outside world.

Ed Cowen arrived as a junior broker with C.E. Heath. His first thought was that there was a puzzling lack of work. Cowen would be dispatched from the broker's offices to Lloyd's, do the rounds of the underwriters and their deputies, and return to his offices and read a book. His elders seemed to make a great deal of fuss about doing an absurdly easy job; and raised their eyes if he did not disappear promptly at 3.30 pm for tea. This did not seem to the young Cowen to be in keeping with the spirit of enterprise on which Lloyd's was founded.

The same inertia permeated the higher levels of the working membership. Lloyd's seemed to some to be operating its own kind of disincentive scheme. It was widely believed that the influence of freemasonry was powerful and even that the Lutine Lodge decided who would and would not be Chairman. Others hinted darkly about a cabal of born-again Christians reputed to exercise a stranglehold on key business. Ian Posgate was among those convinced that the masonic influence was pervasive to an unhealthy degree. His critics pointed to the fact that as a practising Catholic Posgate was congenitally undisposed to freemasonry; and that he was merely jealous in that he was still an active underwriter for a syndicate of fewer than thirty members at the time.

But Posgate reserved his real spleen for his own generation of the 'second, third and fourth-generation Lloyd's men.' To him, too many fathers working in Lloyd's had made their sons working members. In 1900, Posgate liked to say, a second son at public school would go into the Church of England. In the 1920s and 1930s he would go into the Colonial service or the Malayan rubber plantations. But after World War Two the options narrowed; Rhodesia and Kenya no longer seemed such safe bets. So the fathers sent their second sons into Lloyd's, and made them working members, and they had a good and easy life.

Even in his most outspoken moments, some people could not quite work out whether Posgate meant this as a criticism or a compliment.

Robin Warrender believed that the seeds of the subsequent scandals in Lloyd's were sown at this time. The new found wealth of the 'Broker Barons' was not generally matched in the underwriting community, except by those who were also share-holders in Lloyd's brokers or the largest underwriting agencies. Leading underwriters tended to have very high incomes which were heavily taxed and without the opportunity for capital gains enjoyed by the brokers. This caused envy and jealousy, and a few underwriters, apparently aided and abetted by some brokers and accountants, started to look around for ways to redress the balance. This led them to the dark alleys of tax mitigation schemes and, thinly disguised as reinsurance, arrangements offshore.

Another problem was that the most successful brokers were the boldest salesmen (although they would have hated to be described as such). Even the best salesmen had few financial or managerial skills; and yet because the insurance business was booming they were growing more and more powerful all the time.

In such a climate it was becoming increasingly possible for brokers to badger and bully underwriters into accepting risks with the threat that they would otherwise take their business elsewhere; and for the underwriting power of the brokers to turn into a massive time-bomb that no one would notice until it was too late.

'I don't want to be quoted on this,' said one man on the way up as a successful broker in those years, 'but when they were subsidiaries of brokers, the members agencies tended to be populated by failed brokers, or the cousin of the chairman who couldn't get a job anywhere else.'

By 1965 Lloyd's had 6,000 members on 300 syndicates, underwriting risks placed by 240 firms of approved Lloyd's brokers. This was the year in which one natural disaster shook up brokers, underwriters and membership: Hurricane Betsy.

Hurricane Betsy struck the Gulf of Mexico late in the year and did billions of dollars' worth of damage to offshore oil and gas drilling rigs. This was the end of a year which had already seen a spate of fires, shipping losses, air crashes and disasters befall other drilling rigs. The rise in premium income from the preceding year was wiped out and worse was to come. Betsy cost the members an average of £6,000 across the market and a further £3,000 in the following year: a total of over £50 million.

One or two new members had their losses carried by their syndicates, as the R.W. Sturge agency carried losses of the shipowner and budding impresario Eddie Kulukundis. Other members like Robin Kingsley survived in spite of losing the equivalent of ten times their annual salary. For some members it was the end of the road; both external and working members were bankrupted.

There was also a noticeable tightening within the non-marine market. Before Betsy, a junior broker could take a risk to a box and have it stamped by more or less anyone. After Betsy, many underwriters appeared at a loss as to what to do. Some would only act after referring to R.W. Sturge, whose young underwriters were Ralph Rokeby-Johnson and David Coleridge. 'What's Rokeby-Johnson doing?' they asked.

In such circumstances reputations were made and not easily broken. Rokeby-Johnson may have had long lunch hours; he may have liked a drink from time to time; he may have been an abrasive customer. But he was there and he was underwriting and he was doing so in the face of considerable pressure. The downside of Lloyd's self-proclaimed 'unwritten rules' and 'relaxed schoolboy atmosphere' was a craven-hearted lack of individual initiative. In the absence of visible leadership, Rokeby-Johnson did more than anyone else to hold together the market.

Others plotting and shaping their careers at this time were nothing if not individualists. Peter Green, by this time a prominent active underwriter, succeeded his late father Toby as chairman of Janson Green, and the departure took place from Janson Green shortly thereafter of Peter Dixon and Peter Cameron-Webb. PCW, their new company, would act as both a members agency and a managing agency.

Twice as many members resigned over the years 1965–8 as had resigned over the previous eight years. Conspicuous among the newly elected external members in 1966 was the publisher and Labour MP for Buckingham, Robert Maxwell.

Unlike the Conservative party, very few Labour MPs would ever endorse Lloyd's brand of capitalism red in tooth and claw. But then there were very few Labour MPs like Robert Maxwell. It would have suited Maxwell perfectly to 'show' sufficient audited assets without actually having to make them available in liquid form.

But Hurricane Betsy had stopped the influx of new members and their capital. Insurance premiums were rising but the underwriters lacked the syndicate capacity to respond. The Committee of Lloyd's realised it had to do something to reverse the flow. In late 1968, a commission of enquiry was set up under the former Governor of the Bank of England, Lord Cromer. The brief was simple: to decide how Lloyd's should develop and the means by which new members should be attracted to achieve this.

The Cromer conclusions were clear and simple. First, Lloyd's had to admit foreigners. Second, it had to admit women. Third, it had to admit the 'mini-name' – a new category of member, often the wife of an existing Name, who had to show assets of only £37,500 (the downfall, some said, of many frightened old ladies twenty years later. Many people at Lime Street, however, when they heard, did not like the sound of this at all.

Paul Dixey, who was Deputy Chairman, was not among their number. Dixey said he wanted both women and foreigners and he wanted them soon; there simply were not enough new members to be found among the British rich.

Dixey's stock was high at Lloyd's after the triumph he and Merrett had enjoyed in Djakarta. But Dixey was not one of the bigger underwriters and he was also a socialist. Lloyd's unique status as a tax shelter meant it did well under the punitive tax policies of Labour governments, but socialism was not a personal quality much in favour at Lime Street.

Ralph Hiscox, the Chairman of Lloyd's, was of the old school. Dixey and fellow Committee member Jackie Mance wanted to change things. Hiscox said he recognised change was needed. Foreigners were all very well and some of them were perfectly decent fellows. Women were quite another matter. There was the problem of lavatories for a start; not to mention legal and fiscal considerations. Women had only had the vote for fifty years in Britain; surely they could wait a little longer?

On 26 November 1968, a parliamentary delegation of Danish MPs visiting Britain were invited to lunch at Lloyd's. At the last moment it was discovered that the party included a woman MP, Mrs Clara Munck. Mrs Munck's invitation to lunch was hurriedly withdrawn; a woman had yet to darken the threshold of the Captain's Room.

The first foreign non-Commonwealth members of Lloyd's of London, including two Americans, a Swede, an Italian, a Lebanese and a Kuwaiti, began underwriting on 1 January 1969. Six weeks later, Lloyd's announced it would accept women as candidates for election. There were still legal and fiscal and lavatorial problems to be ironed out, and the women members would not be admitted until 1 January of the following year. They would have to be of British nationality (the combination of foreigner and woman was still unacceptable), and they would only be allowed as external members. They would have to sign an undertaking not to transact business in The Room or at Lloyd's in general.

Even Jackie Mance was not sure where this would all lead. After nearly 300 years of risking fires, floods, sinkings, hurricanes, tidal waves and wars, women, he nonetheless said, were 'a very big step.' For women actually to transact business at Lloyd's, said Mance, would be 'a change of organisation.'

Mance was obviously aware that the word 'organisation' sat ill in the Lloyd's context – but he was still uncomfortable all the same.

So he tried a different analogy. 'You would not play mixed teams at hockey,' he said.

The 1960s were turbulent years for Lloyd's and for the world's insurance markets. The higher insurance premiums brought with them higher claims and deeper losses, in a decade which saw not only a series of natural disasters, but also the prospect of a ship that could possibly be salvaged succeeded by that of the commercial airliner which could change in seconds from an item insured for millions of pounds, dollars or yen to a pile of worthless scrap. The admission to the club of foreigners and women was forced on Lloyd's by commercial pressures which would otherwise have further diminished its underwriting share of the market. The reduction of the asset requirement from £75,000 to £50,000 was another recommendation which was eagerly accepted.

But the Cromer Report contained other important conclusions about the structure of Lloyd's regardless of the race or sex of its members. They included criticism of the high pay and low performance of members agencies and the need for members to have greater information about syndicates. 'We feel it would be a mistake,' wrote Cromer, 'to disregard the degree of bitterness felt by some outside Names drawing heavily on their personal capital to meet underwriting losses while seemingly the earning power of underwriting agents and brokers is less affected.'

Cromer also proposed the appointment of a Chief Executive.

The Cromer Report received little or no attention from external members. The reason was simple: the Committee of Lloyd's decided not to publish it. In the boom years of the 1970s that followed everyone grew rich at Lloyd's and the Cromer Report was buried deeper than HMS *Lutine* in the sands of the Zuider Zee.

Occasionally Paul Dixey would take out the Cromer Report and read it and marvel at its accuracy and clarity of purpose. But by then he would be long retired, and the time-bomb that had started ticking in the 1960s would have exploded with a force and a fury that were terrible to behold.

THREE

THE BROKER BARONS
AND THE FISHER REPORT

In the early 1970s Lloyd's underwrote the insurance cover of a
specially marked Vancouver salmon against being caught before
it reached its anticipated destination. The cover was for 5,000
Canadian dollars and the premium was 250 Canadian dollars; a
casualty risk of one in twenty or 5%. History does not record if
and where the salmon was caught but there was little chance of
a renewal.

To the underwriter at his box this was just one more risk to
be assessed and stamped and recorded and cross-referenced and
entered in the books before the end of the day. The reputation of
Lloyd's for insurance innovation – whether it was a footballer's
legs or a chief executive's brain or a movie star's breasts – was
not matched by the latest technology. The wooden boxes were
positively Dickensian and however much money they were making the furthest the underwriters generally travelled in the course
of duty was to Lloyd's and back from their homes in the suburbs
and shires around London.

The brokers on the other hand were living a life of travel
and adventure on an increasingly glamorous scale. They were
always up to date in their knowledge of international and inter-
continental airline schedules. They crossed time zones as easily
and with the same sense of purpose as they crossed the floor of
The Room. They broked policies for clients in over one hundred
countries. They did nearly half their business in North America

and a further quarter in other parts of the world. The foreign business they placed was a major part of Britain's balance of payments.

The brokers were becoming ever richer and it was not long before people began to complain that their Rolls-Royces were blocking Houndsditch, Fenchurch Street and Lime Street. The underwriters at Lloyd's could only take business from the brokers. But the brokers could place business not only with the underwriters at Lloyd's but with any of the insurance companies in what was known as the London market. This meant not only Lloyd's but also the likes of Guardian Royal Exchange, Eagle Star and Sun Alliance.

But even the brokers had trouble placing the biggest risks and when they did so they risked higher premiums if the business blew up in the faces of the underwriters. This happened during the Jordanian civil war in 1970 when four jumbo jet aircraft were hijacked and blown up in Cairo and at Dawson Field in Jordan. The three main Lloyd's underwriters for risks of this type were Ian Posgate, Peter Cameron-Webb and Roy Merrett.

Cameron-Webb loved to write the big risks that brought big premiums and big investment income for himself and his members; but after Dawson Field even he came out of the aviation market. Posgate too was heavily exposed and did not know if he could take the heat.

He confided as much in Roy Merrett. 'No, dear boy,' Merrett told him, 'don't get out. We'll put up the rates and do it on an hour by hour basis.'

Posgate listened and agreed to follow everything Merrett underwrote. Within three months they had made back all their losses. 1970 was one of Posgate's best years ever.

In the same year the Committee of Lloyd's decided to place another obstacle in Posgate's path. They accused him of 'writing on the back of the Central Fund.'

To Committee members like Paul Dixey this was a cardinal

sin; it jeopardised the members by exposing them to risks beyond the range of their underwriting. It cynically relied on the Roylance precedent to bail them out with the Lloyd's 'lifeboat' fund.

Posgate, said Dixey, was not only writing on the back of the Central Fund – he was writing risks that would not be signed for two years and keeping back the premiums. Posgate replied that he was only doing what everyone else was doing; what was more, he was making a lot of money for his members. Was that not why they were all here?

Dixey, said Posgate, was picking on him because Posgate was not one of the second or third generation freemasons who were preventing Lloyd's from entering the twentieth century.

Posgate, said Dixey, was an unscrupulous bully who did not like the fact that he had been caught out. The second generation excuse was nonsense; Eric Pieri, the head of Dixey's company, was the son of an Italian immigrant.

Several people on the Committee of Lloyd's wanted Posgate thrown out of Lloyd's forever. But the publicity would have been bad and even Dixey admitted that for all Posgate's lack of scruples he was a brilliantly successful underwriter. Who was to say that the two characteristics did not necessarily go together? How would the members interpret the expulsion of such a man?

Eventually a compromise was reached. Posgate could stay in Lloyd's but on their terms. A notice was posted in The Room like the reprimand of a naughty schoolboy.

NOTICE

As from the 1st January, 1971, in accordance with the directions of the Committee of Lloyd's, Mr Ian Richard Posgate will cease to act as an Underwriting Agent at Lloyd's and will cease to be a shareholder in or Director of any Company or a Partner in any Firm acting as an Underwriting Agent at Lloyd's.

Mr Posgate has been severely censured by the Committee

for the way in which he has conducted the affairs of Syndicate 128/9.

Mr Posgate has given an undertaking not to underwrite for more than one Managing Agent, who would be approved by the Committee of Lloyd's.

Negotiations are proceeding which may enable a Managing Agent approved by the Committee to commence a new Syndicate as from the 1st January, 1971, with Mr Posgate as the Active Underwriter.

BY ORDER OF THE COMMITTEE

The 'Managing Agent approved by the Committee' was none other than Alexander Howden (Underwriting) Ltd., the underwriting arm of the Alexander Howden group. The chairman of the Howden group was Kenneth Grob.

'The Grobfather', as he was nicknamed, and his trusted lieutenant Ron Comery (known at Lloyd's as 'Mr Commonry') presided over a classic example of a growing Lloyd's phenomenon – a big broker in search of more muscle for its underwriting arm.

The gentlemanly free-for-all – or lack of regulatory structure – that existed at Lloyd's was making it possible for big brokers to create and operate their own syndicates and underwriting businesses. The advantages to the broker were immense: syndicates could be very profitable and a big broker also had the resources to ease the passage of its syndicates through a bad year in the hope of better times to come.

Some independent underwriters feared this would enable brokers also to dump risks on syndicates whose managing agents they controlled, in the knowledge that those syndicates could not refuse to accept the business. Others feared that the brokers would keep the best business for their own underwriters, instead of broking it freely on the floor of The Room.

Others were worried about the effect this would have on the members who provided the capital that enabled the underwriting

that enriched the broker who owned a managing and a members
agent. To what extent would such a members agent still be able
to fulfil the so-called 'fiduciary duty' to its members traditionally
enshrined in their contract?

Incredibly, because of the disappearance of the Cromer Report,
there was still no standard reply to these questions – except that
everyone agreed that no one knew the answer.

These were the circumstances in which Ian Posgate found
himself in the early weeks of 1971. To Paul Dixey he was an
unscrupulous bully who should have been shown the door. To
Kenneth Grob he was just the man they were looking for. To
Posgate this was a chance to resume his career.

The most brilliant risk-taker ever to walk the floor of Lloyd's
was rehabilitated by one of its most powerful and sinister figures. The Committee of Lloyd's thought this was a good idea.
Was Posgate a convenient scapegoat, or a Faustian figure who
had at last found his Mephistopheles? Either way, the legend of
'Goldfinger' was born.

As the underwriting power of active underwriters like Posgate
climbed, so the asset requirements for new members fell with the
falling purchasing power of the pound. The £75,000 in effectively
liquid form of the 1950s and 1960s had been replaced by £50,000,
and then by £37,500 for 'mini-names' – at the same time new and
existing members were allowed to write a premium income of not
four or six, but ten, times their deposit. Thus a member with a
deposit of £100,000 might 'write' business of up to £1 million.

This meant potential losses were higher; and the selling pitch
for Lloyd's that began in the 1970s did not fail to stress the
downside. But after the bad years of the 1960s, the market was
on the rise and suddenly everyone wanted a place on the Lloyd's
gravy train. Members enjoyed higher lines for their deposits; they
enjoyed lower asset requirements; and they enjoyed better and
better tax breaks in return for that vital contribution to Britain's
balance of payments.

The word spread quickly that again Lloyd's was a good place to be; and this time it percolated through a network of bank managers, accountants and solicitors, to the ranks of the professional classes.

For the first time membership of Lloyd's was sold as a sound investment. Farmers were persuaded by rising land values to stake their farms as collateral. Sportsmen and women saw an income for the future as they neared the end of their careers. Members of Parliament saw a second income in case they lost their seats. Another factor united all these prospective members. The old class barriers may have been breaking down, but the new money was still susceptible to the snobbery that came with the cachet of Lloyd's membership. As for the motives of the members agents and their *de facto* recruiters, nobody ever mentioned money.

In they came . . . boxing promoter Jarvis Astaire and recently retired heavyweight champion Henry Cooper; elected in 1971 through Oakeley Vaughan. In 1972 came the Penarth racing man Wilfred Sherman, who also joined through Charles St George and the Oakeley Vaughan agency.

Peter Nutting knew nothing about Lloyd's but was a director of a merchant bank that had bought an interest in the old-established Lloyd's agency, R.W. Sturge; his fellow directors thought it was a good idea if he became a member.

Paul Marland, a farmer and budding Conservative MP, was elected in 1973. Jeffrey Archer was a PR man and back bench Conservative MP. And then there was Christopher Thomas-Everard.

Dulverton, Somerset, 1973

Three-quarters of Somerset was under water and the rest was in Lloyd's; at least this was how it seemed to Christopher Thomas-Everard.

Thomas-Everard lived on a farm his family had owned since

the Domesday Book. The weather had not changed a great deal since those days either. Wind-lashed moor and sodden meadow were good for nothing except sheep and Thomas-Everard had 1,000 of them. Thomas-Everard looked after his sheep. A man trimmed their feet and sheared them and Thomas-Everard did the selling. Thomas-Everard had heritage coming out of his ears but it was hard making a living as a sheep farmer.

The Ministry of Agriculture and Fisheries kept telling farmers to diversify. Thomas-Everard had not interpreted this to include becoming a member of Lloyd's, but quite a number of his friends seemed to be doing exactly that.

They would take him aside after dinner. 'There's something I want to talk to you about. It's only a possibility, of course . . .'

To Thomas-Everard it was quite obvious that these pillars of county society who were offering to do him a favour were on some kind of commission. There had to be an element of self-interest in what they were suggesting that compromised their judgement. But they were right about his lack of money.

He decided to take independent financial advice. He went to see his bank manager. 'Oh, yes,' said the bank manager, 'and I know just the people you should talk to . . .'

Thomas-Everard was sold on the idea. He was also reassured. After all, the bank already had his farm overdraft. This way they were bound to look after him. Thomas-Everard was elected to Lloyd's and from 1 January 1974 he began underwriting as an external member of Lloyd's.

*   *   *

In that same year the Lloyd's broker Peter Nottage of Adam Brothers met a Dallas entrepreneur called Charles Christopher. Christopher had a smart idea.

A former encyclopaedia and waterbed salesman, Christopher would buy computers from manufacturers with the aid of bank loans. The computers themselves were the collateral. He would then lease them to corporations and government agencies. The monthly payments from the leases would cover the bank repayments.

The problem was that after three or four years the lessees were entitled to break the contracts and the banks were unwilling to lend money for more than that period. The reason was that they were terrified that IBM would bring out a better model. Christopher had to find a way of persuading the banks to lend him money beyond that period. He found the solution in an insurance policy.

This stated that, if a lessee broke the lease immediately after the expiry of the obligatory non-cancellation period, then the insurer would pay Christopher any balance due to the bank on the purchase cost of the computer. This way the banks were happy to lend him huge sums and ensure him equally huge profits. Christopher persuaded the broker to broke the policies at Lloyd's. When other computer-leasing companies heard this they too headed rapidly for London.

A total of 57 Lloyd's underwriters concluded on the basis of Christopher's information that IBM would not bring out a better computer in the near future. They underwrote 14,000 policies covering potential claims of over $1 billion. The lead underwriter was Peter Green, to whose Janson Green box Adam Brothers had previously broked this kind of risk; the others included Murray Lawrence, but not Ian Posgate or Peter Cameron-Webb.

Green, Posgate and Cameron-Webb were the big active underwriters, writing bigger and bigger lines with their growing syndicate capacities. They were rivals but they also had their own areas of speciality. Green was strong on direct liability business – after Hurricane Betsy he too turned a demoralised market round by raising premium rates. Posgate was known for his love of war risks and the growing field of kidnap and ransom. Cameron-Webb too wrote high risk direct business and 'long tail' risks such as asbestosis and pollution which might not turn into claims for many years to come. He would reinsure these and from them he made huge premium income and capital gains for his syndicate members; these included external Names like Clive Bemrose and working Names like Michael Church and David D'Ambrumenil.

Posgate, Green and Cameron-Webb were big enough to resist bullying brokers; if anything they themselves were accused of being the bullies. Posgate would say to a broker: 'You haven't shown me your war risk. If you don't, I'll undercut you on that other account.'

Cameron-Webb would receive young brokers like Robin Kingsley late in the day in his plush offices, sitting at his desk in shirt sleeves with red braces and his jacket hanging over the chair. He was unfailingly courteous but just as they were about to do business the telephone always seemed to ring about his yacht.

Kingsley would broke his business and depart. He was learning a good deal about the different underwriters and filing away the information in his head. He rarely saw Cameron-Webb's partner Peter Dixon, and remarked to friends that perhaps the latter was kept locked away somewhere cooking up clever schemes to make even more money; a prophetic remark, although nobody realised this at the time.

The Chairman of Lloyd's by this time was Posgate's old adversary Paul Dixey. Dixey retained his respect for 'Goldfinger's' mathematical ability and his distaste for what he saw as his utter lack of scruples. He also suspected Cameron-Webb of being less interested in meeting future claims than he was in the huge amount of cashflow his underwriting generated. But like everyone else inside and outside the market Dixey had no idea why.

Dixey was an honourable man who proclaimed the right of the active underwriter to take risks unfettered by decisions made in boardrooms by people who were not players in the market. He revered the memory of Roy Merrett and admired Raymond Sturge, a past Chairman who had done a good job in spite of the fact that he commanded little respect because of his humble background. When the Sturge organisation ran into trouble during Dixey's chairmanship, he attended a meeting and expressed his support for one of the younger directors, David Coleridge. Dixey even offered to become a member of the Sturge syndicates. Dixey was only a small active underwriter himself but the fact that he was Chairman of Lloyd's carried the day.

He deplored the growing trend towards ownership of managing and members agencies by brokers but there was nothing he could do about this. Instead he used his authority to tackle individual problems. One of these concerned a 'misunderstanding' between Dixey and Charles St George's broking and agency business, Oakeley Vaughan.

The Chairman of Lloyd's invited the Chairman of Oakeley Vaughan to his offices. He indicated his displeasure at what was going on and requested that Oakeley Vaughan clean up their act.

A week later Dixey received a letter from Charles St George. It described a forthcoming polo party to be attended by the Duke of Edinburgh. St George was glad that their little 'misunderstanding' had been sorted out. In the circumstances, would Dixey care to come to the party?

Dixey was thought very unkind when he replied that he too was glad their little misunderstanding had been sorted out and he had no intention of attending the party whatsoever.

St George continued as Chairman of Oakeley Vaughan and would expand with his sons James and Mark into managing their own syndicates. While his sons trawled the ranks of their Downside schoolfriends for new members, St George Senior, by now a brilliantly successful racehorse owner, attracted many famous sporting names to become members. These included his close friend the champion jockey Lester Piggott, who narrowly failed to win the Prix de l'Arc de Triomphe for St George on Ardross, but would win the 1976 Derby. But Paul Dixey would never overcome his misgivings about Lloyd's and the turf.

Another of Dixey's little misunderstandings as Chairman was with the meteorically successful young broker Christopher Moran.

Dixey's private diary read in 1974:

'I saw Christopher Moran about a policy. He complained that he had not been able to get the claim settled. I pointed out that he had not yet paid the premium. I also pointed out that his wagering policies were not legal in the UK and were illegal in the USA. As he was not dealing in pennies he should perhaps look at it more closely. To which he disarmingly and charmingly agreed.'

Ten years after he left school Moran was the millionaire proprietor of a publicly-quoted broker. Moran's forte was the broking of reinsurance for wide-bodied passenger jets and oil rigs. Dixey regarded Moran with the same combination of respect and distaste as he did Posgate. Moreover he did not like it when Moran parked his Rolls-Royce directly outside the main entrance of Lloyd's. Dixey liked it even less when he found his own parking space occupied by CJM 1.

Moran's broking company was making millions of pounds in profits a year and his seven syndicates all made money. The old guard at Lloyd's could not stand him. 'You're not one of us – get out,' one future Chairman told him.

'First generation don't even speak in this place,' said another.

Moran's view, like that of Posgate, was that he was not doing anything anyone else was not doing – including many of his fiercest opponents. But his face did not fit and never would. This would eventually lead to his downfall. There were those at Lloyd's, however, who were unwise to make an enemy of Christopher Moran.

The wagering policies to which Dixey referred concerned the chances of a collision between ships of a certain tonnage, and were also known as 'tonners'; they were a lucrative and controversial form of gambling. It was a 'tonner' broked to him in 1974 by Christopher Moran which a year later was causing a headache to an underwriter called F.H. 'Tim' Sasse.

Sasse had won the M.C. with the Gurkhas during the Second World War and married the wealthy daughter of an active underwriter. He had been elected a working member of Lloyd's in 1951. Like Charles St George he had a share in the bloodstock syndicate that owned Rheingold, a winner of the Prix de l'Arc de Triomphe. As Moran had shrewdly calculated, Sasse was a gambling man who always seemed to need money. Paul Dixey did not have much time for Tim Sasse either; he was another racing man.

But there were those who were attracted to Sasse's raffish style and his office outside Lloyd's decorated with nude pin-ups and racing prints. Sasse's syndicate 762 had 110 members, many with aristocratic old money, for whom he was rumoured to make a good capital appreciation, and it was supported by many long-established members agencies.

Sasse had been one of the 57 underwriters who wrote computer leasing risks. He needed to go on underwriting high risk business to sustain his various operations, and the loss brought about by the 'tonner' was not helping him to do so. It was in this frame of mind that he was approached early in 1975 by John Newman, a broker from Brentnall Beard, bearing the offer of further business from America.

Newman helped Sasse give what was known as a binding authority to an American agent called Den Har that enabled Den Har to place property and fire risk business with the Sasse syndicate. Sasse's partner Thomas Turnbull, another Second World War veteran, signed the authority that enabled syndicate 762 to underwrite the business.

What neither Turnbull nor Sasse nor Newman knew was that Den Har was not an 'approved' Lloyd's agent; and that some of the business placed through Den Har came from a source Lloyd's

US lawyers Leboeuf Lamb Leiby and MacCrae euphemistically described as 'traditionally a problem for underwriters.'

By the time they did find out, they would also find out that the Committee of Lloyd's had known about the irregularity for some time and had apparently done nothing more about it than sweep it under the Adam Room carpet. But meanwhile Tim Sasse was pleased with the business the Den Har binder had brought him, especially after the headache caused by the 'tonner' broked to him by Christopher Moran.

The Lutine Bell tolled once again at the beginning of 1976 for the loss of the supertanker *Berge Istra*, gone to the bottom of the Mindanao Trench, at six miles one of the deepest chasms in the oceans of the world. This was to be a bad year for shipping losses, but they and the consequent rise in premiums would be spread across the market.

Paul Dixey had retired as Chairman and was succeeded by Havelock Hudson, shortly to be knighted, whose wife Cathleen was one of Lloyd's first woman members. In the year the bell tolled for the *Berge Istra*, other new members included Margaret Clark, a widow living alone in a Sussex village, Lady Victoria Leatham, châtelaine of Burghley, and John Clementson.

Clementson was an oboist with the London Symphony Orchestra. Years earlier he had worked for a Lloyd's broker. His father had been a legal printer and had tried to join Lloyd's; for some reason Lloyd's believed him to be an enquiry agent and turned him down on the grounds that this was an unsuitable job for a member.

Clementson had been approached by his accountant. He was not a wealthy man but in time he would inherit a house and some money from his mother. He was single and a fairly high earner. Income tax was high and there was no knowing how long he would enjoy a successful musical career: 'There's something I want to talk to you about. It's only a possibility, you understand . . .'

Clementson felt his election to Lloyd's redeemed his father's memory. He joined through Bowrings with a modest premium limit of £110,000 and was soon receiving cheques for £5,000 a year.

Tim Sasse, by contrast, was receiving bad news almost daily. By the middle of 1976 the Den Har binder had turned into a nightmare. Not only was the North American cover holder not 'approved' by Lloyd's, but neither the Non Marine Association nor Sasse, whose job it was, had noticed this fact. The property and fire risks placed through Den Har turned out to be rigged at every stage. Premiums had been skimmed off by organised crime members on cover for decrepit tenements in the South Bronx which were then torched by paid arsonists. By the time Sasse and the broker cancelled the Den Har contract it was too late. Syndicate 762 was looking at a risk overwritten by twenty times the original figure – and now that risk was turning into a claim. It looked and smelled like fraud.

The first reaction of the Committee of Lloyd's was to keep the whole affair quiet. Apart from the broker, the underwriter and the people who had supplied the business, nobody was to know. If they did, it would be bad for the market. The good name of Lloyd's was at stake.

Incredibly, the Committee then went a step further and invoked the spirit of Cuthbert Heath: 'Pay all our policyholders in full irrespective of the terms of their policies . . .'

For Tim Sasse the real nightmare was that this was actually happening. For the 110 members of syndicate 762 the nightmare would be all the worse for the fact that nearly two years would pass before anyone bothered to let them know.

Why were the Sasse members – and many more like them over the years – kept so long in ignorance of a catastrophe that already concerned them? The three years it took to 'close' an underwriting year were not the whole story. One reason was that their interests were placed beneath that unmistakable yet indefinable entity known as 'the interests of Lloyd's.' Unlike the shareholders in a public company, the notion that Lloyd's should be publicly accountable to its members was a heresy to many members of the Committee.

A second reason was that there were only 110 Sasse members among a total Lloyd's membership of 10,730 in 1977, with 4,500 people waiting to join on 1 January 1978. On the one hand they were a valuable 1% of the membership who had to be kept in. On the other hand they could not be allowed to jeopardise the morale of the other 99% by publicly 'rocking the boat.'

In the event, the sweeping of Sasse under the carpet would result in precisely that. Worse, the members of other syndicates would begin to question the lack of information that might be crucial to their own wellbeing. But many more would not have wanted to hear bad news in a market that was rising with a premium income approaching £1,500 million a year.

They were too busy increasing their lines and receiving bigger and bigger cheques for doing so; and saying to carefully-chosen friends: 'It's only a possibility, you understand. But it might just be the answer to your problems. Are you interested?'

In they came ... General Frank Kitson, pioneer of low intensity operations and GOC of the 2nd Armoured Division, elected in 1977. So were Dave Gilmour and Nick Mason of the Pink Floyd. Edward Molesworth was a Downside contemporary of James St George and became a working member as assistant to the rising underwriter star Dick Outhwaite.

John Pearson was a company pensioner living in Malta whose investment manager recommended Lloyd's membership and just happened to know a Lloyd's members agent. Philip Francklin was a retired naval commander with a distinguished war record whose solicitor was also able to recommend Lloyd's membership. Mary Archer was an academic scientist whose husband Jeffrey was doing well as a novelist and member of the syndicates of Ian 'Goldfinger' Posgate. Giles Curtis had four daughters to educate and was taking the plunge into self-employment from the firm for whom he had worked since leaving university. He was elected through a members agent owned by a broker and also went onto the Posgate syndicates.

Posgate was fighting his way back towards establishment respectability; in that year he joined the main board of Alexander Howden and became a shareholder in the new agency of Posgate and Denby.

Everyone wanted to be on Posgate's syndicates. He was making so much money that he used to pay out to his members not once but twice a year (this was the only way he could soak up all that premium income). New members desperate to pass Lloyd's solvency requirements so that they too could have a slice of 'Goldfinger's' profits would promise to produce audits of their assets by the biggest accounting firms, and then come up with accounts signed by some tiny outfit of whom no one had ever heard. All these people and more were elected members. And then there was Earl Alexander of Tunis.

Freeport, Grand Bahama, 1977

The Bahamas are an archipelago of 700 islands north of Cuba and east of Florida. Contrary to popular belief they are not a tropical paradise but they do have many delightful features. Their location, more or less equidistant from Havana and Miami, and within range of Colombia and Panama, has also led to their being known over the years as 'a sunny place for shady people.'

Grand Bahama is the largest island, 87 miles long and 14 miles wide at its broadest point. Parts of it are white sand, blue lagoons, palm groves and mangrove swamp, and the population is equally exotic. After years of white colonial rule the black Bahamians had won representation and then independence under their 'Moses', the Prime Minister Lynden Pindling. But at the same time a small part of Grand Bahama remained as a reminder of the colonial days in so far as it was run as a de facto state within a state by the Grand Bahama Port Authority. This curious place, organised for profit by white businessmen in return for financial 'support' for the black nationalist government, was Freeport, Grand Bahama.

Lord Alexander had been brought up in a fine tradition. His father was the great British war hero Earl Alexander of Tunis, who had become Governor-General of Canada. Lord Alexander had been educated at Harrow and in Ottawa. After five years in the Irish Guards he had gone into business. He had knocked around in America and Canada. In 1963 he had bought 600 acres of land on the Bahamian island of Exuma. He had interests in property, pretty girls and the jazz piano.

In 1977 Lord Alexander's interest in property resulted in an invitation from the Grand Bahama Port Authority to visit Freeport. The two key players in this enterprise were the expatriate Briton 'Union' Jack Hayward and the lawyer and Maltese-born businessman Edward St George. Lord Alexander's girlfriend was St George's secretary. St George wanted to know if Alexander was interested in a property development on Grand Bahama.

Alexander worked with an architect and armed with his pilot's licence flew at the Port Authority's expense to inspect developments on other islands like Treasure Key and Eleuthera. Interest in the project cooled but relations remained warm between Alexander and his girlfriend. So did the contact with Edward St George.

Like his more publicity-happy brother Charles, Edward St George had come a long way since the family moved from Malta to the Curragh. Educated at Downside, he had read law at Merton, Oxford. He had gone on to write the constitution of Bhutan. An Oxford contact had led him to the Bahamas to become a magistrate in Nassau.

In 1961 Robin Warrender was visiting Nassau. He was amazed to see that the person standing outside the house flying the Union Jack was none other than his old contemporary from Oxford.

'Edward,' he said, 'what on earth are you doing here?'

'I'm the acting Solicitor-General,' came the reply.

After several years in England and in the Middle East St George had developed close links with the Hayward family and moved back to the Bahamas, where he became a director of the Port Authority. He married, for the second time, an American, and then, for the third time, Lady Henrietta Fitzroy, daughter of the Mistress of The Robes to The Queen, one of the most senior positions at Buckingham Palace.

St George was an astute judge of character in all its strengths and weaknesses. He was managing to rise in business with Jack Hayward and remain on the right side of Lynden Pindling; he also avoided being tarnished by association with suspected Mafia figures such as Lou Chessler who were involved in the development of the Bahamas in the 1950s and 1960s.

In 1967 Edward St George had been elected a member of Lloyd's through Oakeley Vaughan (Underwriting) Ltd, the Oakeley Vaughan members agency and managers of the Oakeley Vaughan syndicates. In 1971 he was a director for six months of the same company. By 1972 he was a director of Oakeley Vaughan & Company Ltd, the Oakeley Vaughan holding company and broking house, and would remain so for the next sixteen years.

In 1977, years after the collapse of the Grand Bahama property project, Edward St George introduced Lord Alexander to his brother Charles, Chairman of Oakeley Vaughan. 'There's something I want to talk to you about. It's only a possibility, you understand. But it might just be the answer . . .'

Lord Alexander had a distinguished background. Charles St George had been a Coldstream Guards officer. The leading underwriter Peter Green was just one of many Lloyd's men who, like Lord Alexander, had been to Harrow. Henry Cooper, the British sporting hero and Oakeley Vaughan member, was a mutual friend. So was the Chairman of Lloyd's, Sir Havelock Hudson. There were tax advantages; Lord

Alexander was not a wealthy man but his accountant was enthusiastic.

Besides, his brother Brian was doing well after being elected a year earlier.

Charles St George took Lord Alexander round the marbled halls of Lloyd's in Lime Street. He showed him the Captain's Room. Lord Alexander was impressed. He was so impressed that on 1 January 1978 he became not only an underwriting member but also a director of the Oakeley Vaughan members agency, whose offices were near Lloyd's at Fetter Lane, London EC4.

A titled director and war hero's son was an asset to the board of a members agency. To Lord Alexander in turn there was an advantage; as a director he had access to the agency's own syndicates. He grappled with some of the complexities of insurance but soon became familiar with the names and numbers. In time they would become branded on his memory.

Thus it was that a visit to the Bahamas led Lord Alexander to Lloyd's and to the Oakeley Vaughan syndicates 168, 420, 423, 862 and 551.

* * *

Tim Sasse had no choice but to obey the Committee of Lloyd's and pay out on the bad business placed with him through the Den Har binder. Worse still, the Brazilian reinsurer involved refused to pay its share. Sasse was left with claims of hundreds of thousands of dollars and rising. The consequences for his solvency were inevitable. In late 1977 and unknown to the Sasse members, the Committee of Lloyd's suspended syndicate 762 from accepting business in The Room.

The Committee was much preoccupied at this time with the Lloyd's image. The Sasse affair, they hoped, could be kept quiet; but other stories detrimental to the reputation of Lloyd's were appearing in the press. Brokers were squabbling over a possibly fraudulent claim involving 301 Fiat cars supposedly damaged by fire on board the Italian cargo ship *Savonita*. Nineteen syndicates specialising in cargo insurance and led by the eminent active underwriter Henry Chester were blaming a broker for misleading them over the melting of a £7 million butter mountain in a warehouse fire in Elst, Holland.

Lloyd's enjoyed some glory when its inquiry agents exposed a swindle involving the shipping of non-existent Filipino cement. But the general mood was one of siege as brains were racked to work out a response to phrases like 'Internal Mafia' and 'Broker Barons' being bandied about in the press.

As Chairman, Paul Dixey had had a healthy respect for the media which was not shared by his successor, Sir Havelock Hudson. Hudson's successor Ian Findlay did not have a great deal of time for the press, either, but during his reign Lloyd's did feel compelled to issue a public relations booklet:

> The insurance broker is a key figure in the Lloyd's market. Lloyd's underwriters have no other contact with the insuring public and their premium income is entirely dependent on the initiative and enterprise of Lloyd's brokers in obtaining business throughout the world. The Committee of Lloyd's insist on the highest professional standards from the several hundred accredited brokerage firms permitted to place risks in The Room.
>
> The Lloyd's broker's prime duty is to negotiate the best available terms for his clients. To this end he is free to place risks wherever he thinks fit . . .
>
> Spreading a risk as widely as possible is one of the cardinal principles of insurance which enables Lloyd's and the London market to withstand the pressure of heavy claims which might otherwise be ruinous. The famous preamble to an insurance Act of Parliament passed during the reign of Elizabeth I puts it succinctly '. . . it cometh to pass that on loss or perishing of any ship there followeth not the undoing

of any man, but the loss lighteth rather easily upon the many
than heavilie upon the fewe . . .'

Probably nowhere in the world is there so much
collective underwriting expertise under one roof as at
Lloyd's. Although syndicates compete with each other there
is a wealth of shared experience within the market. This
subtle blend of competition and co-operation combines
with an unshakeable belief in the old insurance dictum of
'utmost good faith' to give Lloyd's its unique quality.

Good faith undoubtedly characterises the relationship
between broker and underwriter who each place considerable
trust in one other. An underwriter's signature on a slip is
absolutely binding – in honour if not in law – and the broker
can be confident that a valid claim would be settled even if it
were presented before a policy had been issued. For his part,
the underwriter knows that the broker will have disclosed
all material facts accurately and fairly. Without such mutual
trust, Lloyd's would not long survive.

One matter on which there was agreement at Lime Street was
that Lloyd's would not long survive in its present headquarters.
This was a source of pride to some Committee members and
embarrassment to others. Another building would be Lloyd's
fourth this century.

A sub-committee was formed to investigate the options. Among
the parties involved were Courtenay Blackmore, head of admin-
istration, and Peter Green.

Green was a complex and intriguing character: like his father
Toby he was a Lloyd's man through and through, a buccaneering
and acquisitive tough guy, sceptical of outsiders and representative of an inward-looking culture.

On the other hand Green had a provocative streak that loved
to shock and he was a master of the strategically-uttered profanity.
He approved the presence of women working in The Room and
was the first underwriter to accept a risk from a woman broker.

He despised the hypocrisy of those who had wealth and power and would not occasionally flaunt it; it was as if he sometimes had doubts about this himself, but would have fought to the last to prove those doubts also existed in his contemporaries. He was just the kind of man Lloyd's needed to push through the commissioning and construction of the headquarters it was hoped would fix the image of Lloyd's into the 21st century.

By the summer of 1978 Peter Green and his associates had chosen the man who would make that image real. He was Richard Rogers, the ultra-modernist architect of the Pompidou Centre in Paris. Rogers soon came up with a model that he showed to Green and his sub-committee. Green and his sub-committee showed it to others. After the initial shock, they were united in one respect: it was different.

The hunt continued by members agents for new Names and syndicates on which to place them.

Lord Alexander had spent a year working for Oakeley Vaughan during which time he brought in one or two friends before resigning as a director. He wanted to pursue other business commitments, but he remained a member of the Oakeley Vaughan syndicates.

Alexander built up his reserves and took out 'stop-loss' insurance against bad underwriting years. He would also join other syndicates through the Oakeley Vaughan members agency. He remained on good terms with Charles St George after he lost regular contact with Edward St George and the girlfriend in the Bahamas. In 1981, after Lord Alexander's marriage to Davina Woodhouse, a Lady in Waiting to Princess Margaret, Charles St George would become godfather to one of their daughters.

Edward Molesworth, the working Name who had been at Downside with James St George, left the employment of Dick Outhwaite for Oakeley Vaughan. Molesworth had had his doubts about Oakeley Vaughan. They seemed a raffish crowd and, even though his problems were not yet known, Tim Sasse had rather

set the tone for the kind of person at Lloyd's who was involved
in racing. But the syndicate underwriting figures looked good and
James St George assured him there was no need to worry. After
its amateurish start in life Oakeley Vaughan was here to stay. He
offered Molesworth a solid deal: a directorship, company car,
perks and a higher salary.

Molesworth's job was to bring names from other members
agencies onto the Oakeley Vaughan syndicates. To this end he
assiduously dined with members agents like Brian Bell, David
Evers and Sir Francis Dashwood. Molesworth brought in £5 million in underwriting capacity to the Oakeley Vaughan syndicates,
splitting the commission with the agents in question.

Wilfred Sherman, the Penarth sporting man who had become
an Oakeley Vaughan Name several years earlier, was also doing
well from his membership and from the St George connection.
Although he was not a director, Sherman was dispatched on trips
around the world armed with an American Express card and an
expense account.

In New Orleans, he met the oil millionaire Jim Stone and
his family. In Houston, Texas, he met Jay D. Hirsch, once
Adjutant-General to the US Armed Forces. In Chicago he met
Jerome Glaser, millionaire head of the Glaser steel group, and
Glaser's accountant.

In Sydney, Australia, he met John Attridge and the Woodhouse
family, Bill Woodhouse, his son Robbie and daughter Louise, his
brother Jack and Jack's son John; all of them signed up with
Oakeley Vaughan. The syndicate underwriting figures looked
good and even modest Oakeley Vaughan Names like Mark and
James St George's friend Richard Overall were receiving cheques
for £3,000 a year.

Robin Kingsley had used his considerable experience as broker
to build up a mass of information about the various underwriters
in the market. He knew the high fliers and the ones who flew too
high, and the ones who would write a risk drunk in the afternoon
that they had turned down sober in the morning. He knew the

ones who were flattered rather than suspicious when the brokers clustered around their boxes. He knew the ones whom the brokers could soften up with a few drinks and a pretty girl at the Rififi club, a notorious West End watering-hole often used for this purpose.

He knew the softening up process at first hand now that he too was setting up in business as a members agent. Oakeley Vaughan's Guy Walmsley took him to lunch in the Captain's Room. Afterwards, Kingsley said: 'That was very nice, Guy. But what do you want from me?'

'Oh,' said Walmsley, 'I've been told to make sure you support our syndicates.'

Kingsley would decline the invitation on this occasion but there were other managing agents and syndicates whom he had observed favourably during his years as a broker and on whom he was happy to place his growing list of members. These included the oldest Marine syndicate, Secretan 367, John White's Spicer and White 895 and Derek Walker of the Gooda syndicates, which had weathered Hurricane Betsy and existed since the 1930s.

Kingsley got on with Derek Walker. As a broker Kingsley had placed quite complicated aviation business with him to the satisfaction of both parties. Walker himself had a light aircraft which he never flew too high or too far, and only flew in fair weather. You noticed these things, as a members agent with a fiduciary duty to your Names who were providing the capital for underwriting. As the Gooda syndicates grew, so did Kingsley Underwriting Agencies.

Kingsley had a theory that had evolved out of the growth of the unit trust investment and which he had refined over his years as an underwriting assistant and then a broker. Instead of concentrating his members' underwriting capacity on a small number of syndicates in the traditional fashion, he would spread the risk over a larger number. This way he perceived he could reduce the risk and increase the chances of a steady return. When he had first tried to apply the theory to his own narrow spread of syndicates as a working member, he had encountered no official opposition.

He had gone upstairs in the 1958 building to the second floor and consulted the Corporation staff in charge of the syndicate participation. Here he had made a simple discovery. The opposition to the idea of a wide spread of syndicates seemed to be founded simply on the fact that there was not enough room to list them on the existing forms.

In those days a new.members agency could be started up with only a few names, a suitably experienced underwriter on the board, and the approval of the Committee. Kingsley had started out by placing new members through Spicer and White, a members and managing agency with which he had close links. His own first members had been his wife Camilla, his brother-in-law Martin de Laszlo, de Laszlo's sister Lavinia and Wing-Commander Eustace 'Gus' Holden DFC.

Then came John Pearson, the company pensioner living in Malta, and the retired naval commander Philip Francklin. In Bermuda they included cymbal manufacturer Robert Zildjian. In the Bahamas they included the retired surveyor Michael Oakes, brought to Lloyd's on a Wimbledon tennis court, a game of which Kingsley himself was a keen exponent. Virginia Wade, the immensely popular 1977 Wimbledon Ladies Champion, was another Kingsley member.

Kingsley was careful to show all his prospective new Names accounts and syndicate results going back several years and to explain the rationale behind his risk-spreading strategy. Not only did they find this attractive, but many of his existing members increased their underwriting as the cheques came in and improvements in their circumstances made them willing to take a bigger participation on Secretan, Gooda Walker, Spicer and White and other many syndicates.

None of them saw it as a gamble; not even Kingsley. Kingsley's idea of a gamble was the loser paying for tea after a tennis match. What was more, his risk-spreading theory seemed to be working.

Not only were his names making money; so was Kingsley. He moved to Sudbrook Lodge, a magnificent Carolean house as old as Lloyd's itself on the edge of Ham Common, an area of Surrey patronised by stockbrokers and film stars. Kingsley Underwriting Agencies was becoming one of the success stories at Lloyd's in the late 1970s and early 1980s.

By now the annual ups and downs of Lloyd's underwriting results were well and truly obscured by the lower solvency requirements and enormous tax advantages of membership. Nothing could stop the flood of new members. Robin Kingsley was merely one of the more successful members agents. In the same year, many more members were elected via many other members agencies in exactly the same way.

In they came ... Melvyn Bragg was a writer and television presenter and staunch supporter of the Labour government whose punitive tax policies were making Lloyd's membership so attractive. Edward Heath MP had opposed such policies during the years 1970 to 1974 when he was Prime Minister. Tony Jacklin was a world-famous golfer who had won the English National PGA tournament the preceding year. Camilla Parker-Bowles was a confidante of the Prince of Wales and a familiar figure to the Royal Family.

Her Royal Highness the Duchess of Kent and His Royal Highness Prince Michael of Kent were some way down the Civil List of royal 'salaries' and were grateful for the chance of additional income they hoped would come from Lloyd's membership. General Sir John Hackett was a highly decorated soldier and successful author. Marmaduke 'Duke' Hussey was a newspaper magnate married to a Woman of The Bedchamber to The Queen; Hussey had lost a leg during the Second World War but had no plans to lose his cufflinks at Lloyd's.

The Reverend Allan Murray Maclean and Mrs Maclean were clearly unworried by the proverb about the rich man and the eye of the needle. The Earl and Countess of Lichfield were custodians of an expensive stately home and he was a successful photographer. Geoffrey Rickman had practised as a solicitor and was a Surrey landowner. Rickman's own solicitor recommended membership, and just happened to have good contacts with a reputable members agent. After election and a good lunch in the Captain's Room Rickman went onto the much-sought-after syndicates of Posgate and Denby.

Clive Francis was a former RAF Squadron Leader who had become wealthy through property dealing. Francis believed in trust, decency and what he liked to think of as 'the Baden-Powell virtues.'

Francis had a house in Gloucestershire with gardeners, and his dinner guests could see he lived well. After dinner one of them said over the brandy: 'Clive, old boy, I can get you into the most exclusive club in the City.'

'What on earth are you talking about?'

'It's strictly between ourselves, of course. But it might just be a possibility. Are you interested?'

Francis was interested and flattered. He had previously associated the name of Lloyd's with that of a high street bank.

At the 'Rota' interview as it was called, where new members were met by members of the Committee of Lloyd's, Francis and the other new members were reminded that they could be subject to unlimited liability.

'You know you can lose your shirt on this,' someone murmured.

There were twelve new members standing there. Francis would always remember how they all simultaneously burst into a jocular chuckle. The first profits went into his reserves and he was glad to be a member of the most exclusive club in the City.

At the same time that Lloyd's members agents were trying to bring in new members from all around the world, including America, the Committee of Lloyd's was trying to keep the Americans out.

The American brokers had seen the power of the Lloyd's

'broker barons' and they wanted a piece of the action. This was the only way even the American insurance giants could achieve direct access under the archaic arrangement whereby the Lloyd's approved broker acted as sole agent for the underwriter in his box. The Americans also objected to the degree of commission they had to share with Lloyd's brokers on the £1 billion of business they directed to Lloyd's each year. But the Committee of Lloyd's, which contained brokers and underwriters but neither foreigners nor women, did not like this at all.

However mere conservatism was ultimately not the Committee's motive. There were already 800 Americans out of 14,134 Lloyd's members and as much as 40% of Lloyd's overseas business (which was 75% of all its business) came through America. Thanks also to the little-publicised dollar trust fund that had been set up in New York to protect policy-holders in the event of Hitler invading Lime Street, there were thousands of millions of dollars sitting there ready to meet US claims; only the profits went to London. This cash mountain in Manhattan would have made the nucleus of a formidable Lloyd's of New York City.

What worried the Committee was that there was little legislative equipment for them to move confidently either way. First they discovered foreign ownership of brokers was already a reality to a far greater extent than they realised. Then, when they were asked to produce a copy of the rules relating to foreign ownership of brokers, they discovered no such rules existed.

Under pressure, the Committee reacted wildly and made a serious tactical mistake. They announced that henceforth no outside interest could own more than 20% of any Lloyd's broker. Even the Chairman of Lloyd's Ian Findlay admitted later that he was embarrassed by the decision. Frank B. Hall, the American company already in negotiations to buy a stake in Leslie & Godwin, and Marsh & McLennan, who were trying to do the same with Wigham Poland, were furious, as were other American brokers involved in similar overtures.

First the Brits invited you to play ball and then they started moving the goalposts. In a spiralling game of broker poker, the Americans threatened to set up their own exclusive New York reinsurance exchange.

The British correctly believed they were bluffing; in a naturally volatile market such a move could soon end in disaster for a new institution with none of Lloyd's fabled reserves. At the same time, however, insurance was an international business and Lloyd's could no more afford to be excluded from a New York reinsurance exchange than America could afford to be excluded from Europe.

Furthermore, in Europe the big players like Munich Re (Munich Reinsurance, premium income $2.2 billion) and Swiss Re ($2.7 billion) already did more business than Lloyd's. In a market where the competition was becoming tougher the ostrich position was that of the loser.

Eventually the Committee of Lloyd's climbed down, or rather found a complex set of means by which the American insurance giants could be said to stay within the 20% rule and yet still buy substantial stakes in Lloyd's brokers. The Americans replied deadpan that Lloyd's-approved UK brokers would be welcome to apply for admission to any notional New York reinsurance exchange. Soon Marsh & McLennan had C.T. Bowring, Fred S. James had Wigham Poland and Frank B. Hall had Leslie & Godwin.

This left another American company, Alexander & Alexander, still looking long and hard at the Lloyd's broker into which they had been contemplating buying for the last few years. Again they came close and again they backed away. But somehow they still could not quite summon up the decision. Was it just a question of money; or was there something more?

Either way, Alexander & Alexander could not make up their minds. Yet all the time they edged closer to 'the Hanging Gardens of Howden', whose Nebuchadnezzar Kenneth Grob was looking to retire to the South of France and the fabulous villa he had bought from Gregory Peck. 'The Grobfather' was ready to sell

Howdens at the right price, lock, stock and barrel – in the knowledge that, whatever the other new American broker barons had, they did not and would not have 'Goldfinger' Posgate, the rehabilitated Lucifer of Lime Street.

One of the complex means by which the Committee saved their faces over the American invasion was the citing of a whole raft of structural defects for which they hinted reforms were imminent. Chief among these were the conflicts of interest inherent in the ownership of agencies by brokers, the bickering between brokers and active underwriters over the Elst butter mountain meltdown, and the need to slow down the growth of the membership in a tightening market.

To this end Ian Findlay and the Committee announced they had commissioned the compiling of the first report since Cromer ten years earlier. This was the Fisher Report, headed by Sir Henry Fisher, son of the late Archbishop of Canterbury. Sir Henry was a former High Court judge and director of Schroder Wagg; he was then a non-executive director of Thomas Tilling and Equity & Law.

Findlay – not Fisher – added a few comments of his own: 'I do not expect any fundamental changes in Lloyd's rules and regulations, just an updating in the existing practices and rules.'

The Chairman went on: 'We would not necessarily publish its results in full, some of it could be highly technical, but we would hope to produce a summary.'

Findlay could hardly have been expected to promise the heads of incompetent underwriters on plates and the bodies of broker barons swinging from the lampposts in Lime Street. But this did sound as though, no sooner had counsel begun questioning the witnesses, the judge was instructing the jury.

The first signs came to the outside world that all was not well with Sasse syndicate 762. One by one the members opened the envelopes from their members agents, sat down and felt sick.

Tim Sasse meanwhile assumed everything would be all right. Stephen Merrett, son of Roy Merrett and a rising underwriter, had undertaken to try to sort Sasse out. Merrett was happy to do so because there was a chance he could buy the Sasse Turnbull agency for his own firm of Merrett Dixey. But when Merrett discovered the extent of the Den Har horror he realised he could no longer even keep on the table the offer of £20,000 that Tim Sasse had reluctantly accepted. Sasse Turnbull was insolvent and Tim Sasse's underwriting career was destroyed. The only Names to be taken off Sasse's syndicates in time were those placed on them by Oakeley Vaughan and Charles St George. St George had helped Sasse start up a bloodstock agency and was irritated to learn that Sasse had expressed his gratitude by undercutting Oakeley Vaughan on an important American account.

St George was so ill-disposed to the Sasse Turnbull agency that he ordered all his names to be taken off the Sasse syndicates immediately. Not long afterwards St George was in the lavatory off The Room when Stephen Merrett appeared at the next urinal.

'Do you know your friend Sasse is in a lot of trouble?' asked Merrett.

St George would never be able to convince him that sheer chance and not a brilliant feat of prescience had enabled him and his members to dodge the century's worst underwriting scandal to date.

Merrett reported to the Committee that syndicate 762's losses for the years 1976 and 1977 could be as much as £20 million. The Committee considered it essential that Lloyd's be seen to be honouring claims, especially on business done in America. The letters had gone out to the 110 members; £48,000 required from Lady Middleton in Yorkshire and £258,000 from Paddy Davies in Sussex. For many these sums spelled likely bankruptcy: between £120,000 and £700,000 in today's terms.

The Sasse members were honourable folk and counted many retired Brigadiers, Lords and Ladies among their number. Paddy Davies went to see the Chairman of Lloyd's. He was not begging for special treatment, he said, he was simply asking for more time. After being kept in the dark for so long after things had gone so badly wrong, the least Lloyd's could do was give them time to assess their losses on a more informed basis.

Davies came out of the Chairman's office with Findlay's response still ringing in his ears: 'Bad luck, old boy. Wrong syndicate, bad luck!'

Davies had already calculated that, if he continued in Lloyd's and it was profitable the whole time, he would still need to live to the age of 160 to wipe out the debt. He was also a businessman and did not believe in bad luck except as a convenient excuse. What happened next marked a turning point in the history of Lloyd's and its members. The Sasse members decided they were not going to pay.

To exacerbate matters, Tim Sasse's underwriting had included a substantial amount of the computer-leasing cover. But Sasse was only one of the 57 underwriters who had taken a risk on the basis of information provided by the plausible Dallas whizz kid Charles Christopher. All 57 were now acquainted with the worst possible news. IBM had indeed brought out a better, faster, and much cheaper computer. In the words of IBM President John Opel, the new 4300 offered 'up to seven times more bang per buck than its predecessors.'

As the lessees promptly broke their contracts the insurance claims rolled in and Lloyd's was suddenly facing a bill of $225 million and rising – already twice the size of Hurricane Betsy. Unlike Sasse, this was a clear case of Lloyd's facing the downside of a fair business risk. The settlement of claims was complicated by controversy over some of Christopher's more doubtful activities and the inevitable blizzard of lawsuits. But as Murray Lawrence, a top underwriter with Bowrings and one of the 57, put it: 'If we didn't have losses we wouldn't be in business.'

Later the computer-leasing disaster would be publicly held up as an example of the folly of underwriters who wrote risks

without any of the research facilities enjoyed by the large insurance companies. It was a high price to pay for a reputation for
'innovation', another term increasingly used as a euphemism for
a doubtful risk underwritten for a quick profit. But there were
revealing private conversations and secret responses that gave a
truer flavour of life at Lloyd's cutting edge at the time.

As the computer-leasing bills reached $450 million it became
imperative to send someone to Boston to negotiate a limit to the
damage. This was a job for the best negotiator – and the best
salesman – of his time. The ad hoc committee set up by Lloyd's
unanimously chose Peter Cameron-Webb.

Cameron-Webb exacted a high price for the honour of doing
battle in Boston for his colleagues at Lime Street. He insisted
on travelling by Concorde to New York with his girlfriend
– later his wife – and her two daughters. He insisted on their
being accommodated at the Carlyle Hotel. The following day
they were to be transported to Boston by private aircraft. All
the while there were regular seven-hour flights direct from
London to Boston.

Ian Posgate was a member of the committee which sent him.
Posgate would later cite the computer-leasing disaster as an example of the hypocrisy of his old bête noire, the second generation
Lloyd's establishment. How could they criticise and censure him
for writing direct high risk business when the computer-leasing
affair showed that even 57 supposedly 'safe' syndicates could end
up going to the Central Fund?

But the most telling comments in retrospect came from Dick
Outhwaite. Outhwaite was not a second generation remittance
man. He was a highly intelligent self-made Yorkshireman whose
syndicates were doing increasingly well. He had first been spotted by Roy Merrett and begun his professional life working with
Stephen Merrett, the idea being that they were joint-heirs apparent. But Merrett junior was an abrasive character who could not
tolerate this arrangement and Outhwaite set up on his own.

Eddie Kulukundis was an Outhwaite Name and wrote one of

the biggest lines of any member of Lloyd's. Every time he had lunch with an active underwriter of whose syndicate he was a member, he would nervously inquire whether or not they had underwritten the computer-leasing business.

Outhwaite said: 'Eddie, I'm not involved.'

Kulukundis breathed a sigh of relief. 'Thank God,' he said and sat back in his chair.

'I'll tell you why,' Outhwaite said. 'Peter Green was the leader and they wanted me to be the second lead. But, when I saw that the banks wouldn't finance the computer-leasing unless there was insurance, I said this was not for us.'

Kulukundis started to say something complimentary, when Outhwaite cut him off. 'But Eddie,' he said, 'if I had been eighth on the list, and seen Peter Cameron-Webb or someone else leading . . . I would have been there.'

In other words, Outhwaite was saying, he had been given a chance to read the contract and it was only luck that he had decided not to become involved. Kulukundis admired Outhwaite for this and made a mental note to support his syndicates all the more in future.

The Fisher Committee went about its work and the new Lloyd's building was announced. The Sasse members were sued by Lloyd's and Lloyd's was sued by the Sasse members. Lloyd's announced profits of £122 million for the 1976 underwriting year on £1.7 billion of premium income and this was judged to be a poor performance. A committee of enquiry led by former Chairman Paul Dixey was set up to look into alleged irregularities on the part of his old adversary the broker Christopher Moran.

Dixey was well aware that his case was less than likely to be helped by the most recent available legislation, the Lloyd's Act of 1871.

The prospect of the new building for all its eccentricities shone like a lighthouse in the gathering gloom. Peter Green, now Deputy Chairman and strongly tipped to succeed Findlay, enjoyed nothing more than extolling its controversial qualities.

For a start the inside appeared to be on the outside, which confused many observers even in the looking glass world of Lime Street. The Room itself was intact but had become a vertical rather than horizontal space. Underwriters would be whisked heavenwards to their offices in lifts encased in glass tubes connected to the outside of the building. Save Britain's Heritage called it a costly and unnecessary folly. The Royal Fine Art Commission said it would be 'one of the most remarkable buildings of the decade.'

Most people who inspected the model expressed relief that it was not just another steel and glass box.

Blackmore and Green had wanted a 'world class building' and in Rogers' bold concept they had one that would push an image of Lloyd's to the forefront as never before. That image was ultra-modern, highly technological and indefatigably innovative; yet it rested on solid foundations. Green likewise would need all the credibility he could muster as Chairman and architect-elect of Lloyd's image for the new decade.

The Lutine Bell tolled for the loss of the giant ore carrier *Berge Vanga*, sister to the ship for whom the bell had tolled three years earlier. Peter Green's appointment as Chairman was confirmed and tribute was paid to his forceful public personality and long market experience. Here surely was the man who could maintain Lloyd's best traditions and at the same time unite underwriters and brokers in the face of pressure to change working practices.

Or as Green characteristically put it, 'It will appear to be incestuous,' speaking as an active underwriter playing down the power of the broker barons, on the board of one of which, Hogg Robinson, he also sat as a director, 'but you don't have to practise incest, even if you live with your mother and she's the only other person there.'

Green was guardedly in favour of a successor to the 1871 Lloyd's Act although he did not agree with the mandatory separation of brokers from managing agents; this would have obliged him among others to sell out of the broker of which his own company, Janson Green, was a subsidiary. As an active underwriter involved he was honest enough to be philosophical about the computer-leasing losses. He was in favour of the raising of the minimum wealth requirements for new members, a measure which was also implemented in 1979. This was to stem the flood of new members that in a shrinking market threatened Lloyd's with over-capacity. Henceforth new members had to show a minimum of £100,000 or £50,000 for 'mini-names.'

Yet there were so many ways in which this figure could be reached that access to Lloyd's was as easy as before to the middle-class professional with property and equity investments. The rising value of property in particular meant that a guarantee secured at the bank's discretion was often enough to pass the asset requirements. Lloyd's in turn did not require details of the assets behind the guarantee in question, which conveniently enabled it to maintain the illusion that it did not accept a person's house as a guarantee of solvency.

In a stable or rising market this was all very well, but many new Names were no longer afforded the protection against a stock market crash or property slump that had once been guaranteed by the £75,000 entry requirement – £750,000 by the standards of today. If they then belonged to syndicates that made a loss they were doubly hit by the decline in value of their principal assets and by Lloyd's cash calls.

This was the fuse of the time bomb that had started ticking with the shelving of Cromer. A series of catastrophes could easily light the fuse and once this had happened nobody would be able to put it out. The question was, would Fisher find and defuse the bomb in time?

In they came . . . tennis player Mark Cox and Air Vice Marshal Sir Nigel Maynard and Her Royal Highness the Princess Alexandra.

Richard Micklethwait had 400 acres of grazing and woodland and an ancestral house overlooking the Bristol Channel. Land values were rising and the cash-poor farmer had two friends who had done very well out of Posgate. Dominique Osborne was another new member; a banker friend of impeccable honesty recommended Lloyd's membership as a source of independent income and happened also to be a Name with Kingsley Underwriting Agencies.

Marjorie Walsh was a widow in indifferent health whose elderly friend thought highly of Lloyd's and insisted she join. She knew very little about Lloyd's and happily left her affairs in the hands of her members agent.

Bridget Milling was a young widow with children whose husband John Milling had been killed in a helicopter crash off the coast of Oman, a mysterious incident which later formed part of Sir Ranulph Fiennes' best-selling book *The Feather Men*. Mrs Milling knew little about financial affairs and was therefore grateful for the advice she received from David Bentata of Charterhouse Japhet.

Bentata had an old colleague from Charterhouse Japhet called Brian Bell, now one half of the Lloyd's members agent Cox and Bell.

Through the offices of Bentata and Bell this young widow with no job and two children was put up for membership of Lloyd's of London. With eight others she went through the Rota interview.

She had £80,000 in the world. 'Don't you worry your pretty head,' Bell told her, 'I'll look after you.'

Thus it was that, in the year when Lloyd's was increasing its members deposits and entry requirements, Bridget Milling was elected to Lloyd's and placed on the Oakeley Vaughan syndicates, on Secretan 367 and on Pulbrook 334.

In Fulham, a secretary earning £100 a week had sold her Notting Hill Gate flat to an employee of Peter Cameron-Webb. Letters continued to be sent to her old address and a number of them were opened by the new occupant. One was a bank statement showing she had recently received a modest sum of money – in fact it was a legacy from her father.

At her new flat in Fulham she was surprised to receive a letter from the Cameron-Webb agency inviting her to lunch. Intrigued, she accepted the invitation.

The Cameron-Webb organisation had prospered mightily under the umbrella of the broker baron J.H. Minet. The Cameron-Webb marine syndicates like 810, 840, 930 and 869 and the non-marine 918, 157 and 940 were the stars in the Cameron-Webb galaxy and to many brokers it was so important to have 'PCW 918' on their slips that they would sometimes queue for days on the little benches around the great Cameron-Webb box.

Nicky Samengo-Turner was a young broker with Howden whose family had a boat in the south of France. Samengo-Turner was used to life in 'The Hanging Gardens of Howden' and often saw the Grob yacht and the Howden corporate jet at Cap Ferrat. But even he was unaware of the scale of the Cameron-Webb lifestyle, until he went into a bar frequented by the yacht skippers at Cap Ferrat. 'Oh, you work at Lloyd's,' one of them said to him. 'You must know Mr Dixon and Mr Cameron-Webb . . .'

The Fulham secretary was impressed by the plush offices and the manners of the staff. She took it for granted that they were gentlemen. She did not know of course of the existence of the Cameron-Webb 'baby syndicates' 954, 988, 986, 893 and 138. These were the secret syndicates which for the past ten years and contrary to Lloyd's code of gentlemanly conduct had skimmed off the best business and the highest profits for Cameron-Webb, Dixon and a select group of members composed of their wives and senior staff. She did not know that the business was brought to the baby syndicates by an inner ring of brokers who were members of the baby syndicates in question.

She did not know of course that baby syndicate 954 alone had made £1,400,000 profits in 1979, £100,000 each of this going to Dixon and Cameron-Webb. She did not know of the work

Dixon did in his office behind those seemingly locked doors. She did not know that at the same time the external Cameron-Webb members were bearing the higher risks for lower profits. She did not know that membership of baby syndicates – insider dealing – was common among 'high fliers' and even Committee members of Lloyd's at Lime Street.

The Fulham secretary was impressed; but she had read in the papers about Sasse. She asked one question of the people who were least likely to give an impartial answer, the associates of Peter Cameron-Webb.

'What happens if I have losses?' she asked.

'Oh, no,' they said, 'that virtually never happens.'

Don't you worry your pretty head . . .

Then there were Betty Atkins and Sylvia Hatton.

Fenchurch Street, London, 1979

The firm of C. Rowbotham & Sons had started life as an insurance agency and shipping company. A few of the directors had become members of Lloyd's through the obvious marine connection. By 1979 operating from their offices in Fenchurch Street they had become a fully-fledged members agency.

Betty Atkins and Sylvia Hatton were secretaries. By 1979 Mrs Atkins had been with the firm for 25 years and Mrs Hatton was approaching retirement. Mrs Atkins had spent her whole working life at Rowbotham & Sons and lived with her husband in Greenwich. Mrs Hatton was a neat, petite person married to an East End coal merchant. He had come home and had a bath and then taken her out on his cart when they were courting.

The two secretaries earned modest salaries and had modest pension schemes. It is not hard to imagine their surprise, and delight, when their boss Mr R.A. 'Dick' Rowbotham invited them into his office.

'Betty,' he said, 'Sylvia, sit down, there's something I want to talk to you about . . .'

They had both done a wonderful job. The firm wanted to do something in recognition of their many years' service. They were going to make them members of Lloyd's.

Mrs Hatton was grateful and nonplussed. Mrs Atkins had the practical questions. She too had read about Sasse in the papers.

'What happens,' she asked, 'if I have losses?'

'Oh, no,' he said, 'we'll put you on the best syndicates. We'll take out stop loss too. The firm will see you all right . . .'

Mrs Atkins and Mrs Hatton were strongly given to understand that the firm would supply the necessary bank guarantee in order that they could meet the membership requirements; something neither woman could possibly have done by herself. Nor would either ever have contemplated joining Lloyd's had they not been given to understand that this was the arrangement. After all, if the agency was not going to vouch for them, it surely would not even have contemplated putting them into Lloyd's at all.

Mrs Atkins and Mrs Hatton thought about it and talked about it and there really was no one else outside the firm or in their circle of friends whom they could consult. After all, why did they need to consult anyone when they had so clearly earned this reward for so many years of service? This was how Mrs Atkins and Mrs Hatton thought of Mr Rowbotham's kind offer – as a reward.

So Betty Atkins and Sylvia Hatton became probably the lowest-paid working Names in Lloyd's history. Through her employer (and now her members agent) Betty Atkins was put on four syndicates: 463 McKay Forbes; 254 Marchant; and, the biggest prize of all, a £20,000 line on R.H.M. 'Dick' Outhwaite's syndicate 317/661.

Betty Atkins and Sylvia Hatton were very grateful to Mr Rowbotham; even though they both knew full well how loyally and how hard they had worked for him for so many, many years.

* * *

The Sasse saga was wound up with exactly the kind of public embarrassment Lloyd's had hoped to avoid. The Sasse members still lost an average of £80,000 each on one underwriting year alone, but their losses were even greater on the others. When Peter Green and the Committee offered a partial settlement they accepted and dropped their legal action.

Lady Middleton, a Sasse Name, was the prime mover in the group of external Names that became the Association of Lloyd's Members. She reserved a patrician contempt for Tim Sasse. 'I always wondered,' she said, 'why the bloody man had so many racehorses.'

But instead of accepting the Sasse saga as a lesson in failed self-regulation, one of the principal areas of the enquiry at that moment being conducted by Sir Henry Fisher, many insiders still seemed to reserve a similar contempt for the idea that the underwriting done at Lloyd's was any business of the people who made it possible: the members.

Ian Findlay spelled this out at the general meeting of members in November, 1980. 'Our experience of the problem of Syndicate 762 has revealed a number of misconceptions,' he announced to the assembled Names. 'It is no part of the Committee's function to intervene in matters of day to day underwriting judgement and it is not in members' interests that the Committee should do so. Indeed, were such a control to be imposed over the underwriter by the Committee or any other body, Lloyd's would . . . cease to keep its place among the leaders of the world's insurance markets. To those who work at Lloyd's all this is a truism. But these facts need emphasising to those many Names who have joined in recent years and who may not as yet fully appreciate how Lloyd's functions.'

After the Sasse disaster and the computer-leasing fiasco and a spate of air crashes, this was just what many members frightened by recent losses did not want to hear. Charles Sturge was one member who was not taken in by this patronising statement served up so blithely that the speaker himself was probably unaware of it. Sturge was an external Name but he was also a member of a Lloyd's dynasty; his managing agency was the family firm of R.W. Sturge.

Sturge had had a bright idea for making money for himself and all the external members; surely an idea in keeping with the spirit of the forthcoming Fisher Report. Sturge and his friend John Rew intended to research and publish a set of *Lloyd's League Tables*. Produced in conjunction with the new Association of Lloyd's Members these would analyse the annual performance of individual syndicates and form a valuable guide to new and existing members. To this end, Sturge began his researches, talking to syndicate managers in the market.

Sturge did not get very far before news of his activities reached the ears of his own managing agency. He was hauled in before them like a naughty schoolboy. They told him in no uncertain terms that if he persisted in this offensive activity he could expect to be dismissed from their syndicates.

Rew too experienced a similar reaction. 'We'll cut your throat,' said another leading player.

Sturge could not believe his ears. If this was the attitude of one of the biggest firms in the market, then it was clear to him that the need for the *League Tables* was all the more overdue. Sturge told the family firm what they could do with their syndicates. He took his underwriting business to another agent and continued his researches into the 1977 underwriting year, the results of which were then emerging. By the time he began research into the 1978 year he had the co-operation of over 100 syndicates in the market. The first edition of *Lloyd's League Tables* quickly sold out when it was published in the spring of 1981.

The Fisher Report, *Self-Regulation at Lloyd's*, found Lloyd's wanting in all aspects of self-regulation; as expected by many if not by the Chairman who had commissioned it.

Chief among Fisher's findings were the following:

- There should be a new Lloyd's Act.
- There should be a Council of Lloyd's which would pass bylaws and oversee regulation of the market.
- The brokers should divest themselves of their underwriting interests within the next five years.

'We have no doubt,' the Report said, 'that Lloyd's would be best served by a properly conducted system of self-regulation. Indeed we do not see how it could function in anything like its present form under any other system of regulation.'

Whether or not this meant Lloyd's should continue 'in its present form' Fisher did not say.

The new Chairman, Peter Green, and the Committee locked themselves up in the London Hilton for a weekend and worked out a response. Green had taken to his new role with his customary brio; at Lime Street the rear end of a stuffed racoon protruded from the wall above his desk, and a table presented the visitor with the backsides of a litter of toy piglets.

At the press conference Green declared that he was wholeheartedly in favour of the Fisher findings even though they were going to cost him a lot of time and money. Green also gave a copy of the Fisher Report to every member with a letter expressing the same views.

The Fisher Report was published, which was an improvement on Cromer, but in concentrating on the divestment question from the point of view of the market it paid little attention to the point of view of the 18,000 providers of the market's underwriting capital.

In spite of the fact that working members were only one fifth of the total membership, the Council would still contain twice as many working members as external members. New disciplinary procedures would be introduced and existing ones tightened up, but there was still no standard agreement as to the nature of the 'fiduciary duty' owed to Names by their members agencies. Paul Dixey would never take the Fisher Report down from the shelf and admire it in the same way as he had done with Cromer.

In they came ... Desmond O'Neill was a retired engineer with a small farm and a smaller house he had built for himself and his wife overlooking the beautiful Bay of Tralee in south-west Ireland. O'Neill liked to sit and watch the fishing boats return at dusk before he lit the fire and sat with his wife and chatted. He had had to obtain a bank guarantee on the house to meet the deposit and he had a diminishing retirement income, which his wife had worried about. O'Neill reassured her he was going into Lloyd's with the highly reputable members agent introduced to him by a friend in Dublin. The name of the agent was Robin Kingsley.

Dr John Mathias was a dentist who lived in a wealthy suburb of Boston, Massachusetts. Like Desmond O'Neill Dr Mathias liked fox hunting and one of his wealthier hunting friends told him about Lloyd's of London. The friend explained that in spite of the American tax laws there were still substantial gains to be made from membership; furthermore he too just happened to know a highly reputable members agent called Robin Kingsley.

Ken Lavery was a successful accountant living in Ottawa. 'I started out with zippo,' he said to himself, 'and I figure I am a pretty smart fellow.'

A couple of Lavery's friends told him how he could be even smarter. Lavery joined Lloyd's through the members agency of C.E. Heath, whose founder had done so much to secure the reputation of Lloyd's for fair dealing at home and abroad.

Lloyd's had a new Chairman, a new building on the way and a new set of rules by which it was going to regulate itself. From Eire, America, Canada and many other countries new members around the world looked forward to a greater prosperity in their lives courtesy of a unique financial institution with a 300-year-old history of honourable dealing. Lloyd's had finally got its act together. For the next couple of years it seemed from the outside at least that Lloyd's could do no wrong.

FOUR

PROFITS WITHOUT HONOUR

The new Lloyd's Act recommended by Sir Henry Fisher and accepted by Peter Green had to pass through both Houses of Parliament like any other bill. The trouble was that Lloyd's was not like any other institution.

For a start, 55 of its members were also Members of Parliament. These included Sir Marcus Kimball, the future Scottish Secretary Ian Lang, the future Northern Ireland Secretary Peter Brooke, the future Arts Minister Timothy Renton, Michael Jopling, who was Government Chief Whip and a Member of the Thatcher Cabinet, Bernard Weatherill, soon to be Speaker of the House of Commons, and the Leader of the House of Commons who was about to become Foreign Secretary, Francis Pym. Many others, like Lord Alexander, were in the House of Lords.

Then there were the terms of the bill. Crucial among these were the clauses to the effect that Lloyd's should regulate itself, that the brokers should sell their agency interests, and clause 11, which said that the members of the new Council should be immune from legal action.

This last clause was slipped in quietly and went unnoticed by many members – but not by Lady Middleton. She had been stung into action after the costly experience of the Sasse disaster and was determined that the clause should be changed. She had no confidence in the so-called 'fiduciary duty' of members agents on salaries which did not fluctuate with the fortunes of their members. She wanted to be able to sue Lloyd's if necessary for failure to look after the people who supplied its capital.

With the fledgling Association of Lloyd's Members she set about changing the bill. In this she acquired an unlikely ally in the form of a man of whom she had always thought less than favourably: Ian 'Goldfinger' Posgate.

Posgate's position was as ambiguous as that of Lady Middleton and the 55 MPs and members in the House of Lords. On the one hand he supported the proposed divestment of agencies from brokers, because he saw it as a way of removing the conflict of interests. On the other hand, he himself was trying to break away from Alexander Howden and set up on his own; a move he knew would be facilitated by the successful passage of the bill. Posgate also knew by then that all was not well within Howden: a fact that was not known outside Lloyd's and would have explosive consequences when it became public.

Thus an unlikely alliance was formed. Posgate and Malcolm Pearson, the broker who had been embroiled in the *Savonita* Fiat cars affair, put up £37,500 each to mount a petition against the bill. This was a lot of money but Posgate was rumoured to be the highest paid man in Britain and Pearson too was a wealthy man.

Lady Middleton and her external members lobbied Parliament and Lloyd's denigrated her as a madwoman who was simply trying to insure herself against unlimited liability. The MPs and peers tied themselves in knots over the ambiguity of their positions. Most people outside Lloyd's did not understand what all the fuss was about. Thus in the early months of 1981 the Lloyd's Bill went on its way.

Peter Green had no time for Lady Middleton and made this uncompromisingly plain whenever she turned up with her barrister Archie Hamilton at the Chairman's office at Lime Street. But Lady Middleton was not the only visitor who spelled trouble for Green in the early months of 1981. On 13 February he had a visit from Christopher Moran.

Moran was then in the middle of the disciplinary hearings brought under the 1871 Act by Paul Dixey's subcommittee. He was in deep trouble and he resented the fact. Five out of ten counts on which he was being charged would be thrown out and he persisted in maintaining that the other five offences were committed by many others in the market. His detractors later said that his action at this time was intended to deflect Lloyd's energies when he himself was under heavy fire.

Moran told Green and his Deputy Chairman Alec Higgins that he had evidence of irregularity at the Lloyd's brokers Oakeley Vaughan. He told them Oakeley Vaughan had been 'netting' premiums and claims on business underwritten 100% by Oakeley Vaughan aviation syndicate 862, a practice which was illegal at Lloyd's because it enabled agencies to exceed their permitted underwriting limits and conceal the true volume of premiums they were writing. This exposed syndicate members to serious danger in the event of losses. Moran handed over copies of various slips, a schedule, working papers and premium advice forms. He said they had been passed to him by a man called George Mountain.

Moran made a second secret visit to Higgins four days later. This time he handed over a slip placed by Oakeley Vaughan and underwritten 100% by Oakeley Vaughan non-marine syndicate 423. This slip also contained irregularities according to Moran. Higgins had no choice as to what to do. He telephoned Charles St George and requested his presence immediately.

St George had been diagnosed as having stomach cancer and given two years to live; as a racing man he knew the odds against his survival had been put at 16 to 1. He also knew George Mountain. Mountain had been an employee of Oakeley Vaughan with a serious drink problem. St George had tried to straighten him out and failed. Mountain had left Oakeley Vaughan to work for Christopher Moran.

Higgins stared at St George across his Deputy Chairman's

desk. 'Charles,' he said, 'your men have been overwriting. It's got to stop.'

St George returned to Oakeley Vaughan's Fetter Lane offices and discovered that his underwriter Barry Bowen had indeed been writing on the back of the Central Fund.

The Deputy Chairman then called him in again. 'Charles,' he said, 'I'm afraid it's gone further. Some of your files have got into the hands of the *Financial Times*.'

This was bad news. The *Financial Times*' John Moore was an ambitious journalist and would become the bane of Lime Street. With the press already alerted to the row over the bill and Oakeley Vaughan stories beginning to appear, Green and Higgins had no choice but to institute an enquiry. The man they chose to lead it was the veteran Lloyd's underwriter Henry Chester.

While Chester proceeded in strictest secrecy, the press stories were causing the Oakeley Vaughan members some alarm. It was no doubt to allay their fears that they received a letter dated 6 March 1981 from Mark St George:

> Syndicate 862
> You may have become aware of some recent publicity
> with regard to one of the syndicates managed by us and
> as featured in two daily newspapers . . .
> The Committee of Lloyd's, in the interest of its
> Members and the Lloyd's community, investigates any
> formal complaint and/or any matter which it feels could
> potentially give rise to concern. As such in a market the size
> of Lloyd's enquiries of this nature are not unusual . . .
> . . . if there is an issue to be answered, it is of a purely
> technical nature . . .
> We would conclude by stating that we would consider
> all the syndicates under our management are progressing
> satisfactorily relative to the Market conditions . . .

In fact this letter was highly unusual. First, it was amended and approved by Lloyd's before it was sent out. Second, it was far from common to have what was now a formal enquiry. Third, Lloyd's already knew that the Oakeley Vaughan syndicates were not progressing satisfactorily.

But the members who received this letter, half of whom lived abroad, were not to know. It was at this stage, with Charles St George in hospital, that Mark St George's uncle Edward once again came into the picture.

Edward St George had continued his quiet ascent to power and influence in the Bahamas. Like him, his wife Lady Henrietta was a name on the Oakeley Vaughan syndicates. St George and the Grand Bahama Port Authority were also investing in hundreds of thousands of dollars of 'loans' to the Bahamian Prime Minister Sir Lynden Pindling.

The loans were said to be for the purposes of creating housing and employment but were spent by Pindling and never repaid. Pindling's Progressive Liberal Party (PLP) continued to support the Grand Bahama Port Authority.

St George's senior associate 'Union' Jack Hayward had always been thought of as the majority partner in the Port Authority; rumours were circulating in the Bahamas that this was no longer so. But St George was a charming and witty host at home at Greening Glades and Lady Henrietta was a devoted patron of the Grand Bahama Children's Home. St George would always stand up for Pindling. 'He's the best Prime Minister the Bahamas could have,' he liked to say.

He was similarly loyal to his brother. He had a special telephone at which he had only to shout 'Charles!' and it dialled Charles St George's number. Early in 1981 the telephone was used with increasing regularity, when Charles St George became ill and the Chester inquiry into Oakeley Vaughan began. At this point Edward St George flew to Britain.

The Chester team met on nineteen occasions and asked numerous uncomfortable questions of the key players: these included Charles St George, James St George, the Deputy Managing Director Michael Whitelock and the underwriter of syndicates 862 and 432, Barry Bowen.

Charles St George, Chester concluded, had been misguided in leaving so much of the day-to-day running of the company to James St George and Michael Whitelock. James St George had been aware that the company accounts were not entirely accurate. Whitelock 'conducted his business in whatever way suited him best without regard to the proper operation of Lloyd's procedures', and a man of his market experience should have known better. Bowen, Chester decided, was also a party to net accounting and did not make proper disclosure to the auditors.

The collective conclusions of the Chester Report were a damning indictment of mismanagement, breach of directors' duties and account-juggling on a scale embarrassing both to Oakeley Vaughan and to Lloyd's in this crucial year.

But the Chester inquiry was only one of three attempts to unravel the affairs of the Oakeley Vaughan syndicates and broking company.

Bob Bishop, a former City of London Fraud Squad officer, was appointed to investigate a flow of bad marine insurance business from America via Uniguard, a joint-venture company 49% owned by Oakeley Vaughan. Bishop reported confidentially in April 1981.

After Chester had also reported unfavourably and revealed further areas of concern beyond its remit, Ken Randall and Jim Morris were commissioned to investigate those areas of Oakeley Vaughan on a 'semi-informal basis.' These were specifically the overstatement of profits for past years and the means by which this was done. A detailed questionnaire was prepared by Lloyd's and Oakeley Vaughan was invited 'to provide comprehensive answers.'

Ken Randall was a trained accountant and Head of Lloyd's

Regulatory Services. The Randall & Morris Report, like Chester and Bishop, made interesting reading; or would have done, had anyone been able to obtain a copy:

> 'In complying with Mr St George's wish not to send in an investigation team to inspect the books of the company, it has not been possible to investigate these matters at first hand; much reliance has been placed on information supplied by Mr Edward St George and his staff . . .
> 'Mr St George . . . added that there had been "lots of misdemeanours and he had little doubt he could dig up a lot more . . ."
> 'On several occasions . . . he has expressed the view that the profits of the company had been overstated (Mr Edward St George has said, "We plead guilty and throw ourselves on the Court's mercy").

'I will now be most interested to hear the outcome of your own enquiry,' St George wrote to Peter Green in July 1982, 'and feel that in all probability your Committee's conclusions will coincide with mine.'

While Bishop, Chester and Randall and Morris had pursued their inquiries, Edward St George had indeed conducted his own investigation into the company of whose broking arm he had been a director for some years and of which he was temporarily Chairman. He had come to a swift and drastic conclusion. The sooner the company was sold, the better.

Unfortunately for him the disciplinary process, however well deserved, was getting in the way. Whitelock, Bowen and James St George were suspended by Lloyd's for two years. Green then informed Charles St George that he too would have to face disciplinary action. Edward St George meanwhile had found a prospective buyer who was keen to make Charles St George Chairman of the joint company, and now Lloyd's was rocking the boat.

Edward St George recommended a compromise: Peter Green would 'privately reprimand' his brother. His brother disagreed with the terms of the sale and did not like this at all. When the prospective buyer backed out, pleading lack of funds, Charles St George, having beaten the odds of 16 to 1 against his survival, went back to Lloyd's and managed to have Oakeley Vaughan rehabilitated under the supervision of Colin Yellop, an underwriter whom Lloyd's regarded as a benign influence. Edward St George flew back to the Bahamas.

The Oakeley Vaughan mess was swept under the Committee Room carpet and the syndicate members kept in ignorance of the time bomb that was ticking away. Lester Piggott, Henry Cooper, Jarvis Astaire, Wilfred Sherman, Lord Alexander, Jim Stone, Jay D. Hirsch, John Attridge, Edward Molesworth, Bridget Milling and many others went on underwriting. Not only that but more sheep ripe for shearing would find their way into the fold. Like much of Cromer, the Bishop, Chester and Randall & Morris reports went unpublished and unread by the people who most needed to know their conclusions.

The suppression of the evidence by the Lloyd's authorities and the participation of such colourful and controversial figures as Peter Green, Charles St George, Edward St George and Christopher Moran ensured that the spectre of Oakeley Vaughan would come back to haunt Lloyd's with the same certainty as the disaster which was to be visited upon the Oakeley Vaughan members.

During the time he was busy with Oakeley Vaughan and the St Georges, Peter Green was also much concerned with the affairs of his contemporary and old rival Peter Cameron-Webb.

Cameron-Webb had expressed a sudden desire to resign from Lloyd's and retire to Switzerland. There were standard procedures to enable a member to resign, but Cameron-Webb seemed to be in something of a hurry; he was ever a man for the broad brush rather than the fine detail.

Cameron-Webb resigned and Peter Dixon, Cameron-Webb's partner, remained as a principal director of the PCW companies. Apart from the fact that they had all become working members of Lloyd's in the immediate post-war years, a complex network of business relationships had enveloped Peter Cameron-Webb, Peter Dixon and Peter Green since their days together around the Janson Green underwriting box. Dixon was also the Green family accountant. All these things and many more would be noticed and taken into account after Peter Cameron-Webb flew to Switzerland in January 1982.

In they came ... David Becker was an architect introduced to Charles St George by 'the sporting baronet' Sir William Piggott-Brown. St George took Becker to lunch at the Savoy Grill and afterwards to Lloyd's, and the far from wealthy architect was impressed by what he saw. Andrina Colquhoun was a former girlfriend of the missing Lord Lucan and friend of Jeffrey Archer, whose literary career was now in the ascendant and who had done so well out of Ian Posgate. Susan Hampshire, star of *The Forsyte Saga*, was one of Britain's favourite television actresses, and had recently married Eddie Kulukundis: 'I'm not going to give you housekeeping money,' he told his new wife, 'I'm going to make you a member of Lloyd's.'

Rupert Hambro was Deputy Chairman of the family bank and sat on the board of a company whose Chairman was a working Name and extolled the advantages of Lloyd's membership. Hambro knew little about how Lloyd's worked but trusted his members agent; like Betty Atkins he was told how lucky he was to be placed on Dick Outhwaite's syndicate 317/661.

Dr Gavan Griffith was a rising star on the Australian legal circuit. Elizabeth Harker joined through Wing Commander Eustace 'Gus' Holden DFC, an RAF colleague of her husband and close friend of Robin Kingsley, through whose agency she became a member. She lived far away in Taupo, New Zealand, and relied on her members agent all the more to look after her interests. Then there was Dale Jenkins.

Tuxedo Park, New York State, 1981

Tuxedo Park is a pretty village of a few hundred people in a rural setting. There is a lake and one of only eight real tennis courts in America. A cross-section of folk live in Tuxedo Park. There are the rich, and the not so rich: the Chairman of First Boston and the partners in law firms, and the lady who hangs wallpaper to make a bit of extra money.

Dale Jenkins and his family lived in an average-sized house and planned to stay there – the view was beautiful and the air was clean after New York City. When he received a mailing about membership of Lloyd's, Jenkins was curious and not a little flattered. The returns looked good – some syndicates would achieve up to 20% in a good year and total returns could be between 8% and 10%. A shrewd man of much experience in the corporate world, Jenkins also wanted to know more about the downside of such an apparently attractive investment.

Kingsley Underwriting Agencies appreciated Jenkins' concern before he made a commitment. 'A syndicate is only as good as its reinsurance,' they told him, and added that the syndicates on which they placed their names always adequately reinsured their insurance risks. Kingsley also stressed that members were placed on a wide spread of syndicates in order to minimise the risks. Jenkins was right of course to ask about unlimited liability, and Kingsley spelled out the implications. But no one Jenkins knew in America had ever had a cash call, let alone lost their cufflinks.

Jenkins was sold on the idea, which is why, in the autumn of that year, he too was elected a member of Lloyd's.

*   *   *

As the Lloyd's Bill made its slow and controversial progress through Parliament early in 1982 it became clear to Peter Green that he was going to need all his famous powers of toughness and diplomacy to pull this one off.

Not only were Ian Posgate, Malcolm Pearson and Lady Middleton cluttering up the stage with their unholy alliance, they had been joined by the unprepossessing spectacle of Ron Comery and Kenneth Grob. Posgate and Pearson wanted divestment and Lady Middleton wanted to throw out Clause 11 and be able to sue the new Council of Lloyd's where necessary. As leading broker barons, Grob and Comery wanted to keep the right of brokers to own managing and members agencies – a system under which they had prospered greatly and the abolition of which was a central plank of the Fisher Report.

Worse still for Green, Posgate had managed to be elected to the Committee of Lloyd's, the body which had suspended him ten years earlier. The sight of 'Goldfinger' piously preaching divestment among the second-generation establishment whom he so despised was almost too much for some of them to bear.

As Posgate's status grew in the politics and the market of Lime Street, so did his desire to leave Alexander Howden. He had the loyalty of his syndicate members and he saw no reason why he should share the profits with people whom he no longer trusted. This was in spite of the fact that they had originally been cast in the role of minders and he was the delinquent.

This was also complicated by the fact that in January 1982 Alexander & Alexander suddenly bought the Hanging Gardens of Howden for $300 million. Posgate was not consulted and two months later he resigned from the Howden board.

For $300 million, Alexander & Alexander might have delayed signing the deal until after they had carried out a thorough audit. But they did not do so, and, although this would cause pain to all concerned, the likelihood is that a pre-takeover audit of Alexander Howden would not only have changed the mind of Alexander &

Alexander. It would also have blown the Lloyd's Bill clear out of the water.

While Alexander & Alexander carried out their audit Posgate, Pearson, Lady Middleton, Grob and Comery continued their various assaults on MPs at Westminster. Many of those bemused by the ramifications of the proposed bill were also Lloyd's members. The issue of how outsiders might help regulate such an apparently arcane market-place conveniently obscured the question as to why such external regulation might be necessary.

But the divestment issue was so straightforward, particularly to Labour MPs such as Michael Meacher bent on exposing conflicts of interest in the City of London. Posgate and Pearson were so effective in their representations to Parliament, that the proposal for divestment of underwriting agency ownership by brokers carried the day.

Lady Middleton and her small band of external Names failed in their attempts to rescind Clause 11 and the Council of Lloyd's became immune to legal action from members. The burden of regulation fell largely on the people who were major players in the market.

Even then there were problems appropriate to the enacting of a bill concerning such a unique institution. Equally appropriate were some of the bizarre solutions. Sir Marcus Kimball, who had joined as an external member in 1953 and received a lecture on hound breeding, was a noted figure in hunting, shooting and fishing circles as well as a Member of Parliament. When it came to the vote, Kimball mobilised the many MPs and Names at Lloyd's who were members of the British Field Sports Society. The Lloyd's Act received the royal assent on 23 July 1982.

In keeping with the peculiar goings-on behind the scenes at Westminster, and in the light of the failed attempts to rescind Clause 11, a number of interesting meetings took place elsewhere during this time. The first of these concerned the recently-retired Peter Cameron-Webb.

Among the many Cameron-Webb enterprises was the reinsurance of part of the PCW marine syndicate through a brokers called Seascope and then a second company called Unimar which was registered in Monaco. Rumours were going round the market that the commission from the reinsurances in question had not only been above the normal rate but also that it had been diverted at Cameron-Webb's instigation from the syndicate members to a bank in Switzerland. Since Cameron-Webb had resigned from Lloyd's and also gone to Switzerland he was unavailable for comment.

Seascope and Unimar were closely connected, and a key player in the setting up of Unimar and the broking of these reinsurances was a director of Seascope, David D'Ambrumenil. D'Ambrumenil was a big Name on the PCW syndicates as well as a Cameron-Webb broker. The son of a past Chairman, he had known Cameron-Webb and Green for years and was a prominent part of what passed for a Lloyd's ruling establishment. He was surprised to be summoned to the current Chairman's office.

D'Ambrumenil was further disturbed when he saw a clerk sitting there ready to record their conversation.

'Do we have to have him here?' he asked.

'Yes,' said Green, 'I'm afraid we do.'

D'Ambrumenil explained how the Seascope-Unimar enterprise worked – or, rather, how it did not work, since it had not generated the amount of medium risk marine business he and Cameron-Webb had expected. According to D'Ambrumenil Unimar had however generated some income which had not been spent and which Cameron-Webb had been told was available to be refunded any time he liked. Cameron-Webb had apparently suggested they go on trying to implement the arrangement.

'Look,' said D'Ambrumenil to Green, '*can* we have an off the record chat?'

Green agreed and the clerk was sent away. The meeting was

over. A few days later Green called at D'Ambrumenil's house in Chelsea.

'You know me,' D'Ambrumenil told him, 'you know the banker involved in setting up Unimar. We may be stupid at times but we are honourable.'

'I know,' Green replied, 'but I have to say it was a pretty stupid idea.'

D'Ambrumenil was glad they had had this off the record chat. To him Unimar was a business venture which had simply not worked out. Green too recorded the verdict that 'there was no dishonesty on the part of anyone connected with the transactions.'

D'Ambrumenil had regard for Green as Chairman and a man of the market. Green likewise accepted the word of D'Ambrumenil as someone he had known for many years. Unusual though it may appear for a Chairman of Lloyd's single-handedly to have conducted his own private enquiry into two long-standing colleagues from the market, neither Green nor D'Ambrumenil gave the matter a second thought. Nor did they question the role of Cameron-Webb.

The second interesting meeting took place at Leeds Castle, a favourite Lloyd's venue, and concerned asbestosis – or, more specifically, the awards this created in American courts and the insurance claims that were likely to arise from it in the next few years.

A San Francisco attorney, Peter Keen, had already expounded on this subject to Lloyd's non-marine association. 'You guys,' he said, 'had better wake up. Asbestosis is going to be the most diabolical thing that has ever hit the insurance industry.'

Asbestosis risks were traditionally underwritten as 'long tail' business at Lloyd's. An asbestosis claim might not come in for many years, during which time the risk underwritten would generate handsome premiums. The tactic of the active underwriter was to reserve heavily, take out adequate reinsurance and hope by the time the claims came in to be safely out of the way.

Keen reported to Lloyd's that asbestosis claims were running at 400 a month and could reach 50,000 by the end of the decade. A new US arrangement, the Wellington Agreement, was to be put in place to settle these claims on a less complicated basis. This and the changes in US Tort Law meant that henceforth they would be settled more quickly and on a big scale; a piece of information of burning importance to any asbestosis risk underwriter.

At the Leeds Castle meeting the asbestos committee, including Ted Nelson, a leading underwriter of American non-marine reinsurance business, and Deputy Chairman Murray Lawrence, also a leading non-marine underwriter, considered the implications of Keen's information. As underwriters of long-tail business and, in the case of Lawrence, as a director of Bowrings, the big broker, they were also directly concerned as players in the market. Nor were they the only players who stood to win – or lose – a fortune according to how they reacted to the latest information.

But Lloyd's was about broking and underwriting and there was no way the asbestosis business already broked and underwritten could be withdrawn from the market. The only course of action for an underwriter was to 'run off' his asbestosis business with another underwriter who, for the right money, was willing to take the risk.

Thus it was not as Deputy Chairman, or as a member of the asbestos committee, but as an active underwriter that Lawrence arranged for his asbestosis business to be run off through Bowrings with the syndicates 317/661 of Richard 'Dick' Outhwaite. Nor was Lawrence the only underwriter to do so; a total of twenty syndicates paid Outhwaite millions of pounds to take on a total of 80% of the asbestosis business in the market. The other 20% was run off by syndicates such as Pulbrook 90/334 onto the likes of Outhwaite's long-standing rival Stephen Merrett's 418.

To Outhwaite and to a far lesser degree to Merrett, neither of whom were on the asbestos committee or at the Leeds Castle meeting, the asbestosis run-offs represented a handsome slice of business to add to their already very successful syndicates. Both men subscribed to the maxim of 'Lead, Follow or Get Out of the Way.' There was no room at the top of Lloyd's for anyone but leaders.

Everyone respected Dick Outhwaite and the clamour by out-side members to be placed on his syndicates 317/61 was unabated. The outside members did not know what sort of business he was underwriting, nor was it part of the ethos of Lloyd's that they should do so. All the outside members knew was that Outhwaite's syndicates made money and that Outhwaite was no soft touch for a broker. If Dick Outhwaite took a risk, which was what he was there to do, he did so on the basis of considerable experience; and of course on the best available information at the time.

The third interesting meeting concerned Charles St George and Oakeley Vaughan.

Having beaten the odds of 16 to 1 against his survival St George was displeased to be hauled into the Deputy Chairman's office at Lime Street. Under the terms of his private reprimand St George was already under pressure from Lloyd's to walk away from the Oakeley Vaughan business. Murray Lawrence, the Deputy Chair-man, had further bad news: the underwriting had yet again gone beyond acceptable levels. St George's response was immediate: he said he was going to close down the business.

St George returned to the Oakeley Vaughan offices in Fetter Lane and announced his decision to the staff. These no longer of course included James St George, Barry Bowen or Michael Whitelock, all of whom had been suspended. Nor did they include the unfortunate George Mountain, who had returned to the employ of Christopher Moran. Moran in turn had been thrown out of Lloyd's forever: 'Lloyd's is like the loose thread in a sweater,' he said, 'you pull it and the whole thing starts to unravel.'

Undaunted, Moran married a former beauty queen and bought

50,000 acres of Scottish mountain and grouse moor. But he could no longer park his Rolls-Royce outside the main entrance of Lloyd's and irritate the Chairman. His wife was photographed with a pet deer, and the joke at Lloyd's went that her husband had other plans for it. 'Do you know what they call that deer?' they said. 'They call it Dixey.'

Charles St George received a telephone call from Richard Bowes of Willis Faber. Bowes had heard he was in a spot of bother. He suggested salvation might lie in the person of one Robert Napier. Napier, said Bowes, was just the man to sort out Oakeley Vaughan.

St George went back to Murray Lawrence with the proposal. Lawrence was surprised. But while St George was in the Deputy Chairman's office the buzzer went and Lawrence excused himself for a moment.

He reappeared having spoken to Peter Green. 'Yes, Charles,' he said, 'Napier is a splendid fellow. He sounds like just the man.'

St George was initially surprised at this change of heart. But he was relieved. Closing down the business would have meant 'running off' the syndicates until all the claims were exhausted and then shutting them down, and that would have meant bad publicity. St George knew that the Lloyd's view was that all publicity was bad publicity unless it was controlled by Lime Street. St George – and Lloyd's – had had enough bad publicity over Oakeley Vaughan already.

St George sold Oakeley Vaughan to Robert Napier for the tellingly small sum of £1,000. The Oakeley Vaughan members, still ignorant of the Bishop, Chester and Randall & Morris reports, as Lloyd's refused to allow their publication, received a letter from Charles St George telling them that the Oakeley Vaughan syndicates were being transferred to Robert Napier as a result of divestment under the 1982 Lloyd's Act.

There were exceptions however. Edward St George cut down

his underwriting on Oakeley Vaughan and concentrated on another set of syndicates run by an underwriter for whom the market had the highest regard. Other Oakeley Vaughan Names were also on the syndicates in question. Like Edward St George, his wife Lady Henrietta and his brother Charles, Lord Alexander, Wilfred Sherman and Edward Molesworth were all pinning their hopes on Dick Outhwaite's syndicates 317/661.

To the outside world these meetings were invisible and it was felt essential that they be so. This was not just because they were considered to be none of the outside world's business, although it was undoubtedly in keeping with the ethos of Lloyd's that, in spite of the Sasse disaster, the lids on Cameron-Webb, Unimar, asbestosis and Oakeley Vaughan should be kept tightly shut. The passage of the 1982 Act may have given Lloyd's immunity from suit but not from scandal. The ink was barely dry on divestment and on the new self-regulatory procedures and the Council that had been proposed by Fisher, enacted by Parliament and entrusted to the recently-knighted Sir Peter Green.

Green had fought as hard for the bill as he had fought against it, once he accepted it was inevitable. He had been knighted for his efforts and he was a wealthy man at the height of his career. His name was synonymous both with the business of underwriting and the reputation of the market within which he was a major player. Just as he stood to gain more than most, if anyone stood to lose by the failure of that market to work on the terms it had set itself, he did. Sir Peter Green was all the more disturbed therefore to learn just as the act received the royal assent that everything was far from wonderful in the 'Hanging Gardens of Howden.' Alexander & Alexander had at last carried out their audit.

What Alexander & Alexander and their auditors discovered in Alexander Howden was no less than a multi-million-pound hole in the group's complex and considerable finances. Grob and

Comery and their associates Page and Carpenter – now dubbed 'the Gang of Four' – had been secretly arranging reinsurances with offshore companies which just happened to be owned by Grob, Comery, Page and Carpenter. One of these companies, Southern International Re (as in Reinsurance), had then purchased a Swiss bank called Banque du Rhône et de la Tamise. Opulent houses, Impressionist paintings and preferential loans had also been purchased and arranged in this way.

None of these transactions had been reported to the underwriting members of Howden or anyone else for that matter. The auditors for Howden's new American owners were talking of sums of up to $55 million missing from their $300 million purchase.

The news could not be contained and at Lime Street it caused a sensation. Many simply could not or would not believe that plunder could have taken place on such a cynical and sizeable scale. 'I am absolutely utterly amazed and dumbfounded that these allegations have been made' was the verdict of David Coleridge of R.W. Sturge; a response he was to repeat ten years later to some critics of Lloyd's when he was Chairman.

Alexander & Alexander wanted the missing money. The Gang of Four were eased out and Posgate was not only fired from Howdens, but also suspended from the Committee of Lloyd's and forbidden from working in the market. This time his career would never fully recover. The delinquent who had rehabilitated himself was brought down by his association with the very men who were meant to secure his wellbeing.

Posgate was underwriting for over 5,000 members and while he and his names protested his innocence the downfall of 'Goldfinger' caused a sensation in the press. His syndicates were taken over and many members were encouraged to leave and join other syndicates; such as those of Richard Outhwaite.

After the Securities and Exchange Commission had reported, the Department of Trade stepped in, closely followed by the City of London Fraud Squad. The press were now shooting pieces off Lloyd's in all directions. Worse was to come for Sir Peter Green. He was soon to be faced with the fact that the trail of fraud, theft and falsehood, that led to and from Grob and his cohorts, also led to Peter Cameron-Webb.

Cameron-Webb's resignation, achieved with Sir Peter Green's permission, had placed him beyond Lloyd's disciplinary procedures. How much Green knew then of what was to be made public as a result of the Howden disclosures it was impossible to gauge; no comment would be forthcoming from either Green or Cameron-Webb.

The Alexander & Alexander investigations revealed the connections between Howden and Cameron-Webb's parent group, the broker baron J.H. Minet. They further revealed that Cameron-Webb and Dixon had owned a share in the Banque du Rhône et de la Tamise, and that low-risk, high-profit reinsurance premiums from syndicates run by Cameron-Webb and Dixon had been diverted to companies owned by the two men in the Isle of Man, Guernsey and Gibraltar.

The sums of money were staggering; over the past few years a total of £40 million had been withheld from PCW syndicate members in this way. Worse, the PCW non-marine underwriters had written such unprofitable business that their losses were thought likely to exceed any monies recovered from the offshore companies. When Dixon heard of the Alexander & Alexander discoveries he immediately announced his resignation and secretly made arrangements to flee Britain: 'He was always very polite,' said Dixon's expensive private dentist, 'but I knew he was a crook the moment he sent me his Philipino servants. They could have had treatment just as easily for no cost on the National Health . . . except that they were illegal immigrants.'

The Department of Trade promptly announced an enquiry into J.H. Minet. A short while later the Chairman of Minet, John Wallrock, a highly respected figure, stunned an already shaken market by resigning after it was revealed that he too had had a $2 million interest in the secret PCW reinsurance companies.

But there was an unpleasant twist to all this for Sir Peter Green. Only a year earlier he had pronounced Cameron-Webb innocent after his own private inquiry into Unimar. Now he was faced with the fact that Cameron-Webb was guilty of stealing members' funds on an epic scale. Furthermore, the vehicle used to do so was one which Sir Peter himself had used: the offshore reinsurance scheme.

This was a means by which an underwriter could reinsure risks accepted by his own syndicates through offshore tax haven companies in which he also had a personal shareholding. The capital growth on these holdings, even when the interest was paid back to the members, was still considerable.

Cameron-Webb and Dixon had done this via a number of companies and on a huge scale, without even bothering to pay their members the interest. Sir Peter Green too had a personal shareholding in a Cayman Islands company called Imperial, which his father Toby Green had founded many years earlier in the Bahamas. Sir Peter felt impelled to explain that he had tried and failed to find a buyer for his shareholding when he became Chairman of Lloyd's; as a result of which he still stood to benefit.

Sir Peter Green should have been basking in the afterglow of the Lloyd's Act. Instead, in an overheating climate, voices were suggesting that his own involvement in reinsurance and offshore tax havens had led him to tread softly and look none too carefully when it came to investigating the affairs of Peter Cameron-Webb.

What other secret connections, they asked, existed between the two men? Just when Green might have hoped this question would remain unanswered, the reply came all too publicly. He was among the members of a baby syndicate run by Peter Cameron-Webb.

The Brooks and Dooley affair was the final straw for Green in what had become a terrible year. The underwriters of marine syndicate 89, Raymond Brooks and Terence Dooley, were also discovered to be the controllers of a reinsurance company called Fidentia based in Bermuda. £6.2 million of syndicate money had been diverted this way.

'Fidentia' was a reassuring word that meant 'faithfulness'. Brooks and Dooley took it to mean that they could purchase property in Cyprus and indulge in other unsuccessful speculative ventures at the expense of their syndicate members. They were unable to refuse an invitation to make amends by a committee of disgruntled Names, which included members of the legal profession.

But the Brooks and Dooley affair was small beer compared with Cameron-Webb and Howden, and the stories of the members' missing millions became front-page news. No sooner, it seemed, had Parliament allowed Lloyd's to regulate itself, than Lloyd's was showing itself manifestly unfit to do so.

Kenneth Grob, Ron Comery, John Wallrock and Ian Posgate had all testified in the Parliamentary hearings. They were now known to have done so in the knowledge that they were directly or indirectly involved in wrongdoing on a massive scale.

The MPs who had voted against (and in many cases for) the Lloyd's Bill felt angry and deceived. The Howden audit alone was enough for them to start talking about repealing the act before the gentlemen of Lloyd's did any more damage to the reputation of Parliament.

Green, meanwhile, was assembling a working party after the Cameron-Webb and Howden scandals had revealed defects in the auditing arrangements. He wanted a chairman for the working party who could show the role accountants had played in enabling the crooked practices to take place and in condoning dubious tax arrangements.

More specifically he wanted an accountant capable of tracking down the tricks of other accountants, and, the bigger the tricks, the better an accountant he had to be.

Ian Hay Davison had been Managing Partner of Arthur Andersen & Co., one of the biggest accountancy firms in the world. As a Department of Trade inspector he had detailed experience of investigating fraud. Davison was a highly intelligent self-made man and an accomplished public performer who knew how to talk to the press.

In November 1982 he was on business in New York. After a game of squash at the University Club on Fifth Avenue he was taking a shower when he heard the telephone. The Chairman of Lloyd's wanted to know if he would run the working party.

Davison agreed to do so and returned to London shortly afterwards. He soon discovered that Lloyd's had no standardised accounting procedures and syndicate accounts contained little or no useful information. Baby syndicates, though theoretically contrary to the regulations, in practice were all too easily run for the enrichment of insiders.

One of the Davison working party's first recommendations was that syndicate accounts should contain full details of reinsurances and of the ability of reinsurers to meet liabilities. Reinsurances themselves would be controlled and there should be a code of accounting methods.

The Committee of Lloyd's did not like this. One member said they 'were inappropriate since they would lead to members being overburdened with too much potentially confusing information.'

Don't you worry your pretty head . . .

Davison and his working party persevered, in spite of these ominous signals from the Committee. Thus it was, in the dying days of the year, that Ian Hay Davison received another telephone call. This time it was from the Governor of the Bank of England.

FIVE

THE HERALDS
OF FREE ENTERPRISE

First Cromer, then Fisher, then Richardson. In a little over a decade three distinguished men, two of them Governors of the Bank of England, had become involved in attempts to regulate the affairs of Lloyd's of London.

Gordon Richardson was the latest in this distinguished line. Richardson had supported Ian Hay Davison when the latter was made Chairman of the Accounting Standards Committee; Davison owed him a favour.

Richardson and Davison sat in the Governor's office at the Bank of England in Threadneedle Street. The Governor came straight to the point. Davison was obviously making progress with his working party. Had he considered applying for the position of Lloyd's new Chief Executive?

Davison said he had not considered this. 'I am not a member of Lloyd's, for a start,' he said.

'That's a qualification,' said the Governor.

'But I don't know anything about Lloyd's,' said Davison.

'That's another qualification.'

Davison considered this.

'I'm not asking for a life sentence,' the Governor told him. 'Three to five years will do. After that,' he looked at Davison, 'all sorts of things will be possible for you.'

Davison left the Governor's office telling himself he would not make up his mind until he had considered the matter over

Christmas. But he already knew the answer in his mind. The Governor of the Bank of England was a persuasive man.

The newly-formed Council of Lloyd's met early in 1983.

Davison's appointment, on his own terms, was presented to them by Sir Peter Green as a *fait accompli*. Some Council members were horrified at this. They immediately set up their own committee to 'interview' Davison for themselves.

It was a futile gesture. Sir Peter Green was more aware than any of them that the new Chief Executive had been imposed on Lloyd's by the Governor of the Bank of England. The Governor had intervened and appointed Davison as a condition of Parliament not repealing the 1982 Lloyd's Act.

Green had fought tooth and nail against the appointment; but he was a realist and made it plain he would support the new man all the way: 'You came like Daniel into the lion's den . . .' he wrote to Davison later.

Davison was concerned that there was no precedent for his role except that of Secretary to the Committee, a comparatively lowly post. As Chief Executive he would be seen as being on the wrong side of the green baize door. Although it was 1983 in the rest of the world, at Lloyd's these class distinctions still counted.

Davison wanted to be Deputy Chairman and Chief Executive.

Some Council members resisted this but Green seized on the point: 'Absolutely right,' he said, and looked around at the others present, 'and the trouble is too, this term "Chief Executive." It's an Americanism; we don't understand it in England . . .' there was amusement at this, 'but I think this may be the solution. We do have two Deputy Chairmen . . .

'The Deputy Chairman,' Green went on, 'is a well-established position. Everyone respects a Deputy Chairman; we all know what he does and what he stands for. I think if Ian is to have any respect in the market we should call him Deputy Chairman and Chief Executive.'

This was music to Davison's ears. There was no doubt in

his mind that this was a platform from which he could launch the reforms proposed by Sir Henry Fisher. The decision was eventually ratified by the Council and Ian Hay Davison became Lloyd's first ever Deputy Chairman and Chief Executive.

Some Council members still differed as to what this meant. Peter Miller, a successful broker, believed Davison's first duty was to the external members and told him as much. Others saw in Davison an accountant who had no experience of the cut and thrust politics of Lime Street. Others saw a possible conflict of interests between his role as Deputy Chairman and as externally-appointed regulator.

At least one Council member had a vision of an elephant trap. There were bamboo spikes at the bottom and Davison had fallen straight into it. But Sir Peter Green was supportive of the new man and, as long as this was the case, all might be well.

Davison had to send signals to the press as well as to the market. One of his first declared aims was to ensure disclosure of the interests of working members: 'It may be,' he said, 'that the Council will see fit to recommend certain conflicts should be forbidden . . .'

But some members of the Council, and of the Committee of Lloyd's, which was already seeing an erosion of its traditional authority, were displeased with what Davison had to say. 'We are going to dip into the barrel and pick out every rotten apple that is there,' he said at his first press conference.

This remark infuriated some members of the Committee. Frank 'the Bank' Barber was a prominent underwriter and Deputy Chairman of Lloyd's whose nickname reflected his success in the market. In Barber's opinion Davison's appointment was a standing disgrace to Lloyd's and the sooner he left the better. Barber took the view that the business of Lloyd's was Lloyd's business and nobody else's.

Davison had great respect for Barber (who subsequently succeeded where others had failed, and came to a deal with the
Inland Revenue) both as a man of principles and as a man who
made money for his members. But the very presence of a Chief
Executive was anathema to Barber and others bred and raised
in the club-like ethos of Lime Street. To others Davison was
a mystery or a matter of indifference: 'the chap the Governor
found.' He was Sir Peter Green's problem and Sir Peter Green
knew how to look after himself.

Green himself was in contact with the Governor of the Bank of
England over another matter. That spring Green and Richardson
met with Green's tax adviser. The fact that Peter Dixon was the
Green family accountant, and the extent of Green's offshore
reinsurance interests had attracted the curiosity of the Inland
Revenue. The presence of the Governor of the Bank of England
at this meeting, when it became known, raised eyebrows in
Parliament.

But Green was as ebullient as ever, not least when in The
Room at Lime Street he was presented with Lloyd's highest
award, the Gold Medal. 'When I heard they were going to give
me this, you could have buggered me through my oilskins,' was
the Chairman's considered reply.

Sir Peter was indeed rudely surprised to learn that both the
Department of Trade and Members of Parliament were making
suggestions that he might be seeking special tax treatment for
himself at a time when a microscope was being applied to the
tax affairs of Lloyd's as a whole.

He was happier to be able to announce that total profits for
all Lloyd's syndicates for 1980 – the most recent year available
under the three-year accounting system – were over £225 million,
an increase of 50%.

The PR releases of the time too spelled out that Lloyd's
could be not just profitable, but fun. Among the risks broked
and underwritten was a grain of rice with a portrait engraved
on it of Her Majesty the Queen and the Duke of Edinburgh,

insured for $20,000. A killer whale called Namu, captured off the Canadian Pacific coast and towed to Seattle for display in an aquarium, was insured for $8,000 against various contingencies, including rescue attempts by other whales. Cutty Sark whisky had offered £1 million to anyone who could capture the Loch Ness Monster alive, or produce a flying saucer; and had insured at Lloyd's against both eventualities.

But behind the cute PR were some sobering figures. Of the £225 million profits announced by Sir Peter Green, only £13.5 million actually came from underwriting; around 6%. 94% of the profits came from investment income and capital appreciation of syndicate funds. Furthermore, the tax breaks of the 1970s had become less attractive as the Labour government had fallen and with it had fallen the high levels of personal taxation. Wealthy people and high earners no longer needed to look to Lloyd's for a unique escape from tax.

The smaller underwriting profits also meant a greater likelihood that recently-elected medium-sized members would see this as an inadequate reward for risking everything. Something had to be done if the members were to continue to be attracted and the agents were to go on enjoying their considerable commissions and salaries.

Later, arguments would rage as to when what was known as 'Excess of Loss' reinsurance at Lloyd's began to spiral out of control and even be artificially 'churned' to a dangerous degree. The allegation was that the London Market Excess of Loss (LMX) market was forced into generating extra business for itself in order to use its spare capacity. Others rejected this idea. But there was no doubt to market insiders that the level of reinsurance was rising and underwriters were laying off risks with each other to a greater and greater degree.

Excess of Loss reinsurance (EOL) was an established practice at Lloyd's; without the ability to reinsure themselves even the biggest underwriters and their syndicates risked going out of business. The bigger a risk, the bigger the excess; that part of it not covered by the first layer of insurance. There was nothing whatsoever wrong with Excess of Loss reinsurance – unless it was taken to excess.

The way Excess of Loss worked was theoretically simple. But, as one experienced market man put it: 'You could ask six different people to explain it and the only thing of which you could be sure is that you would get six different explanations.'

A risk broked of £100 million might carry a premium of £3 million for the underwriters. If the broker placed that risk with the first layer of twenty underwriters the premium between them would be worth £3 million. But a big risk like this needed big reinsurance and the first layer of underwriters would find a second layer with which to reinsure themselves in turn. To the second layer the premium would be worth £2.7 million between them – £3 million less the 10 per cent excess – and a total of £5.7 million had been paid out in premium so far. To a third layer of underwriters the premium would be worth £2.43 million – £2.7 million less the 10 per cent excess – and a total of £8.13 million had now been paid in premium . . . and so it went on, and the amount of premium payable to each layer diminished until there was none left and the risk could not be reinsured any further.

But the original risk broked was still £100 million and it was still just as likely or not to turn into a claim. If it did, the first layer of underwriters were well covered by reinsurance, but the progressive diminution in premium meant that this reinsurance cover too was diminished as the risk passed from layer to layer. A further complication was that the same syndicates might and often did reinsure these kinds of risk backwards and forwards with each other several times or more. In the event of a big risk turning into a big claim, the later layers of underwriters could be wiped out – which was why, each time a catastrophe risk came round again, the underwriter who took it on did so on the assumption or sometimes merely in the fervent hope that he in turn would be able to reinsure himself. In its most extreme and crudest 'spiral' form this kind of business was like a game of 'pass the parcel' – except that the floor of The Room at Lloyd's was not the place for a children's party.

The risks broked and insured and then rebroked and reinsured in this way were the big catastrophe risks: earthquakes, hurricanes, forest fires and the like. Aircraft and oil rig risks were also common. The premiums could be high and the likelihood of claims was relatively low – it just depended on the layer of which you were a part.

A second attraction was that with each reinsurance the broker and underwriter took another cut. There was nothing illegal about this kind of business and it was broked by many companies including Sedgwick, one of the biggest brokers in the Lloyd's market. One broker in particular, Bill Brown of Walsham Brothers, would grow fabulously rich in this way without having to travel further than the distance to Lime Street from his offices in Fenchurch Avenue.

A third attraction was that this kind of business benefited both syndicates and members agents. More premium paid to an underwriter meant that his syndicate could take on more members, and each member paid the managers of his syndicates an annual fee of 1% of his or her underwriting capacity. The incentive to increase capacity was clear. In the case of Gooda Walker 298 alone these fees grew from £3,850 to £443,000 from 1982 to 1989.

Many members agents owned by brokers were under pressure after the 1980 Fisher Report and 1982 Lloyd's Act to sell themselves to new owners within a certain time limit. Other independent agencies wanted to grow with the idea of selling themselves as a longterm aim. Either way, to make themselves more attractive the present owners had a strong incentive to increase the number of members they handled. This was difficult in a stagnating market where few syndicates were increasing their capacity – except those dealing with Excess of Loss and what was to become known as the LMX 'spiral.' Thus it was that syndicates like Gooda Walker, Feltrim and Rose Thomson Young and members agencies like Gooda Walker, Stancomb and Kenington and Lime Street were the fastest growing ones of their kind in the middle and late 1980s.

The members looked at their copies of *Lloyd's League Tables* and saw which syndicates had the fastest rising capacities. The bigger the capacity, they said to themselves, the bigger the potential profits. The members would telephone their agents and ask to be placed on Feltrim and Gooda Walker and think themselves clever and lucky when their agents obliged.

Other members were steered by their agents onto the syndicates in question. Oddly enough, there were relatively few working members on these syndicates. Gooda Walker 290 had only seven per cent compared with a market average of 12 per cent and up to 54 per cent on the most profitable syndicates. Many of these furthermore were clerical staff of the managing agency or senior staff of the agents who supported the syndicates placed there to reassure members. The number of 'voluntary and informed insiders' on these syndicates was therefore even lower.

But in any case, in keeping with the secrecy which surrounded so much Lloyd's activity, neither the external members nor their agents nor *Lloyd's League Tables* could tell exactly what sort of business these syndicates were underwriting. Nor did many members think to ask – for what did it matter, as long as the cheques kept coming?

And in they came ... the cheques and not the claims. On the Bay of Tralee Desmond O'Neill received a cheque for £12,000 from Kingsley for profits on syndicates including Warrilow and Gooda Walker. In Fulham the secretary who had come via such an unusual route to the syndicates of Peter Cameron-Webb received a cheque for £5,000 which was nearly half her annual salary.

But there were no cheques for the members of Spicer and White 895, once a venerable and conservative syndicate run by Robin Kingsley's friend John White. A new underwriter called

Bryan Spencer took over. The quantity of underwriting went through the roof; and the quality of business reinsured went through the floor. Spencer's apparent willingness to underwrite virtually anything led to his being known to the brokers, who clustered round his box like crows around carrion, as the 'nodding donkey.'

Before they were stopped, Spencer and 895 cost the 200 members £13 million, the highest loss since Tim Sasse ten years earlier.

Among them were many Kingsley Names including Virginia Wade. But at least Kingsley's risk-spreading theory meant she was on a wide variety of the syndicates in the market: such as Gooda Walker 164 and 290, Warrilow 553, Secretan 367 and the much-prized Outhwaite 317/661.

Then there was Michael Church.

Thelnetham, Norfolk, 1983

Thelnetham is a pretty village even by Norfolk standards and Lower Lodge is one of its prettiest houses. Michael and Mary Church had been happy here, and when Mary became terminally ill with cancer Michael Church took early retirement from his job with the brokers C.E. Heath.

Church was an expert on the insurance of Alaskan fishing fleets and had been a working Name for many years. He was a friend – and a prominent syndicate member – of Peter Cameron-Webb.

Lloyd's was his life. He subscribed wholeheartedly to the famous words of Cuthbert Heath: '. . . there is one thing which is still with us and shines as brightly as ever. It is the honourable feeling that, privileged as we are among traders in that our contracts are those of "*uberimae fidei*", our good faith must also be the supreme law of our existence . . .'

Michael Church nursed his wife and when she died he became close to a Canadian woman he had known as an insurance colleague since the 1960s. Her name was Janis Nash.

In the aftermath of Mary Church's death Janis Nash and Michael Church decided to sell Lower Lodge and move to Minorca. To their excitement they found a house they liked and after two trips to Minorca they made an offer. On their return to Lower Lodge they found a letter. It was a cash call for £36,000 for losses made by the syndicates whose active underwriter was Peter Cameron-Webb.

Church and Nash travelled to London in search of information. They knew Cameron-Webb had recently retired.

Janis Nash did not know Cameron-Webb. She wondered whether there had been foul play by Cameron-Webb against his members.

'No, no, Janis,' Church said, 'you don't understand. I've known him all my working life. We are friends. He would never do anything like that to me.'

Even after two weeks, Church was only just beginning to sense what was happening. His colleagues in the market were also in a state of shock. Most disturbing to him was the reaction of the Lloyd's authorities. They just did not seem to want to know.

Eventually they travelled back to Norfolk. Minorca suddenly seemed a long way away.

* * *

Inside Lloyd's rumours about Cameron-Webb circulated at the highest levels.

Eddie Kulukundis had been one of Cameron-Webb's biggest syndicate members and stood to lose a great deal of money. Kulukundis had heard the rumours. He told his members agency Thomas Miller to take him off the PCW syndicates and advised members of his family to do likewise.

David D'Ambrumenil, whom Green had questioned over Cameron-Webb and Unimar, was an even bigger Name on the PCW syndicates. D'Ambrumenil had socialised with the Cameron-Webb jet set and recognised him as a man who had gone from the bottom to the top and was an intelligent, hard and greedy operator. D'Ambrumenil also knew that many offshore reinsurance schemes had not necessarily been set up for crooked reasons but as a response to punitive taxation and exchange controls. But even he was beginning to suspect that this time Cameron-Webb had gone too far.

D'Ambrumenil was a big Name on the syndicates and he was running out of sympathy. He decided to visit Cameron-Webb in Switzerland. Cameron-Webb was not difficult to track down.

D'Ambrumenil and a director of Sedgwick, the big Lloyd's brokers, flew to Geneva. The three men had lunch in an expensive restaurant. Cameron-Webb tried to explain. He told D'Ambrumenil he was desperately worried about what was happening. 'I tried to build something,' he said 'and now they are destroying it. Nobody understands the facts . . .'

D'Ambrumenil and his colleague flew back from Geneva little the wiser for meeting the man whose name was still little known outside Lloyd's; and Lloyd's seemed keen to keep it that way.

Then there was Wilfred Sherman.

Marbella, Costa del Sol, 1983

Over 100,000 British expatriates live on the Costa del Sol and all of them are there as some form of escape; from the British weather, from the high cost of living, from the stress of an overcrowded island and occasionally from the law.

Wilfred Sherman was not trying to escape from the law and had nothing to hide. Sherman was the Penarth sporting man who had travelled the world meeting prospective members of the Oakeley Vaughan syndicates. Like most Oakeley Vaughan members he was still unaware of the extent of the problems Oakeley Vaughan was facing.

Sherman was seventy-two years of age. His wife was sixty-eight and suffered from arthritis and diabetes. Three years earlier they had moved near Marbella to what they anticipated would be a comfortable retirement.

There were complicated immigration procedures for foreigners settling in Spain and during the process Sherman had made a number of friends in the local legal profession. One of them called in for a beer one day on the way to Marbella from Malaga. He had a friend with him: a young captain in the Guardia Civil.

Sherman too had heard the rumours from Lloyd's, and the news that Peter Cameron-Webb's partner in crime Peter Dixon had arrived in disguise and was now hiding in a heavily guarded villa near Marbella.

'Why do you let these men live here?' Sherman asked the police captain. 'They are criminals. Is there not an extradition treaty with Britain?'

The Guardia Civil man did not hesitate.

'Señor Sherman,' he said, 'I know they are undesirables. I can pick them up any time I like. All I need to know is that there will be a police welcome for them on the aircraft when it lands in Britain. There is absolutely no problem.'

They finished their beers. Sherman was disturbed by what he had heard. Knowing that a Chief Executive had recently been appointed, he telephoned Lloyd's and asked to speak to Ian Hay Davison.

Davison's secretary answered. Davison was away in America, but she assured Sherman she would treat whatever he had to say with the strictest confidence. Sherman repeated to her the conversation he had had with the captain in the Guardia Civil.

A few days later Sherman's telephone rang in Marbella. Ian Hay Davison was back from Lloyd's business in America. Sherman repeated what he had said to the secretary. Davison thanked him and rang off.

Three days later Sherman's telephone rang again. Davison was disappointed. He told Sherman that he had been unable to persuade the Director of Public Prosecutions to issue a warrant for Dixon's arrest on extradition to Britain.

Sherman would always remember the shock of this. So would Davison. Later, he would be offered an informal contract by the Spanish police: for a sum of money Dixon would be delivered dead or alive in London.

The offer was not accepted. Meanwhile, one more British expatriate remained at liberty on the Costa del Sol.

* * *

Sir Peter Green too was increasingly preoccupied with matters beyond the shores of Britain. In his case they were the 'somewhat esoteric' £34 million Imperial reinsurance schemes in the Cayman Islands.

> 'The problem from the underwriting agent's point of view,' he wrote to his syndicate members, 'has been to justify to the Revenue if challenged the reserves for unreported loss are proper reserves and not tax avoidance. Thus schemes to overcome this problem had great attractions to specialist syndicates such as ours with an enormous concentration of risk exposure to wind storm in the Gulf of Mexico, or to long-term environmental or health liabilities arising on our very large third party liability business which is concentrated in the USA . . .'

In other words, Sir Peter interpreted things one way and the taxman interpreted them in another.

A short time later, in September 1983, Sir Peter Green announced his resignation as Chairman of Lloyd's.

Sir Marcus Kimball, the MP and Council member, described the news as 'a bombshell.' But Green's resignation came as no surprise to many. On the one hand Green was the man who had engineered the Sasse settlement, championed the proposed new building and steered the Lloyd's Act through Parliament. On the other hand he was a personal beneficiary of questionable offshore reinsurance schemes and he was too close to Dixon and Cameron-Webb.

The public figure who had been knighted for his services to the market had been brought down by the rough, tough buccaneering market player. The irony – and tragedy – was that these different personas were the two sides of the same coin. They could not have existed without each other and yet at the same time they were expected to have separate existences when it came to the interests of the market and the man. The tragedy for Green was that in his rise lay the seeds of his fall. Only a year after the Lloyd's Act the idea of self-regulation was made a mockery by the resignation of the market's most prominent figure.

Green stated publicly: 'I have been unable to give other than the minimum of attention to my own business and none to my personal affairs or home life.'

But although Green was able to return to running his family company, Janson Green, he was an angry and embittered man. The anger and bitterness would be intensified four years later when he was officially censured and found guilty of 'discreditable and detrimental conduct' over the reinsurances placed with the Imperial scheme in the Cayman Islands.

Nowhere were the paradoxes of his position more obvious than in the reactions of those who knew him best – the key players at the time.

Ian Hay Davison had mixed feelings about the passing of the man who had ironically brought him to Lloyd's in the first place. 'I arrived into a hostile climate and Green was a terrific help,' he said ten years later. 'But, at the end of 1983 when I had been there less than a year, the Bank of England decided he had to go. He was greatly embittered by his prosecution and probably blames me,' Davison went on, 'but it wasn't me. With hindsight I should have told the Bank to delay. He wasn't the only one doing what he was doing and I needed his backing for the time being.'

David D'Ambrumenil, himself first cleared and later suspended from Lloyd's over the Unimar affair, was more outspoken. 'I think he was treated monstrously,' he said in 1991, 'he did a great job for Lloyd's with the bill and everyone knew about Imperial. But it was just like France at the time of the Revolution. If the hounds turned on you they would destroy you. And I think Peter was sacrificed. He seriously thought about returning his Gold Medal. I think he should have done. Who were this establishment who threw him to the wolves? A self-perpetuating clique in England who are very good at saving their own skins. I liken it to the Russian sleigh ride. The wolves are running after them, so they throw out the most expendable person to keep them away.'

Sir Marcus Kimball, later Lord Kimball, was not so sure. 'He had to go,' he told this author, 'he was extremely lucky we didn't ask him to give back his Gold Medal.'

Robin Warrender was less judgemental:

'Peter is an honourable man – a tough buccaneer, yes, and his father Toby Green was a bigger and tougher buccaneer! His green Rolls Royce was a familiar sight in the City in his day. Of course Peter was wrong to keep his shareholding and the involvement with Imperial when he became Chairman of Lloyd's – it was utterly stupid, but I have an idea why he did so. He liked to go each winter on business to the Bahamas and then go deep sea fishing – I don't think it is any more complicated than that.'

But what of Sir Peter Green himself? In reply to this writer's polite letter asking for an interview, he wasted neither time nor words. Nor did he waste paper. He simply sent back the letter with a question that perhaps sums up better than anything else the bitterness, the greed and the tragedy.

Scrawled across the bottom in his handwriting were the immortal words: 'How much do I get paid?'

Before he fled his opulent house in Kensington Palace Gardens Peter Dixon had also posted a letter. In it he gave the impression that the funds diverted to Geneva and Gibraltar had been earmarked for the payment of claims all along and that the money was always going to be returned to the syndicates.

Unfortunately for Dixon the Department of Trade investigators did not believe this letter. Nor did they believe the date on the letter – over two years before it was delivered. Nor did they believe him when he said he knew nothing about any interest in the Banque du Rhône et de la Tamise. Nor did they regard as a valid excuse the remarks about how everyone had indulged in quota share schemes offshore, that Dixon issued through his solicitor Sir David Napley.

Dixon continued to hide in Marbella. In November 1983 Cameron-Webb eventually agreed to meet the Department of Trade men in New York. With no warrant yet issued for his arrest he was on safe ground.

'As to the proceeds of the reinsurance premiums,' he told them, 'the division of responsibility between myself and [Mr Dixon] was that whilst he dealt with the financial, accounting and administrative aspects of our business, I dealt with the underwriting.'

'For tax purposes,' Cameron-Webb went on, 'the routes through companies which the proceeds of the reinsurances in question took, were, I believe, very complex. I have never understood exactly the details of the inter-company structure involved. I was not involved to any significant extent in that structure, or the finances or financial management of any reinsurance company with which any risks originally written by the syndicates were reinsured. All these matters were dealt with by [Mr Dixon].

'As a result I have no detailed knowledge of what happened to the reinsurance premiums paid by the syndicates. Further, and as a result, I am unable to identify which of my assets may represent or derive from the proceeds of such reinsurance. Much of my own personal finance was managed by [Mr Dixon] out of kindness to me and to give me the freedom to devote my entire time to underwriting.'

Dixon's kindness it seemed knew no bounds. The Department of Trade investigators listened to this disingenuous and self-serving nonsense with faces as straight as that of Cameron-Webb.

With Cameron-Webb and Dixon in hiding abroad and Green out of office a blight had fallen on all three of the men who had started their working lives on the Janson Green Box. But Davison and many others knew that the former Chairman was not the only underwriting member of the Committee and Council of Lloyd's with 'rollover' policies tucked away in offshore tax havens.

As Davison remarked with English understatement: 'These arrangements were capable of increasing degrees of refinement in which, in some cases, the line between permissible tax avoidance and criminal tax evasion became somewhat blurred . . .'

Nowhere did the controversy surrounding rollovers pose more of a problem than in the question of Green's successor. Frank 'the Bank' Barber and Tim Brennan, the two Deputy Chairmen, had already indicated they did not wish to stand for office.

Murray Lawrence was strongly tipped for the job and had been Green's choice to succeed him. But Lawrence, though a man of considerable talent and charm, was also a leading underwriter at a time when leading underwriters were attracting the attention of the Inland Revenue.

After the disaster that had befallen Peter Green, the last thing Lloyd's needed was another scandal. Lloyd's needed the polar opposite; someone who was by definition out of scandal's reach. On the Committee and Council of Lloyd's this could only mean one thing: he had to be a broker.

Sir Peter Green and Peter Miller were both second generation Lloyd's men and were close colleagues in the market and on the Council, but in many ways they were polar opposites. Green was a rumbustious larger-than-life figure who enjoyed the good life and was a leading underwriter; Miller was a diminutive figure of a man who liked to keep fit and was a successful broker.

Where Green was fast and free with his choice of words, it was sometimes difficult to fathom Miller's opinions. At a time when the Green factor was weighing heavily on a Lloyd's already staggering under the burden of criticism in Parliament and the press, the Miller factor was seen as bringing back the hope of a newly-confident mood.

Miller also brought back the old attitude to the Chief Executive. At the press conference to announce his election he was asked how he saw their respective roles. 'I am the Prime Minister,' he replied, 'Mr Davison is the head of the Civil Service.'

Davison's fears grew when, within less than two weeks of Miller's appointment, Frank Barber approached him and invited him to consider leaving. In the early weeks of 1984 Ian Hay Davison found himself reviewing the achievements of his own eventful first year.

'My original remit,' Davison told this author, 'was first to catch the crooks, second to write the rule book and third to change the culture of the place so that it was properly regulated. And the third I failed to do.'

Given that he was speaking at the height of the worst crisis in Lloyd's history, his words have a melancholy ring. Yet when Davison had agreed to return the favour for the Governor of the Bank of England he had no illusions about the difficulty of the job.

There was no precedent for his appointment, and his success or failure depended heavily on his relationship with the Chairman. If Davison was not to be a gilded cage bird he was going to have to earn every penny of his salary of £120,000 a year.

In his desire to catch the crooks Davison and his colleagues in Lloyd's Regulatory Services had made considerable progress. They set up an investigations committee which had the authority to prosecute offenders. The prosecutions were heard before a disciplinary panel chaired by a lawyer or externally-appointed QC. The Council of Lloyd's was bound to ratify the panel's decisions.

The suspensions and fines were published in detail. In this way the Chief Executive and his team hoped to send a message to the market: 'You mean, taking members' money is wrong? Yes, it is.'

Davison had a favourite saying which he had used at his first press conference: 'Sunshine drives away the mist.'

Messrs Page and Carpenter of the Howden 'Gang of Four', Dixon, Cameron-Webb, Brooks and Dooley and other misty creatures were all investigated in person or *in absentia* under the new system. The reprimands were challenged by much legalistic squirming but more cases followed. In spite of the apparent reluctance of the Director of Public Prosecutions, Davison still had high hopes that the hand of the law would descend heavily on Dixon and Cameron-Webb.

In writing the rule book Davison and his colleagues had achieved a good deal in a short time. A Rules Committee was set up and proper accounting requirements were imposed for the first time on Lloyd's syndicates. The procedures were tightened governing the management of syndicates and a standard form of agreement was developed between members and agents. But the incestuous relationships between many syndicates were not stopped and the 'baby' syndicates of less than fifty members continued to skim off business. These reforms had to wait for the subsequent appointment of the Neill inquiry in 1986.

Davison would be rightly proud of the achievements of his first year in this intensely inward-looking environment. But in failing in his third endeavour, to change the culture of the place so that it was properly regulated, he was failing in an impossible task. He and his achievements would be assimilated by the club and the proud boast of self-regulation would ring out to the credit of the club and not the outsider who made it happen.

Already the voices were mounting.

'I was a considerable admirer of Ian Hay Davison and I still am,' said one 'Broker Baron'. 'I think he did a brilliant job. But he just did not see the elephant trap – and from that time on he didn't have a prayer.'

'He wasn't an easy man,' said one past Chairman. 'You can't shoot everyone in the corral, you just shoot some of them.'

'A dull man,' barked a patrician commentator, 'no sense of humour. He would have provoked almost anyone into forming a cabal.'

The Corporation staff too resented his salary and were enraged by his (justifiable) questioning of their intellectual calibre.

Now Green and Richardson were gone and the new Chairman Peter Miller was saying he could not believe that 'the shameful behaviour of a very few people is representative.'

The writing was on the wall for the Chief Executive. He may barely have suspected it, but in his zeal to finish his reforms he was moving closer to putting himself out of a job. The sands would close over Davison as quickly as they had done over the *Lutine*, and not until the freak storms of the 1990s would the rotten timbers that he was unable to salvage be exposed again.

With Cameron-Webb abroad and Posgate suspended, R.H.M. 'Dick' Outhwaite was the man on whose syndicates people increasingly wanted to be.

Outhwaite had enjoyed a substantial inflow of premium on the asbestosis business and he was planning to expand the capacity of his blue-chip syndicates 317/661. But, although the normal period of three years had not yet passed, he would feel impelled to write to his members about the 1982 account:

1982 Account
    Even after thirty months it is surprisingly difficult to fore-
cast the precise outcome of this account. This is particularly
a problem with the long-tail section where the outcome is
largely dependent on the updating of reserves normally done

at 31st December. However, the current position in regard to paid and outstanding claims is quite satisfactory.

The carry forward from old years plays an increasingly large part and we anticipate settling between 12% and 15% of the fund of £60.5 million during the year. Again, both the settled and the incurred loss position are reasonably satisfactory. We anticipate a reinsurance to close 1982 account of approximately £75 million (based on the current audit rates of exchange).

Taking all these factors into account and, always providing no serious deterioration takes place in the next six months, we expect a result on the underwriting similar to 1981 account . . .

What Outhwaite was saying was that, contrary to what members may have heard, there was no undue cause for alarm about the results for the year in which he had underwritten the asbestosis business.

This came as particularly reassuring news to Betty Atkins and Sylvia Hatton, the two secretaries made working members for their long service to C. Rowbotham & Sons. They had recently received a letter from Rowbothams telling them that as a result of a merger the business was henceforth to be known as Rowbotham de Rougemont. 'We wish to assure you,' the letter had read, 'that the existing arrangements with this Company will be maintained.'

The last thing they could afford was an underwriting loss; and it was nice to think that their special understanding was intact. Sylvia Hatton was now retired and Betty Atkins was planning to work part-time after so many years' service. Even though Outhwaite was saying there were no grounds for undue pessimism, Betty Atkins and Sylvia Hatton were very relieved.

Outhwaite was the coming man. Posgate was fighting every step of the way to prove his innocence but even the legendary 'Goldfinger' was finding this an uphill task. Meanwhile the mystery of the fallen underwriting star Peter Cameron-Webb had deepened.

Freeport, Grand Bahama, February 1984

The motor yacht was in bad shape when it came in and the crew too were suffering from neglect. The *Nirene* was a distinctive craft and this fact did not escape the notice of John Hinchliffe. Hinchliffe was in any case paid to notice strange yachts in the vicinity, because he was the Port Director.

The *Nirene* was a seagoing motor yacht with a white hull and timber upper works. The crew and captain had not been paid and the vessel needed $250 of immediate repairs from the Freeport Harbour Company's shipwright. The yacht also needed fuel oil and the master and crew did not have the money to pay for this either. Captain Hinchliffe noted all this and made an appointment to meet the Master.

Captain Hinchliffe had been living in Freeport with his wife and children since December 1980. He had been one of the Fred Olsen line's youngest Masters until a road accident cut short his seafaring career. He was a man of robust appearance, unswerving loyalty and uncompromising principles; he saw himself as being first and foremost answerable to Sir Jack Hayward, at whose offices he had been interviewed and accepted for the job in London. He was proud to be a product of the training ship *Worcester*. He joined the Freeport Players Guild and the Rotary Club. He joined the neighbourhood watch and assisted the Red Cross.

Hinchliffe was passionately opposed to the drug trafficking rife in the Bahamas and said so. In June 1983 he had met a US Naval officer and an American DEA agent at the Pier One Restaurant in Freeport and as Port Director had been warned in no uncertain terms of the drugs problem in the Bahamas. To Hinchliffe this was one more piece of confirmation of the growing influence of organised crime in the islands. The Colombian cocaine smuggler Carlos Lehder and the renegade financier Robert Vesco were just two of the Bahamas' less savoury visitors.

Captain John Martin of the recently-arrived motor yacht *Nirene* had an interesting tale to tell. The *Nirene* was en route via Freeport to Miami on the instructions of its owner, Mr Peter Cameron-Webb. Hinchliffe listened and said little. He was all the more interested to learn the name of the person whom Captain Martin had been instructed to contact in the Bahamas.

Hinchliffe had been intrigued by Edward St George ever since he had arrived in the Bahamas. On the one hand he was impressed by the name and the titled connections – St George went on the Royal yacht *Britannia* when the Queen visited the Bahamas. Hinchliffe respected St George as his elder and superior at the Port Authority. He enjoyed the occasional cocktail parties at St George's house in Greening Glades, with its staff and its spacious terrace and jacuzzi.

When Hinchliffe's leg had been crushed between a vessel and a pilot boat at Christmas 1981 St George had arranged for him to be airlifted for crucial emergency medical care in Miami. Hinchliffe had been grateful for this and for the videos he had been given to watch during his recovery and the help St George had offered his family.

But there was another side to St George which sometimes concerned Hinchliffe.

St George had made Pindling those 'loans' at crucial times in the relationship between the black nationalist PLP and the white-dominated Port Authority. Although it would not be made public until five years later in the Nassau *Tribune*, St George had also personally recommended that two suspected Mafia associates take over the running of the government-owned El Casino in Freeport. He had described them as 'upright corporate citizens' – a description somewhat at variance with that used by the FBI.

Captain Hinchliffe was most interested to learn from Captain

Martin of the *Nirene* that Edward St George was acquainted with Peter Cameron-Webb. In fact, unknown to Hinchliffe, St George had been a PCW syndicate member and Cameron-Webb would approach St George with a business proposition in Grand Bahama. St George turned down the proposition. Nor did Hinchliffe know the full extent of the manoeuvres, disguises and repaintings the innocent Captain Martin had been forced to undertake on Cameron-Webb's instructions to remove the *Nirene* from the reach of Her Majesty's Government and take her to Miami.

Edward St George met the costs for fuel oil for the Cameron-Webb yacht when it docked at Freeport. By the time Hinchliffe had returned from leave the yacht had sailed away. In keeping with the general tenor of the Cameron-Webb affair, Hinchliffe ended up paying the Freeport shipwright the $250 repair bill out of his own pocket. As he did with most other things Hinchliffe made a detailed note of this in his log.

Captain Hinchliffe continued to ponder this matter long after the *Nirene* had disappeared to Miami.

* * *

Three months later, the Chairman of Lloyd's, Peter Miller, wrote a letter to members about the growing fears concerning losses on the syndicates once run by Peter Cameron-Webb.

25 May 1984

Dear Member

The Council of Lloyd's is very conscious of the problems faced by the Names on syndicates managed by Richard Beckett Underwriting Agencies Ltd., formerly known as P.C.W. Underwriting Agencies Ltd. Deficiencies must now be covered by those Names in order to meet Lloyd's statutory obligations under the Insurance Companies Act 1982.

The entire Market is aware of the serious allegations that attach to those formerly responsible for managing the syndicates in question. There are also one or two other syndicates, under different managing agents, whose members may equally feel some disquiet at their losses although their affairs would not have attracted the same attention as the P.C.W. syndicates. It is to the Names on all these syndicates that this letter is particularly addressed in order to make clear to them, as well as to the membership as a whole, Lloyd's position in relation to losses such as these.

Lloyd's Acts 1871 to 1982 impose upon the Council of Lloyd's the task of managing and superintending the affairs of the Society and of regulating and directing the business of insurance at Lloyd's. In other words, the Council has a general duty to the membership at large to manage the Society and a specific duty to maintain an orderly market.

It is the role of the Council to ensure that there is a sound and well regulated framework within which individual underwriters can work and Names can subscribe to syndicates. From time to time syndicates and the Names on them can, and do, suffer from the results of poor underwriting judgements. In very exceptional cases, such losses may have been exacerbated by negligence or, in a rare case, by improper conduct on the part of the underwriting agents concerned: in such cases, the Council will act vigorously in the interest of Names through full and expeditious use of its investigatory and disciplinary powers. Furthermore, every assistance will be given to other authorities to enable them to instigate such proceedings as they deem appropriate.

However [Miller went on], it may be that the damage and loss to Names cannot entirely be undone. The primary concern of the Council must be to safeguard Names from further damage, as well as to ensure that an effective underwriting agent is acting on their behalf: that of the underwriting agents will be to attend to and, if possible, repair the damage already done.

It may be that some of the affected Names will wish to discuss this letter with their underwriting agents. It is their agents who will be able to give them detailed advice on any matters of particular anxiety to them, including their legal position and Lloyd's requirements. It is also possible that individual Names or Agents would appreciate general advice and guidance from the Corporation staff, headed by the Deputy Chairman and Chief Executive, Mr Ian Hay Davison . . .

It is perhaps appropriate to remind the membership at large that the Lloyd's Central Fund is maintained for the benefit of Lloyd's policyholders in order to ensure that valid claims are paid in the event of the default of an individual Name. The Central Fund is not available to mitigate any hardship suffered by Names in meeting their several obligations.

What exactly did Miller mean by this letter which would have been drafted and redrafted many times before it was despatched to the thousands of members?

The message was simple. Lloyd's had a duty to regulate itself but when something actually went wrong its first duty appeared to some to be to remind the members of what it could not do for them. Lloyd's could not undo the damage done by wrongdoers. Nor could Lloyd's give detailed advice in this situation; the members should consult their agents. If they wanted general advice they might ask for it from the already overworked Ian Hay Davison. Above all, the members could not expect to receive any help to bear their losses from the Central Fund.

All this was in spite of certain facts of which some members were more aware than others. In the 1920s the Harrison case had been resolved by a levy among underwriting members. In the late 1950s the Central Fund had indeed been used to help bail out the deceived members of the Roylance syndicate. In the late 1970s the market had been persuaded to help bail out the Sasse members by Sir Peter Green. Now members were demonstrating anxiety on an unprecedented scale as a result of the criminal behaviour of Dixon and Cameron-Webb. Yet an unpromising message was now being sent to the people who put up the market's working capital.

What happened next would create a controversy that brought questions in Parliament and bitterness that lasted for years. Less than three weeks after Miller's letter, on 21 June, Lloyd's made an offer to the victims of Peter Cameron-Webb.

The offer was to all PCW Names except of course Dixon, Cameron-Webb and the other guilty parties. Nearly £40 million would be paid out to the members from funds recovered from Gibraltar and elsewhere. In return the members would give up all claims against the companies concerned and, where relevant, their new owners.

The offer was also conditional on acceptance by 100% of the members. The Names were given just four weeks to consider this.

The general reaction was one of dismay. This was neither enough money to cover their losses nor enough time in which to consider. But Lloyd's were adamant. The only concessions made were that the period for consideration was extended and the 100% clause was dropped altogether.

By 24 August over 98% of Cameron-Webb members had accepted the offer. In spite of their continued reservations most were terrified of what would happen if the offer expired.

There was a further factor. As the DTI Report into the affair would note some years later:

'Lloyd's played an important part in encouraging the parties
to negotiate. Lloyd's however expressed no public view on
the offer, although the Chairman, Mr Peter Miller, who was

a Name on the PCW syndicates, announced in a personal capacity his intention to accept . . .'

In this way Lloyd's hoped it had dealt with the problem of legal action from the PCW members. Meanwhile, unknown to those members, all was not well with Davison's attempts to bring legal action to bear on Dixon and Cameron-Webb.

As early as 1983 Davison had had a meeting with the Director of Public Prosecutions at which it was agreed that he would start Lloyd's disciplinary proceedings and they would follow with their own investigation. Davison was proceeding, as were the Department of Trade; but still no warrant had been issued for the arrest of Dixon and Cameron-Webb.

Davison had twice been a Department of Trade Inspector and knew that in these cases it was customary for the Department of Trade to hold fire and not publish its report until the DPP had finished its prosecutions. Davison also knew that, if there were reasons why the Prime Minister wanted the Director of Public Prosecutions to do something, that thing was done.

In 1975 Davison had been the Department of Trade inspector investigating the missing former British Postmaster General John Stonehouse in Australia. Stonehouse had speciously claimed political asylum when he was no more than a common fraudster – a tactic that proved successful for six weeks until he was extradited after pressure from the Foreign Office. Davison knew that there was only one person to whom the Director of Public Prosecutions ultimately listened. Thus it was that, as anxiety mounted over the Cameron-Webb affair, Davison decided to try to interest the Prime Minister.

One of the high points of the early period of Peter Miller's chairmanship was that the Prime Minister accepted an invitation to lunch. Miller had high hopes for this grand occasion which would take place in the Chairman's Private Dining Room at Lloyd's with the white-gloved waiters behind each chair.

Davison had known Robin Butler, then the Prime Minister's Private Secretary, for some time. He spoke to Butler on the telephone:

'No doubt,' he said, 'you will be briefing the Prime Minister for our forthcoming lunch. Perhaps you could interest her in one or two of the following points . . .' and he proceeded to list a few of the more outrageous practices still existing in the Lloyd's market.

The lunch did not quite go as Peter Miller had intended. Mrs Thatcher was no respecter of persons, including the Chairman of Lloyd's: 'Which baby syndicates are you on?' she asked one red-faced underwriter, and called the assembled company to account, quoting chapter and verse. After this, it was no surprise perhaps that her views on City malpractices seemed to change and prosecutions were brought – albeit not at Lloyd's.

* * *

Davison persevered in his efforts to pick out the rotten apples to which he had referred in the first weeks of his appointment. As Christopher Moran had said, Lloyd's was like a loose thread in a sweater; you pulled it and the whole thing began to unravel.

The Brooks & Dooley affair had begotten the affair of Bellew Parry and Raven, a large broking and underwriting agency whose offshore reinsurance schemes were linked to some of the best-known names in the Lloyd's oligarchy, such as Janson Green, R.W. Sturge and Henry Chester. Bellew Parry and Raven were being investigated by a team under the eminent solicitor Sir Edward Singleton.

In spite of his failure to convince the Prime Minister Davison also continued to pursue the case of Dixon and Cameron-Webb. Like much of the missing funds, Cameron-Webb and Dixon themselves remained offshore, as did one or two of their associates, but Davison and the Department of Trade were closing in on some of the smaller fry. Davison also remained hopeful of some sign of action from the DPP.

Relations between Davison and Miller remained outwardly cordial but the tensions were rising between the two men. So too were the voices that fanned these tensions: 'They were like the two towers of the World Trade Centre,' one observer put it, 'each as big as the other and both bigger than anything else in town.'

But, while Davison by his very presence reminded people of the smell of rotten apples, Miller was the embodiment of the new confidence that was rising as fast as the Richard Rogers building on Lime Street. Miller's own confidence as Chairman was growing; as well as personally taking a lead over the Cameron-Webb settlement he had made plain his dislike of Rogers' plans for the top floor offices by bringing in an outside designer.

Clashes between him and Davison over operational matters were becoming more and more frequent. As Miller began to flex his muscles, the vacuum that had existed at the top with the departure of Peter Green disappeared, and Davison began to feel the full wrath of the club.

It was clear that one of them was going to have to go.

SIX

THE KILLING
OF MR CLEAN

The new year of 1985 began with rumours and rebuttals in the market that bad losses would be announced for the 1982 underwriting year. Outside the market, thousands of prospective members were queuing up for election.

Three syndicates which had disastrously exceeded their capacities exploded in their members' faces with the usual recriminations and cash calls. Spicer and White 895 and the 'nodding donkey' had made a loss of £22,780 for every £10,000 their members had underwritten in the most recent year. The new owners of 895, Willis Faber, offered the members a loan to be repaid over five years which would still only cover part of their losses. The deal was that in return they would refrain from taking legal action.

Like Sasse, the 895 members were outraged and decided to go ahead and sue Spicer and White anyway. One elderly gentleman said it reminded him of his schooldays over a half a century ago, when he had first fought back at a bully. 'I got hurt,' he said, 'but it never happened again. If we fight this one it will cost us a lot of money – but Lloyd's won't let it happen a second time.'

Many Spicer and White 895 members like Virginia Wade were also members of Cyril Warrilow's non-marine syndicate 553.

Cyril Warrilow was well known within the market for his willingness to do business after a good lunch. Like the nodding donkey, Warrilow had been replaced as the active underwriter after the agency had changed hands, but the losses he had made remained the losses of his members.

Everyone at Lloyd's had a Warrilow story. One of the favourites concerned Warrilow and the wrongful arrest.

Warrilow had been the lead underwriter for wrongful arrest cover for American police forces. One of the forces taking out such a policy was the San Antonio Police Department in Texas.

The police department sent over a delegation consisting of a supervisor and a woman police sergeant. Within two days Warrilow and the delegation were on convivial terms and after much wining and dining there was a fond farewell at Heathrow Airport. Warrilow even received affectionate letters on San Antonio Police Department writing paper. But for some reason the police department cancelled the cover.

The San Antonio Police Department subsequently incurred more claims under the wrongful arrest cover than almost any other police force in America. If Warrilow had underwritten the policy he would have had to pay out a fortune.

Brokers and underwriters chuckled over this in their favourite watering-holes. Whether or not the members agents laughed was questionable; in terms of the losses they too would suffer. The members agents were supposed to hear and interpret market gossip like everyone else and they would not have liked what they were hearing. The Warrilow members did not know it yet but they were in for an unpleasant surprise.

The members themselves had no idea of the market gossip and relied entirely on their agents to look after them. They signed an agreement to this end:

The Name will pay to the Agent as remuneration for the services of the Agent:
(i) A salary payable quarterly at the rate of one per cent of Premium Income Limit with a minimum of £150.00.

(ii)   A commission of twenty per cent on the profits of
        each year's business.

The agreement contained much about the powers given by the
Name to his agent, but little about the obligations of the agent
to the Name. The agent did however undertake

(e)   to comply at all times on behalf of the Name with the
       requirements prescribed by the Insurance Companies
       Act of 1958 and/or all other statutory provisions for
       the time being in force affecting underwriting Members
       of Lloyd's and with all requirements and regulations
       prescribed by Lloyd's.

Thus it was that, on 1 January 1984, Lord Alexander had
entered into an agreement with the Oakeley Vaughan members
agency and been placed on Cyril Warrilow's doomed syndicate
553.

The Oakeley Vaughan problems had not gone away with the
sale of the business by Charles St George to Robert Napier for
£1,000.
    Napier may have done his best but he and Colin Yellop
had failed to rescue the company. Too many claims had been
rolled forward as part of the defective accounting that had been
identified in the Chester Report. The Oakeley Vaughan syndicates
– 168, 420, 423, 862 and 551 – were heading for run-off, which
meant that they could do no further business. Henceforth they
would simply pay out millions of pounds on claims, until the
claims – and the resources of the syndicate members – were
exhausted.
    Lloyd's had still not published the Bishop, Chester or Randall
and Morris reports. Had they done so it is possible Oakeley
Vaughan members would not have paid their losses. As it was,
some of them complained to Charles St George.

St George had provided bank guarantees for some of his members at the bank and even paid others' deposits so that they could be elected. Now he quietly began 'helping' some of his stricken Names.

He paid money to his close friend Lester Piggott who had ridden so many of St George's horses to victory on the turf. He agreed to indemnify David Becker, the architect who always said he had joined Lloyd's 'for the cachet and not the cash', against past losses if Becker agreed to remain a member. He offered Lord Alexander £4,000 in return for an undertaking not to take legal action or present himself as a creditor in future.

Lord Alexander accepted this money on the assumption that it would enable him to meet all his losses. He had also a degree of stop loss insurance and he was hopeful of better luck with his other syndicates. After all, as well as Warrilow 553 and Aragorn 384, these included the prestigious Outhwaite 317/661

Many other Oakeley Vaughan syndicate members kept quiet for fear of the humiliation and embarrassment that would arise if their identities became known. Membership of Lloyd's was membership of an exclusive club and in keeping with this discreet and secretive ethos they did not know or believe in Ian Hay Davison's words 'sunshine drives away the mist.' Again, if they had known of the Bishop, Chester and Randall and Morris Reports, they might have reacted differently.

Nor did the members know that, within four days of the news that they were facing £4 million in losses, in March 1985, Lloyd's commissioned yet another report into Oakeley Vaughan. The brief of accountants Ernst and Whinney was to check 'the discharge of their duties by all Lloyd's persons involved.'

This covered all aspects of the broking, underwriting and members agency operations and was the broadest investigation into Oakeley Vaughan to date. Four months later, also unknown to the members, Lloyd's suddenly called off the investigation.

Edward St George, who had resigned as Chairman of Oakeley Vaughan & Company Ltd in 1983, was reappointed Chairman on 13 June 1985. Like his brother Charles, Edward St George continued discreetly to offer financial assistance to distressed Oakeley Vaughan members. In the light of the 1982 Lloyd's Act and the brave new self-regulated world this was an extraordinary move; and again, had the members known, they might have acted differently.

The Oakeley Vaughan time-bomb had exploded, as it was always going to do. And, apart from their own greed and gullibility, the members still had no idea why.

In this melancholy climate came the welcome news that a set of syndicates were looking for members to cope with the increased volume of business. These syndicates were Feltrim 540 and 847. Their new underwriter was Patrick Feltrim Fagan.

Feltrim was the name of the small town in Ireland where the Fagan family originated. The two new syndicates were looking for members of course to support their active underwriter and these were duly supplied by the members agents on the normal terms.

The members agents made their own assessment of Feltrim 540 and 847 on the basis of the usual intelligence and gossip that circulated around the market. As usual the members themselves rarely questioned their agents' judgement. If they did, they received a little information.

One highly reputable agent wrote to a member:

Marine syndicate 540 – P.F. Fagan.
A specialist Marine Excess of Loss syndicate formed in 1973.
Its results have been consistently profitable.

When that member, still dissatisfied, pressed for further information about the history of the syndicates, the agent came up with a surprising amount. Patrick Feltrim Fagan had been a small part of an operation run by Peter Dixon and Peter Cameron-Webb.

Fagan had in no way been involved in wrongdoing and the agent added that he would pick the best and reject the worst from the renewals coming through from the old Cameron-Webb business. 'PCW,' wrote the agent, 'had a number of good underwriters and therefore a lot of good insurance business. Mr Fagan, with a smaller stamp, will be able to pick and choose the best of this from the broker wishing to renew. He will not have to cut his rates to attract business as other new syndicates would. His ratio of reserves to premium income is one of the highest in Lloyd's.'

Fagan's reserves of £23.8 million were indeed four times his premium income of £5.8 million. This large fund was a particularly important factor for a new syndicate with a relatively inexperienced underwriter. Members offered a line on Feltrim 540 and 847 by their agents looked at these figures and felt strongly impelled to take it.

Unknown to members and also to the agents, 540 and 847 however had far closer connections than this with the syndicates once run by and for Peter Cameron-Webb. This would not have mattered had the losses of those syndicates been catered for by the 1984 settlement. This had been accepted by 98% of the members after being recommended by Peter Miller.

Richard Beckett, the experienced marine underwriter with no previous PCW connection who had taken over the PCW syndicates, had bad news for Miller and the Council. Beckett had now discovered the extent of the PCW fraud was so great that the PCW syndicates would have to cease trading. The PCW losses looked like exceeding those that had been paid by the 1984 settlement by a terrifying £100 million. The PCW syndicates – and any syndicates linked to them – would be bled dry.

If Lloyd's was going to avoid legal action it was going to have to make more settlements, and, if it was going to make more settlements, it was going to have to find more money – a lot more money. The question was, if no further funds could be recovered from offshore, where was that money to be found?

The PCW members who had accepted the 1984 settlement were horrified when in May 1985 they learned of the scale of the damage from Richard Beckett. They stood to lose £150,000 each on the business they had underwritten up to 1982 alone. The 350 members of syndicate 918 each stood to lose £200,000. Some of the wealthiest members stood to lose more and could afford to pay. Others could not and stood to lose everything.

The Fulham secretary was being asked to pay £260,000; assuming this was the final figure, which was unlikely, she would have had to go on working for over one hundred and fifty years if she was to pay a debt she was being asked to settle by 31 July.

The PCW members were now reaping the full bitter harvest of years of plundered profits and bad underwriting. Asbestos-related diseases and the effects of Agent Orange in Vietnam were just two examples of the long-tail business underwritten for quick profits by Cameron-Webb in the 1970s. Ten years later the claims were coming like a tidal wave towards sunbathers on a beach. At a meeting at the Royal Festival Hall the atmosphere of forced civility soon broke down into recriminations and fear.

'Tell the truth, you devil!' shouted an elderly member at one of the people vainly trying to explain the situation from the stage. There was a silence; then the terrible sound could be heard of hundreds of English men and women similarly losing their self-control.

As the horror sank in, an aura of untouchability enveloped what had been the highest caste of Lloyd's membership. Tony South had been a working member of Lloyd's for many years with Willis Faber and had known and trusted Peter Cameron-Webb. South was one of the 2% of PCW members who had rejected the 1984 settlement; this was beginning to seem a prophetic gesture.

South wanted the market to own up to its failure of self-regulation and spread the losses evenly on the many rather than heavily on the few. He believed this was in the best interests of Lloyd's and its present and future members. He voiced this opinion to a fellow working member on the way home on the train.

The other man was not a Cameron-Webb victim and he had been drinking.

'Let me tell you this,' he spat. 'If you bastards carry on like this, you will bring down the lot of us. You bastards, I'm not bloody well paying to bail you out. Sod you, I say – sod the lot of you!'

The man sat back in his seat and his eyes began to close with the heat and the alcohol.

Pulbrook 90, a venerable non-marine syndicate, was the next casualty of the long-tail furies. The syndicate had underwritten policies which had turned into millions of dollars of claims against the Manville Corporation, one of America's largest companies and a leader in the field of asbestos products. Ironically the founder of Manville had died prematurely of chronic lung disease.

Manville was facing claims which totalled $5 billion and were likely to go on for the next twenty-five years. But the Pulbrook 90 members had another problem from America.

Like Manville's, the other long-tail asbestos policies went back many years. While the present members of syndicate 90 had reaped the profits on the renewals, they had done so at the risk of the renewed policies turning into claims. Now that the worst had happened, many members began to question whether or not they should pay out for claims on policies first underwritten years before they had joined. It was too late for them, of course. People who had made money easily always found it difficult to pay.

Nowhere was this unpalatable truth more starkly evident than in the Rocky Mountain Arsenal, near Denver, Colorado. Owned by the US military, the land had been leased by Shell Oil and others since 1946 and allegedly been used as a giant open-air dumping ground for toxic wastes. The toxic wastes had seeped into the ground and into the water table, which had polluted the rivers for miles around. Shell was facing a $200 million claim for damages.

Why was it that a policy underwritten and renewed year after year could explode in the face of an underwriter and his syndicate members thirty years later?

The answer lay in the changing legislation concerning the environment in America. Underwriters in Britain had gone on stamping the broker's slip year after year after year, without much thought. Year after year, the broker had had perhaps a month to consider the risk before he even brought it onto the floor of The Room. The underwriter had had perhaps sixty seconds to consider and stamp it. A renewal might even be stamped by a junior.

Nothing had changed at Lloyd's. Everything had changed in America. This was the message of Peter Keen from San Francisco. This was the message of the asbestos committee at the Leeds Castle meeting. This was the fate that had befallen Pulbrook 90; and was now to befall the man who had underwritten the biggest book of asbestosis business of all – Richard Outhwaite and his syndicate 317/661.

Gracechurch Street, London, 1985

Richard Outhwaite had told his members in 1984 that there was no undue cause to worry about the 1982 account. Now his colleague Maurice Hussey wrote again to the agents who represented those members with confirmation of the news:

> In view of the many problems faced by Syndicates in
> closing the 1982 year, I thought it advisable to send you
> a note of our preliminary results as soon as possible before
> waiting for the final version of the Accounts.
>
> I am sorry to tell you that the 1982 year has resulted in
> only a marginal profit. This is disappointing as the underlying

results of the business have been quite satisfactory. However, the significant increase in advices from the old years arising from Asbestosis and other causes has led us to take what we believe is the prudent step of increasing our reserves very substantially.

The effective result is to produce a small profit after syndicate expenses but before individual Names' expenses such as US Tax.

The Outhwaite managing agency sent out these letters and enclosed small cheques where necessary. Then Outhwaite did a strange thing. Only two months later he changed his mind: 'Following the publication of our accounts we have discussed with many agents the implications of the qualified audit report. We have reconsidered the matter and have decided to leave the 1982 year open.'

What did this mean, only two months after he had told the members agents to tell their members that 1982 would, albeit on a very modest scale, be a profitable year?

Outhwaite explained:

We arrived at our closing reinsurance after a long and critical examination of the outstanding liabilities in the 1982 and prior accounts. The auditors agreed the figure (without qualification) and we advised all agents and many of our Names accordingly. Some ten days later our auditors informed us that they wished to re-open the position, not because they queried the quantum of the carry-forward, but because they were unwilling to sign the report on an unqualified basis. We decided nevertheless to close the 1982 year . . .

Subsequent discussions have now led us to believe this to have been a mistaken view and we have therefore decided to leave the year open . . .

It is our considered view that despite the common assumption that an open account usually arises because of a

significant loss, the 1982 account will prove to be
profitable . . .

What did this mean?

Normally after three years an underwriting year was 'closed'
and the members of the syndicate were relieved of any further
liability. If a year was left open it was because the anticipated
level of outstanding claims was too great for the underwriter to
quantify and no reinsurer would touch it; as had been the case
with Warrilow and Oakeley Vaughan.

Nobody would have placed Richard Outhwaite in such lowly
company. Yet Outhwaite too was leaving a year open. He was
still insisting that in the end the 1982 year would be profitable
for members. Where that end was, nobody could say.

This letter too was sent out to agents and their members.
Rowbotham de Rougemont passed it on to Betty Atkins and
Sylvia Hatton.

Betty Atkins was puzzled by its contents. She did not know
exactly what was meant by an open year and she was grateful
for the explanation supplied by her members agency. As long as
the firm stood by them, the two women would be all right. The
worst that would happen was that the firm would have to bear
their losses. Betty Atkins hoped this would not happen; it would
be so unfair on the firm after they had shown such kindness in
putting her and Sylvia into Lloyd's.

*　　*　　*

While Outhwaite was feeling the heat Ian Hay Davison was
experiencing the chill: 'I can't get myself heard in this place,'
he told Christopher Moran.

Davison put his feelings in writing in a formal letter to
the Bank of England.

'First,' he concluded '. . . the system of having unwritten
terms of reference for the Chairman could only work in a

climate of self-restraint which we now know cannot always be guaranteed. The experiment of yoking a full-time Chairman to a full-time Chief Executive cannot work without detailed written responsibilities for both, and this must be done for my successor.

'Second, there is a profound misunderstanding between the Committee of Lloyd's and the outside world about the meaning of the phrase "Self-regulation." To most informed observers, and no doubt to most Names at Lloyd's, it means that the rules are made by those to whom they are to be applied. The application of rules, on a case by case basis, would be the duty of the staff (*vide* Fisher above).

'The traditional Lloyd's man sees it differently. He has never known a written rule book, but has relied upon the precepts of the Chairs. To him self-regulation is consonant with self-government. The Chairs decide, case by case, what shall be done. This approach suffers from the lack of clear policy direction, or, at the least, from the lack of proper segregation of policy from execution. Further, those deciding are frequently *parti-pris*, often concerned themselves, may have a conflict of interest, and usually suffer from knowing the individuals socially.'

Or, Davison might have added, through one of Lloyd's three masonic lodges.

'The correct answer,' he went on, 'must be to relieve the elected Chairs from any responsibility for the day to day regulation of the Market, which should be handled by the professionals, expert in the topic, dispassionate and experienced. Rule-making itself, however, should remain in the hands of the elected Council. This would produce a much more effective regime which would still be properly described as self-regulation.

'Third,' Davison concluded, 'given the experiences of the last two and a half years, it is necessary for me to be succeeded by a forceful public figure capable of dealing with a climate of Committee opinion that is still largely unaltered despite the experiences of the last three years. He must be a Deputy Chairman because of the status that brings here, and should be appointed for a five year term, renewable once. He must be independent and must, therefore, come from outside the Society. His appointment must be publicly endorsed by the Bank. And, if self-regulation is to work, he must be supported by a powerful staff of senior colleagues who apply the rules.'

The Deputy Governor of the Bank of England, Kit McMahon, had been a visitor to Davison's house in Somerset. Like Gordon Richardson, McMahon was a friend. Davison came out with it.

'Either Miller goes,' he told McMahon. 'Or I do.'

Lloyd's took what disciplinary measures it could against Cameron-Webb. In the case of Cameron-Webb himself this meant no disciplinary measures at all, as Green had allowed him to resign before they could be taken. He was working openly in Florida on the Insurance Exchange of the Americas.

Peter Dixon was fined £1 million and expelled from Lloyd's. Other lesser confederates were censured, fined and suspended. Dixon was still in hiding in Marbella and made no move to pay his fine. The Department of Trade enquiry ground on. But the Director of Public Prosecutions still made no move to bring about arrests.

James Birkin was a member whose mother was a Cameron-Webb Name. Birkin wrote to the Director of Public Prosecutions. He wanted to know when Cameron-Webb and Dixon were going to be extradited.

A week later, on 24 October 1985, he received a letter from T.J. Taylor, Assistant Director of Public Prosecutions.

'I write to inform you,' Taylor said, 'that the Department has no knowledge or record of either of the two gentlemen about whom you wrote . . .'

Birkin could not believe what he was seeing. He wrote back repeating his request and again Taylor repeated his reply. Furthermore, Taylor said, there was no chance that a mistake had been made or the papers sent to some other department.

Birkin immediately informed the Council of Lloyd's. On 11 November 1985, D.G. Williams, Controller of Fraud Investigation at the office of the Director of Public Prosecutions, wrote that there had been an 'error' in the 'Registry.' The papers were there all the time.

To some PCW members it now seemed that while the innocent were being punished by cash calls the guilty men had been allowed to go free for fear of what they might say were they extradited to Britain. One rumour circulated to the effect that Cameron-Webb and Dixon had even offered to return and give a televised press conference.

Most PCW members were unaware of these rumours. They continued to contemplate their circumstances with varying degrees of shock and asked themselves whether or not they could have foreseen such a calamity.

David D'Ambrumenil, the broker who had visited Cameron-Webb in Switzerland, was at one stage facing losses of over £2 million. He would eventually claw back most of these but his connection with Cameron-Webb over the Unimar affair would cause him to be suspended from Lloyd's. Eddie Kulukundis had had sufficient inside knowledge to get out in time and limited his losses to £8,500, a manageable sum for a Greek shipping magnate. Peter Miller, the Chairman of Lloyd's, had recommended the first settlement but still had a bill for £9,000.

Others further from the heart of the market were less fortunate. Tony South had rejected the first settlement and was still fighting for the losses to be spread thinly and widely over the market. Clive Bemrose had lost a considerable amount and would eventually receive a final settlement cheque for £0.37.5p (he did not cash it). The Fulham secretary had no money and in any case had decided not to pay.

Then there was Michael Church.

Thelnetham, Norfolk, 1985

The shock had worn off from the first cash call and the disappearance of Cameron-Webb, but Michael Church still could not believe he had been deceived by his friend of many years. 'He'll come back,' he told his friend Janis Nash, 'he'll sort it out; you'll see.'

'Why don't you just get out of Lloyd's now?' she said. 'If he could resign, surely you can?'

'I can't,' he said. 'It takes three years, and in any case I told you, I trust him.'

'Michael,' she said, 'that place is a cesspit. Your trouble is you are just too squeaky-clean.'

But she knew when she could and could not press him as he became subject to ever-changing moods. A big man in every sense, he suddenly seemed vulnerable and forlorn. Gone was the man who loved to dress up and sing 'Burlington Bertie.' Gone was the talk of marriage and Minorca.

Then they started talking of marriage again and there was hope. They spoke to the vicar.

He started to fight back against the circumstances into which he had fallen. He managed to find more stop loss insurance to reduce his losses. He joined the PCW 1985 Association and contributed to their legal costs. He went to their meetings. He started talking again about Minorca.

He went to see his accountant.

The accountant advised him against marrying. They would both be ruined, he said, if he did.

They bought a new car, in her name.

They stopped talking about Minorca.

The stop loss ran out and this time he could not find any more.

He tried to find a job and was told he was too old, even though he had retired relatively young to look after Mary.

The accountant said he stood to lose the house, the boat, the money, the pensions, everything.

He sent a Christmas present to a long-standing colleague in the market. The man's wife sent him back a parcel of sale goods – she had not even taken off the price tags.

He could not persuade friends in the market to return his calls.

It was beginning to get to him. It was beginning to get to her.

Lower Lodge had been a happy house for Michael Church and Janis Nash. Now it was a place of shadows in which he prowled about as if it were a prison from which there was no escape. He began to scare people with the way he paced up and down, up and down the drawing room.

Janis Nash was becoming more and more worried. She tried and failed to interest him in other pastimes. She managed to persuade him to talk to the local vicar. She managed to persuade him to talk to a psychiatrist. Everybody liked Michael Church and nobody wanted to see him so depressed. Meanwhile the letters kept on coming, and Michael Church kept on paying the cash calls for the losses on the syndicates of his old friend Peter Cameron-Webb.

* * *

The press sniffed around the fringes of Lloyd's and the news leaked out about the baby syndicates, through which insiders had creamed off the best business for themselves, their associates and their families.

Cameron-Webb had been the unrivalled exponent of these but they were commonplace at the heart of the market. In a year when Lloyd's would announce record underwriting losses, the members who bore them were outraged to learn that one baby syndicate run by the leading underwriter Henry Chester (of the Chester report into Oakeley Vaughan) had made an average profit of £8,600 per £10,000 of business underwritten for his members. Chester's baby syndicate 485 was the second most profitable syndicate in the entire market; its members were Henry Chester, Mrs Henry Chester and a friend.

The Chairman of Lloyd's himself, Peter Miller, was filmed for a BBC TV *Panorama* programme and casually admitted that he too was a baby syndicate member. It was put to Miller that it was hard to find working members to police the market who did not have a vested interest in the market they were supposed to be policing.

Miller's reply was revealing.

'Isn't that,' he said, 'the very heart of self-regulation?'

The item did not appear in the subsequent broadcast.

Other baby syndicates went on trading for the time being. Syndicate 973 consisted of David Coleridge and Ralph Rokeby-Johnson of R.W. Sturge, Ian 'Goldfinger' Posgate and Messrs Bellew, Parry and Raven.

Coleridge only made a total of £216 out of this syndicate, but baby syndicate 207, whose parent was Sturge 206, made him a profit in 1982 of £5,700 for a £10,000 line.

Baby syndicates were not illegal at Lloyd's at this time, but the outrage unleashed by the news of their existence meant that they soon would be; a fact that would bring some embarrassment to Coleridge when he was Chairman of an embattled Lloyd's in the early 1990s.

In the autumn of 1985 Lloyd's announced its worst-ever underwriting loss of £188 million for the 1982 year. Peter Miller added that Lloyd's had made an overall profit of £57 million which was cause for some satisfaction. But, as Charles Sturge and John Rew pointed out in their *Lloyd's League Tables*, the profit commission payable by members to their agents would be between £50 million and £60 million; in other words, Lloyd's had barely broken even.

The £57 million profit figure was vital to Lloyd's at a time when it had suspended 200 members for failing to meet solvency requirements after the losses they had suffered as a result of the activities of Cameron-Webb: twenty times the average number of members usually suspended.

Lloyd's desperately needed more members and more capacity

because the insurance industry was coming out of recession. It had tried to contain the PCW disaster by earmarking £60 million to meet claims from the Central Fund. But £58 million of that was already accounted for and the figure would not stop rising. At this rate Cameron-Webb would make the combined Harrison, Wilcox and Roylance affairs look like rent money spent at the races.

A further blow was that the 1985 Finance Act put an end to the neat little loophole known as 'bond-washing', whereby Lloyd's members and other investors could turn highly-taxable investment income into more lightly-taxable capital gains. This particular dodge involved buying 'gilts' – safe but unsexy government stocks – and reselling them just before they went ex-dividend. The result was a technical change of classification and a lower tax liability. This practice had been widespread at Lloyd's.

The four thousand people waiting to join Lloyd's at this time were not unaware of these problems although in many cases they were ignorant of the finer points of bond-washing. Besides, they all seemed to know ten people who had made profits for every one person who had made losses.

The new mood of confidence was further established under Peter Miller who was proving himself to be an extremely energetic Chairman. The tax breaks were diminished but insurance premiums were rising. The idea of joining Lloyd's was promoted as enthusiastically as ever by members agents, by bank managers, by solicitors, by accountants and 'independent financial advisers.' The membership was expanding yet somehow the club managed to retain its exclusive aura. In this bullish climate it seemed short-sighted, even churlish, to doubt. Yet one or two dissenting voices could still be heard.

Dulverton, Somerset, 1985

Christopher Thomas-Everard, the Somerset sheepfarmer, had done reasonably well since joining Lloyd's twelve years earlier.

The £2,000 or £3,000 a year after agent's commission had come in handy for a farmer with a wife and children who was cash-poor and likely to stay that way.

Thomas-Everard was all too aware that his liquidity could be made drastically worse as well as better by his Lloyd's membership. To this end he took all the precautions to minimise the risk inherent in his unlimited liability. He subscribed to the Association of Lloyd's Members, to *Lloyd's League Tables* and the *Digest of Lloyd's News*. He paid Financial Intelligence & Research for a risk analysis of his syndicates. He studied the annual Lloyd's solvency reports. He read the Fisher Report and the 1982 Lloyd's Act. He assisted the disciplinary investigation into Brooks and Dooley.

He bought the expensive and confidential 'Blue Book' list of Lloyd's members every year and studied where the people with power and influence placed themselves and their families. He wrote regularly to his members agency asking to be placed on such syndicates; they usually wrote back saying that such syndicates, like Frank 'the Bank' Barber's 990, only accepted members who worked in the market.

Once Thomas-Everard had even managed to get himself placed on such a syndicate: Mander 552. He was told after two months that there had been a 'mistake' and Mander only accepted work-ing members. Thomas-Everard had promptly been taken off the syndicate in question.

Among the syndicates Thomas-Everard had been placed on were Feltrim 540 and 847. Thomas-Everard knew that these were Marine Excess of Loss syndicates because his agents had told him so. But Thomas-Everard had been doing some hard thinking. What exactly was Excess of Loss?

There was nothing wrong with Excess of Loss reinsurance per se. But where did it start and where did it finish? If one underwriter reinsured part of a risk taken by another underwriter, did he know how many times that risk had already been reinsured in the market? If he did know, did he care? Thomas-Everard both knew and cared about how Excess of Loss (EOL) could turn into London Market Excess of Loss (LMX), which was a higher level of reinsurance – and risk – altogether. Surely LMX syndicates, though inordinately profitable in fair weather, could in the event of an actual catastrophe go massively and monstrously wrong?

Thomas-Everard wanted small and steady profits rather than fair weather jackpots and this made him think all the harder. If an active underwriter specialised in Excess of Loss, as he had been told Patrick Feltrim Fagan did, then he was treading a high tightrope. Who else was on his syndicates and what did they think about this? How many of them were working members?

Why was it so easy to be placed on Feltrim 540 and 847 and yet impossible to stay on Mander 552 or be placed on Frank 'the Bank's' 990? Furthermore, was Patrick Feltrim Fagan in fact reinsuring the syndicates available to working members but denied to Somerset sheepfarmers?

Though he did not know it, Thomas-Everard was expressing the first doubts about what was to become known as the LMX spiral.

On 10 November 1985 Thomas-Everard wrote to his members agency asking how big his exposure was to Excess of Loss business.

They wrote back on 12 November: 'I am sure you will appreciate that the questions you have raised in your letter will require a considerable amount of work, as this information cannot be looked up in a book.'

Thomas-Everard persisted; after all, this was what he paid his members agent their salary and profit commission to do.

They wrote back: 'I gather you are obtaining a copy of the Chatset (the company founded by Charles Sturge and John Rew) *League Tables* and you will find that these give a breakdown of the Underwriter's accounts in a great many instances. You will also find a certain amount of information in the Syndicate accounts.'

Thomas-Everard bought the latest copy of *Lloyd's League*

Tables. This cost him £7,045 – £45 for *Lloyd's League Tables* and £7,000 for the advice; his agent's fixed annual fee before profit commission.

On page 26 he found that General Marine syndicate 540 underwrote 86% Excess of Loss and 14% General Marine Business. Primary EOL was OK. EOL syndicates shown with the letters 'LMX' denoted the fact that they were higher up the reinsurance spiral; that was not OK. But the letters 'LMX' did not appear against Feltrim 540.

The £7,045 had been worth spending, if only for the peace of mind. Christopher Thomas-Everard was relieved. He had a £25,000 line on Feltrim 540 alone. He might even increase it, for that matter.

*   *   *

Thomas-Everard was not the only farmer asking questions of his members agency.

While many of the gentlemen of Lloyd's had been at Eton and Harrow, Hugh Bourn had travelled from farm to farm in Lincolnshire threshing corn with machinery he carried on his back; thirty years later he still had the scars to prove it. Bourn farmed 3,000 acres of cattle and sheep and had built up a multi-million pound building company. Unlike many farmers he was land-rich and cash-rich. He still repaired his own farm equipment and saw to his own livestock, but after thirty years' sweat and toil the idea that his money could work twice at Lloyd's appealed to him.

Bourn had a friend in insurance who met a Lloyd's members agent on his commuter train. The members agent was quick to strike up a conversation. Bourn's friend had been just as quick to follow it up.

'There's something I want to talk to you about . . .'

At the Rota interview at Lime Street they had made it quite clear that Bourn was liable down to his last set of cufflinks.

Bourn's agent, David Kenington of Stancomb and Kenington, had echoed this. But such was the general atmosphere of conviviality that Bourn had 'a smirk in his brain' when he heard this said. It had not happened to any of his agent's other members and it was not going to happen to him.

That was two years ago. By this time Bourn, his wife Monica and their three sons were all members of Lloyd's. Bourn was on 120 syndicates and his family were on over 200. With so many syndicates there was a correspondingly huge excess clause on the stop loss policies that meant in the event of big losses he would still be seriously exposed. Bourn himself was writing the maximum premium of £2 million.

He had persuaded his wife Monica to join against her better judgement. She was a charitable soul with little interest in material things. Bourn had heard how some syndicates were of a higher risk than others. He was particularly worried about those which specialised in reinsuring chunks of other people's risks; in other words, Excess of Loss.

He invited Kenington, his agent, to Lincolnshire. 'Monica's a bit nervous,' he told him over lunch, 'I just want to be sure nothing goes unnecessarily wrong.'

'Quite understand, Hugh,' Kenington said, 'I'll only put her on low-risk syndicates.'

'That's a relief, then,' Bourn turned to her.

'There is one thing,' the agent added, 'the family are on so many syndicates; is it all right if you have a small line on the same syndicates here and there?'

Bourn saw nothing wrong with this. After all, the family had one of the biggest spreads in Lloyd's. Their agency knew this and they were pleasant and decent people with whom to do business. Bourn himself did not mind taking a risk and was on a number of Excess of Loss syndicates; he had a line of £25,000 on Feltrim 847 alone. He was also on Warrilow and Gooda Walker. But the other members of the family had to be treated cautiously. As long as the risks were spread evenly he felt sure all would be well.

Other people were asking questions in places more public than Somerset and Lincolnshire.

The House of Commons, Westminster, 1985

Brian Sedgemore was a Labour MP and he was not well disposed towards the secretive gentlemen of Lime Street. Under the cloak of Parliamentary privilege, whereby he could say more or less what he liked, Sedgemore and others raised a series of highly embarrassing questions in Parliament. These questions were all the more embarrassing in the light of the fact that only three years had elapsed since the passage of the 1982 Lloyd's Act.

The MPs were particularly keen to know why nothing had been done to extradite and prosecute Peter Dixon and Peter Cameron-Webb. Cameron-Webb was still working freely in Florida. Dixon had fled Marbella and the Costa del Sol for Costa Rica. Dixon had still not paid his fine; even if he did, £1 million was chickenfeed compared to the sums he had embezzled.

Dixon and Cameron-Webb were not the only names mentioned in an unfavourable light.

In a series of questions raised over the next few weeks, the MPs called for the resignation of Peter Miller and demanded to know more about the role played in the various scandals by Sir Peter Green. They criticised Miller over the PCW settlement and made dark noises about the interest accrued on Green's offshore cash in the Cayman Islands. They pointed ominously to the three Lloyd's lodges and the influence of freemasonry. They wanted action from the Director of Public Prosecutions. They called for Lloyd's to be brought within the scope of the new Financial Services Bill; and for the abolition of the 1982 Lloyd's Act.

Why were these questions so confidently asked and left unanswered?

One reason was the nature of the questioners. They could

be dismissed as mere left-wing 'Lloyd's bashers' during the rule of a Conservative government whose ranks contained many Lloyd's members including two Cabinet ministers. Another was the Lloyd's Act itself, whose difficult passage had left a reluctance on the part of many involved to repeat the experience.

But the third and most powerful reason was the enduring lack of motivation when it came to the Director of Public Prosecutions. Elsewhere this became all too plain.

Christopher Moran, the expelled former broker, had sworn to expose what he saw as wrongdoing with a vehemence and a considerable degree of success. He had testified or would do so in the investigations into Oakeley Vaughan, Brooks and Dooley, D'Ambrumenil, Green, and Bellew, Parry and Raven. Moran took his considerable knowledge of Cameron-Webb and Dixon to the Secretary of State for Trade and Industry, Norman Tebbitt.

Tebbitt listened patiently, but his reply was unequivocal:

'Mr Moran,' Tebbitt told him, 'we're lifting no more stones.'

* * *

Davison had seen the end coming since his letter to the Bank of England and his conversations with Kit McMahon. Both had resulted in sympathetic noises but neither had produced a resounding display of support.

The new Governor of the Bank of England, Robin Leigh-Pemberton, was also a member of Lloyd's. At their first meeting two years earlier Davison had found him amicable but somewhat distracted as to whether or not he should remain a member (he did). Thereafter, the Johnson Matthey affair occupied the Governor's full attention and resolving his differences with the Chancellor Nigel Lawson took priority over Lloyd's.

Prompted by an apparent error in Lloyd's accounts, Peter Miller had appointed Sir Kenneth Berrill, a member of the Council, to review the organisation of the staff. Berrill's report had suggested changes in the role of the Chief Executive.

Davison did not necessarily disagree, but he objected strongly to the way the evidence had been collected. He felt Miller was using Berrill as a rod with which to beat his back.

Davison had had enough. He said as much to his former DTI colleague Philip Brown, by this time head of Lloyd's regulatory services: 'I was told three to five years. The three years are up in February.

'But,' Davison told him, 'I'm going to go in such a way as to achieve the maximum of effect. I want to do everything I can for the outside members.'

Davison sat down and wrote the letter that would end his career as Lloyd's first externally-appointed Chief Executive. Davison acknowledged that he had been able to achieve many of the tasks he had been commissioned to achieve. But he also made it clear that he and Miller disagreed over whether or not this meant his job was done.

'My conclusion,' he wrote, 'that now is the time to resign is prompted by the Council's recent initiation of an internal enquiry into the structure of Lloyd's, which has started discussions about changing the Terms of Reference and status of the post of Chief Executive. The preparation of the Council's evidence for this enquiry has revealed divergent opinions about the continuing need for the Chief Executive to be independent and responsible directly to the Council.

'My own views on the paramount necessity of an independent Chief Executive, with appropriate terms of reference, responsible directly to the Council, have not changed and, therefore, I would find it impossible to continue in office were those terms to be significantly altered . . .'

Davison made sure the press received a copy at the same time as the Chairman, a move which infuriated Miller. He also waited to release the news until he had met with the new Secretary for Trade and Industry, Leon Brittan. Unlike the Governor of the Bank of England Brittan was not a Name at Lloyd's. Out of their conversation came the motivation for a new enquiry into Lloyd's under Sir Patrick Neill, which, had Davison not resigned, would not have been appointed.

Miller was quick to play down any talk of trouble. 'Ian Hay Davison seems to feel there is some threat to the independence of a future Chief Executive,' he declared. 'That independence is guaranteed. As of right, he would have a voice on the Council of Lloyd's.'

'But,' Miller added, 'we do not feel that voice should be imposed from outside. To do so would be a negation of self-regulation.'

Within the corridors of power at Lloyd's the reaction to Davison's resignation was swift and uncompromising. Davison instantly became a non-person. In an album later displayed there was a photograph of the Chairman and members of Council sitting in the shell of The Room in the new Richard Rogers building. On the back of the photograph was an outline, with names and numbers.

Against Davison's outline was an asterisk: 'Deputy Chairman and Chief Executive – Alan Lord.' A further asterisk led to a further statement. 'This photograph was taken before Alan Lord succeeded Ian Hay Davison as Deputy Chairman and Chief Executive in May 1986.'

'I am the Prime Minister,' Miller had said at his first press conference, 'Mr Davison is head of the Civil Service.'

Davison's successor, Alan Lord, was a career civil servant who had reached the top at the Treasury during a Labour government committed to state spending on a huge scale. He had then moved to be Chief Executive of Dunlop during that company's decline from prominence. Lord was 58 when he became Chief Executive; Davison had been 51.

Davison let it be known that the one leaving present he did not want was a clock. Miller gave him the biggest and ugliest clock he had ever seen.

Thus ended the career of Lloyd's first Chief Executive. The

truth was that Davison's face did not fit in a culture that still adhered to the axiom: 'First generation don't even speak.'

But, if Ian Hay Davison was truly to go down in the history of Lloyd's as no more than an asterisk, it was up to the club now to prove that it deserved the freedom it had won.

SEVEN

INTO THE SPIRAL

First Cromer, then Fisher, then Richardson, then Neill. The Warden of All Souls and Vice Chancellor of Oxford University was the latest member of the great and the good to grapple with Lloyd's of London.

Sir Patrick Neill's appointment was a direct consequence of Ian Hay Davison's departure and the arrival of the Government's Financial Services Bill. His remit was to examine the viability of self-regulation under the 1982 Lloyd's Act.

The difference with Neill was that his was the first such enquiry to be commissioned not by Lloyd's but by the Government. In the aftermath of PCW and the fact that Lloyd's had just been forced to hand over £34 million from offshore reinsurance schemes to the Inland Revenue, there was considerable hope – and scepticism – attached to Sir Patrick's appointment.

Scepticism rather than hope was the line taken by Ralph Nader in America. Nader, the champion of American consumer rights, launched an all-out attack on Lloyd's, which he said was a major threat to the equitable settlement of environmentally-based insurance claims in America.

Murray Lawrence, the Deputy Chairman, who was well aware of the asbestosis peril, retorted that Lloyd's had paid out on such claims to its own considerable cost. Tell it, he might have added, to the members of Pulbrook 90. But Nader would not be moved.

Lloyd's, he said, was inflating insurance rates and thereby denying cover to the average working man.

Lloyd's was trying to bring about 'a draconian reduction in the rights of injured people in our country. They are particularly focussing on toxic waste exposure and they want to secure a curtailment of the rights of victims.'

It was 'territorial imperialism by Lloyd's that is offensive almost beyond the power of words to describe' ... and as such it was 'highly provocative, highly insulting to our country.'

Rubbish, said Lloyd's. American courts had been awarding higher and higher damages, and the nothing-up-front-percentage-of-the-profits system practised by American lawyers meant that anybody could and did sue.

None of this seemed to put off the existing members or the people who were clamouring for election. Peter Miller's chairmanship had been unsullied, it seemed, by the publicity over Davison's departure. The new Deputy Chairman and Chief Executive was settling in nicely – there were no more remarks about barrels and rotten apples – and the Chairman was becoming more statesmanlike by the day.

Miller had been unwavering in his insistence that his own choice of designer rather than that of Richard Rogers be responsible for furnishing the top two floors of the building. These were the two floors housing the Chairman, Chief Executive, senior staff and the John Adam Committee Room (transplanted virtually in its entirety from the 1958 building). In every other respect however Miller and the Committee and Council had allowed Rogers free rein in his brief: 'To maintain Lloyd's as the centre of world insurance and the unity of The Room.'

At £163 million and £300 per square foot this did not come cheap and the new building was the most expensive under way in the City. Rogers liked to compare it to a castle keep, where towers and staircases separated the served and the servants. Six towers housing lavatories, lifts, staircases and ducting serviced each floor the size of a football pitch. An atrium 250 feet high

topped with a glass vault and crisscrossed by escalators contained
The Room and the rostrum with the Lutine Bell. To some the effect
was like the 'stately pleasure-dome' of 'Kubla Khan' by Samuel
Taylor Coleridge, whose descendant David Coleridge was by this
time Deputy Chairman of Lloyd's. To others, the effect was like
a Grand Babylonian Cathedral made out of materials from an
abandoned central heating project.

The architect was exultant. 'One may recognise in each part,'
he declared, 'its process of manufacture, erection, maintenance
and finally demolition – the why, the how and the what of the
building.'

Some joked that Lloyd's had begun in a coffee house and
would end in a percolator. Others less kindly described it as the
only building in London with the intestines on the outside and
the arseholes on the inside. But whatever people thought and said
about the new building they could not ignore it. Nor could the
inference be escaped that such a forward-looking headquarters
reflected an institution that was looking forward with the times.

The results were beginning to trickle in of the 1983 underwriting
year and they reflected the new forward-looking mood. A modest
underwriting profit seemed likely. Underwriters were enthusing to
members agents about higher premium rates and the agents were
enthusing about this to their existing and prospective members.
Now was the time to increase their premium limits; now was the
time to join.

In they came . . . the doctors and dentists and landowners
and sportsmen and women with short professional lives who
wanted to pay the school fees and make their money last longer.
Those who began underwriting in 1986 included Michael Colvin
MP and his wife Nichola.

Being an MP was an expensive business and the farm did
not bring in much income. Their children were grown up and
off their hands and they took the view that if they went in with
different members agents they would spread the risk.

Mr Colvin went in through Roberts and Hiscox having been

recommended by his solicitor. He used a bank guarantee to obtain his Lloyd's deposit. Mrs Colvin went in like the Bourn family through Stancomb and Kenington, recommended by a cousin. Like Mrs Bourn, Mrs Colvin told her agents that she did not want to take risks; she would be happy if she made a couple of thousand pounds a year. They listened to what she was saying and with her premium of £350,000 of business placed her on a spread of syndicates including Feltrim and Gooda Walker.

Those elected in 1986 would not begin underwriting until the first day of the following year. They included champion jockey John Francombe and David Stirling, the legendary founder of the elite Special Air Service Regiment. Another distinguished and highly decorated SAS figure, Major General Peter de la Billière, had been elected four years earlier through the Secretan agency. Major General de la Billière had been placed on Secretan 367 and had a £30,000 line on both Wellington 406 and 448.

Her Royal Highness Princess Michael of Kent was fond of describing her philosophy to the press. 'I live in the eighteenth century in my mind,' she told *The Times*, 'I see my whole life as a cultivation of taste. If I were asked what is the objective of my life – leaving apart my husband and my children – I would say it was to improve the quality of my life, intellectually, culturally and in the way I choose to live.'

Princess Michael also chose to improve the quality of her life by becoming a member of Lloyd's through the members agency of her friend Sir Francis Dashwood.

Then there was Dr George Pakozdi.

Hamilton, Ontario, 1986

Hamilton, Ontario is the kind of place where the streets are clean and busy professional people live busy professional lives. They are too busy and devoted to their work to indulge in wild business speculations to which they are in any case temperamentally disinclined. Hamilton, and Burlington, and Bracebridge people are typical 'passive investors' – the closest they come to taking a risk is letting the fund manager choose the stocks.

George Pakozdi was a Hamilton dentist. He had a retired dentist friend called Dr Neil Webster. A year earlier Webster told him there was something he wanted to talk to him about.

Webster told Dr Pakozdi that for the last six or seven years he had been a member of Lloyd's of London. He explained how he had made a good income from underwriting. He told Pakozdi that a Mr Robin Kingsley and a Mr Robert Hallam would shortly be in Toronto. Kingsley and Hallam were Lloyd's members agents from Lime Street Agency. Lime Street was their North American and Canadian arm. Webster, who admitted that he received a commission, said he could arrange for Pakozdi to meet them.

Pakozdi had gone along to the Sheraton Centre in Toronto to meet Kingsley and Hallam who had flown in from London. They explained the concept of Lloyd's and showed him how a good spread of syndicates was available since business was expanding and rates were rising. Pakozdi was concerned however by the concept of unlimited liability – that didn't sound right. The two men from Lloyd's explained how this tradition was 300 years old and Lloyd's had done well for over three centuries.

Furthermore, they said, since his underwriting membership would be spread over many syndicates, the losses of one sector of the market would be offset by the profits of others. They projected annual profits for him of between 5% and 7%.

Pakozdi could not make up his mind.

Over the next twelve months Dr Webster came to his house on two occasions to talk about Lloyd's. He said profits were improving because insurance rates were higher since the bottom of the market had been passed. He told Pakozdi he had received

quite a large cheque in June and expected another one the following year. 'George,' he said, 'I expect never to write a cheque
for losses at Lloyd's.'

Any losses, he repeated, would be covered by profits from
other syndicates. Webster reminded Pakozdi that Kingsley and
Hallam would be in Hamilton again shortly.

Dr Pakozdi met them at the Sheraton Hotel, Hamilton, in
March 1986. Again they stated that insurance rates were rising.
They supplied a sample portfolio of syndicates going back several
years and indicated that this was what he could expect in the way
of annual returns. Some years would be a little worse, some a little
better.

Dr Pakozdi was convinced. He put up a letter of credit for
£175,000 through the Hamilton branch of the Bank of Nova
Scotia. He went to London and to Lloyd's for the Rota interview.
He had specifically advised Kingsley and Hallam that he wanted
to be placed on a conservative portfolio of syndicates. Kingsley
assured him he had a well-balanced portfolio without excessive
risk or exposure. Thus it was that Dr Pakozdi came to Lloyd's
and to a spread of syndicates including Feltrim 540 and 847 and
Gooda Walker 290.

* * *

In London, Clive Francis, the former RAF squadron leader turned
property tycoon, had not fared well since his election eight years
earlier. The cash calls of early 1986 were just the latest in a long
line of Lime Street laments; Pulbrook 334, Spicer and White 895
and others had cost him £120,000.

He thought of baling out and told a friend as much. 'Clive,'
his friend said, 'don't do that. If you want to change, I can get
you onto a first class agency.'

Francis joined Sudbrook, a subsidiary of Lime Street run by
Robert Hallam. It was named after Kingsley's Carolean house
on Ham Common. Francis too was placed on Feltrim 540, 542,

847, and the Gooda Walker syndicates. In this way he hoped to claw back his losses and return to profit.

In Hertfordshire, John Clementson, the former London Symphony Orchestra oboist, had done quite well through the syndicates managed by his members agency, Bowrings. But Clementson knew someone who always seemed to do better than him. When Bowrings were unable to give him the spread of syndicates he wanted he used this as his excuse to go elsewhere.

Clementson changed his members agent and went to Archdale, run by Hubert Morris. Here he found a wider spread of syndicates to suit the higher premium he wanted to write. Clementson was placed on Macmillan 80, Poland 104, 105 and 108, Gooda Walker 164, 290 and 298, Devonshire 216, Rose Thomson Young 255, Potter 384 (Aragorn), Wellington 446, Warrilow 553 and others.

The Gooda syndicates seemed particularly attractive because they were growing so rapidly. In 1982 Gooda Walker 298 had had only 61 Names and a stamp capacity of £385,000. In 1984 it was £39,750,000. In 1985 it was £86,700,000. 298 dealt with Excess of Loss business, but there was nothing intrinsically wrong with that. Every risk that came into Lloyd's had to be reinsured. Besides, the Gooda syndicates had been established for very many years and had weathered Hurricane Betsy. Derek Walker, the active underwriter, never flew his private aircraft too high or too far.

Clementson was now writing a line of £500,000. In his first year his agent Hubert Morris told him: 'If you make less than £50,000 this year I shall be very disappointed.'

In fact Clementson made nothing; but within a very short time he was to look back on this year of no profit and no loss as a golden era. Meanwhile it just went to show that, with a little initiative and a copy of *Lloyd's League Tables*, a member could improve his position almost overnight.

In London, Dominique Osborne had been followed by her husband John into Lloyd's through Kingsley Underwriting Agencies.

Unlike his wife, John Osborne had a high earning career, and the Osbornes had property on which they secured bank guarantees.

Mrs Osborne had been making profits of between 6% and 8% a year and had not yet built up substantial reserves. She had been to the party Lime Street Agencies held at the offices of Gooda Walker where they reassured her that the Excess of Loss reinsurance market was unlikely to be hit by a major catastrophe; how often, they asked her, did two jumbo jets collide over New York? How often did California disappear into the San Andreas Fault?

Excess of Loss reinsurance took the pain out of risks underwritten for everyone, they said. It was like a bicycle wheel; the risk was reinsured outwards from the hub up the spokes and was cushioned evenly in the tyre. Mrs Osborne was reassured to hear this, although if asked she might not have been able to explain quite why. She and her husband took out stop loss insurance so that they 'could sleep peacefully'.

Thus it came as an unpleasant shock when her husband received a cash call of £54,000 for Warrilow 553. This was doubly unpleasant since this was for his first year of underwriting.

John Osborne paid up and joined the Warrilow Action Group, founded by the businessman and former MP Tom Benyon. The Osbornes spread out all the information they possessed on all their syndicates on the hall floor. They identified seven syndicates on which they were both Names and told their members agent they wanted to come off those syndicates which they had in common.

Their agent was a little surprised at this and sent them a number of letters questioning the wisdom of their actions. When the Osbornes persisted, the agent slowly began to oblige. He reminded them how lucky and privileged they were to be in Lloyd's at all.

On the Bay of Tralee Desmond O'Neill had paid out losses of £2,000 and £3,000 since the £12,000 he had received on his first year's underwriting. O'Neill was living on a pension and nervous of how his wife might react if she found out there was a problem. He was all the more relieved when he learned that his profits – and losses – were precisely zero this year. Perhaps he would do better next year. If he had any more losses, he would almost certainly have to borrow the money to pay.

Elsewhere the PCW fall-out made its presence felt with increasing rather than diminishing ferocity.

The Richard Beckett agencies set up to manage the syndicates had collapsed and Additional Underwriting Agencies (3) had been formed by Lloyd's to run off the claims. The DTI investigation had come and gone and among the recipients of their advance report was David D'Ambrumenil.

D'Ambrumenil, though closely linked to all three men, had survived the resignation of Green and the disappearance of Dixon and Cameron-Webb. He was running a brokers and was to all intents and purposes a rehabilitated man. When he read the report he was dismayed to see that he was severely criticised for his conduct. D'Ambrumenil knew this meant his backers would probably pull out. He sat down with his lawyers and they demolished the DTI's verdict. The report was republished in altered form. But the word 'discreditable' stayed in. Again he protested his innocence. But for D'Ambrumenil it was time to take the Russian sleigh ride.

D'Ambrumenil sat down in his office at Besso & Co., the brokers he had just taken over, and wrote a letter to Peter Miller. He explained how he had been cleared by two enquiries but he had suspended himself from his duties until this latest problem was sorted out. He looked forward to meeting Miller shortly.

A few minutes later there was a knock at the door of his office. A messenger from Lloyd's had a letter to be delivered to him in person. In effect, its message was: 'You are suspended from Lloyd's . . . We have announced your suspension . . . We will be instituting another enquiry.'

D'Ambrumenil was aghast and immediately protested. He had been a member of Lloyd's since 1951. His father had been Chairman. Lloyd's had exonerated him only a year earlier and now he was being suspended without even a meeting with Peter Miller.

But Miller stuck to his guns and would not see him. Shortly afterwards the Lloyd's authorities telephoned the Deputy Chairman of D'Ambrumenil's company.

'D'Ambrumenil's suspended,' they said. 'Frankly we think you'd better get him out of the office.'

'What can he do?' the Deputy Chairman said.

'Well,' they replied, 'he could make the tea . . .'

D'Ambrumenil remained suspended from Lloyd's after yet another disciplinary hearing. He never returned to his position. He continued to protest his innocence and eventually received an *ex gratia* payment of £10,000 on condition that he undertook not to seek a further judicial review. But he would always maintain that in the absence of the guilty parties he was made a scapegoat. He would never forget how Lloyd's, as he saw it, had thrown him to the wolves; and he would never forgive Christopher Moran.

The DTI would report on Dixon and Cameron-Webb:

> Our conclusion in relation to Mr Dixon is that his actions
> in setting up and operating the schemes were dishonest from
> start to finish. He and Mr Cameron-Webb were the main
> architects of the schemes and the two main beneficiaries.
> He was not motivated by any wish to benefit the syndicates
> for whose well-being he was responsible, but by a desire to
> achieve and maintain an extravagant lifestyle and to provide
> lavish benefits to his friends and associates at other people's
> expense. We can find no mitigating circumstances to excuse
> or condone the systematic, dishonest and cynical plunder
> of the Names' premium over such a period of time and on
> such a scale.

The report went on:

It is right to say that Mr Dixon through his solicitor Sir
David Napley suggested that in the climate of opinion current
in Lloyd's during the 1960s and 1970s nobody would have
regarded the quota share schemes as improper, even though
they did give rise to a conflict of interest . . .

The verdict was the same on Cameron-Webb:

Our conclusion in relation to Mr Cameron-Webb is that,
as with Mr Dixon, his actions in setting up and operating
the schemes were dishonest from start to finish . . .

Cameron-Webb of course was still alive and well and trading
freely on the Insurance Exchange of the Americas in Florida. But
where was Dixon?

Warrenton, Virginia, 1986

Virginia is fox-hunting country and the old colonial town of
Warrenton is ringed by people who hunt across the rolling
lands that link their pillared mansions. Nobody knew much
about the Englishman who had moved here with his attractive
blonde American wife and children except that he liked horses
and dogs and obviously knew how to party. But then Peter Dixon
was a gentleman and when it came to who he was and where he
came from it was obviously not done to enquire.

The Dixon residence was a splendid three-storey white-pillared
house with a magnificent set of steps that would have done justice
to Scarlett O'Hara. The house was surrounded by fir trees and a
six-foot Cotswold stone wall. The gates were electronically controlled from the house and at night they and the drive were lit as
if by daylight. The mail was delivered to a Warrenton postbox.

It was on these magnificent steps that Peter Dixon stood in an immaculate blue blazer and slacks, his dogs at his feet, as he spoke briefly to Brian Vine, a reporter from the *Daily Mail*.

Vine wondered what Dixon's feelings were towards the thousands of people he had systematically defrauded and betrayed.

Dixon did not wish to discuss them.

'Why didn't you turn up in person at the Lloyd's disciplinary hearing?' asked Vine.

'I probably could answer that one,' said Dixon.

'Why don't you come to England? Are you afraid of being arrested?'

'I may be allowed to answer that.'

'What is your side of the story?'

'Hmmm . . .'

'Is it true you and your ex-partner allegedly siphoned off £40 million of syndicate money?'

'I probably wouldn't be allowed to answer that. That matter is the subject of litigation.'

'Is there anyone else at Lloyd's involved?'

'Look,' said Dixon, 'you have to write these questions down formally and I will endeavour to give you my answers in writing should my lawyer approve. I can't do any more than I can do.'

The *Daily Mail* man persisted. Dixon said: 'This house belongs to my wife Sherrill. I have no funds of my own. I have suffered too,' he went on blithely. 'I would like to shield my family from any further damage. That is why I am letting my wife listen to this conversation.'

Still Brian Vine persisted.

'I cannot say any more,' Dixon replied. 'You have put me under wartime attack.' He turned to his wife. 'All I want to do now,' he told her, 'is to look after the children and get on with our lives.'

With that Dixon went back inside. He did not reappear.

This was the position of Peter Dixon in Norfolk, Virginia. In Norfolk, England, it was a rather different story.

Thelnetham, Norfolk, 1986

These were very close and intense times for Michael Church and Janis Nash. They had spent two weeks on the Norfolk Broads and visited a great many garden centres. They had spent a lot of money and told themselves to hell with the consequences. They had been together.

He was still talking to the vicar and psychiatrist. But there was still the terrible fear of the postman, and the next letter, and the next cash call for the syndicates once run by Cameron-Webb.

He had lost a lot of weight. Once he was a big man and now his suits hung off him. They were not, could not, be married because marriage would bring them both financial ruin. But he said to her: 'This honeymoon has to come to an end.'

She gave up her job because of the stress. At Lower Lodge the shadows lengthened and made almost unbearable the light from the outside world.

She had never seen him cry the way he did the day his daughter had her first baby. Two days later she asked him if he wanted to go shopping with her in a nearby town. He said he did not want to come. There was the sound of the letterbox. The postman had come.

The letter was a demand for £20,000 from the Inland Revenue for tax on money he had never seen. He did not know that at this time the Inland Revenue were sending out these 'protective assessments' on the assumption that he and others and not Cameron-Webb had received the profits.

She told him to call the accountant. They could always sell the flat in London to pay for it. She told him not to worry. If it was a mistake then he would not have to pay. She told him she would be back soon.

She left him in the house and drove off in her car to go shopping. On the way she told herself he was going downhill again. She would call his son and the vicar. She had to keep things going.

She returned to the house a couple of hours later. It was early afternoon. She had driven faster than usual down the road.

She went indoors and shouted his name. The animals were in the house but there was no sign of Michael. She unpacked the shopping in the kitchen and went upstairs to the study. She went through the bathroom into the older part of the house but he was not there.

Where was he? She went downstairs again and out of the house. She could not find him in the vegetable garden. She looked across at one of the barns where he had been working. The ladder that was leaning against the door had been moved. The door was slightly ajar.

She walked over to the barn.

He was lying on the barn floor. There was a plastic bag over his head and a pipe ran from his mouth to a calor gas cylinder. They used it when they went camping.

She pulled the terrible items away from him. His face was pink but she could not wake him. She ran into the house and dialled 999. She ran upstairs. She took a pillow and a blanket back to the barn and wrapped him in them. She ran down the lane to the farm and raised the farmer. The farmer came back with her.

Michael's face began to change colour to a dark blue and still they could not wake him. The police came and took him away and would not let her see him again. Still in his pockets were his wallet, keys, small change and credit cards. In the house he had left a letter for her. He did not know, if he was made bankrupt, how he could have faced his son Jonathan and his daughter Sarah. He asked her to say how sorry he was to Sarah, whose own daughter he had never seen.

Janis Nash stayed on at Lower Lodge for a few months on her own. The house was old and had to be kept warm and the children were going to sell it in the spring. She started to drink heavily and take tranquillisers. Her relationship with his children deteriorated under the strain of bereavement. Eventually she had to leave the house in which she had lived with the man she was once to have married.

After the inquest and the funeral she never saw his children again. All his assets were frozen and she had £3,000 in the world. She continued to take refuge in drink and tranquillisers and sleeping pills. Janis Nash drifted away to London and oblivion.

* * *

The death of Michael Church passed virtually unnoticed while the life and liberty of Peter Dixon and Peter Cameron-Webb were proclaimed across the front pages of newspapers for all the world to see. By now it was well-known inside and outside Lloyd's that the two men had perpetrated and got away with the largest fraud in Lloyd's history.

Outside Lloyd's the message was loud and clear; the club had closed ranks to protect its members. Inside Lloyd's, among the greedier and less scrupulous players, the perception was equally simple; crime paid. But to the greedy and unscrupulous there was a further, fatal corollary. If Cameron-Webb and Dixon – and Grob, Comery, Page and Carpenter – had got away with it on such a grand scale, what likelihood was there of punishment for people who merely played the system? After all, in a barely regulated market, there was no great need for conspiracy anyway.

A further aspect of the Cameron-Webb effect was that Lloyd's was forced to publish two sets of results for the 1983 underwriting year: one before and one after Cameron-Webb. The difference between them was striking.

Before Cameron-Webb, on £2.5 billion of premiums Lloyd's made an underwriting profit of £28 million. After Cameron-Webb, this figure became an underwriting loss of £115 million. The overall result, before Cameron-Webb, was a profit of £179

176 FOR WHOM THE BELL TOLLS

million. This became £36 million after Cameron-Webb.

This was twice as bad as the damage done by Cameron-Webb the previous year, but at least it was thought that the worst of the damage had been done.

With or without Cameron-Webb's lethal mixture of fraud and careless underwriting, these results showed how Lloyd's depended four times as heavily on investment income as it did on underwriting for its profits. Yet if it were going to continue to meet claims it also depended heavily on the assets and underwriting capacity of its members. On the one hand it was important to play up the Cameron-Webb effect to distract from the fact that this was a very poor set of results. On the other hand then it was important to play down the Cameron-Webb effect to reassure the members that this was the exception rather than the rule.

Chief among the other problems were the claims arising out of the 'long-tail' business written from North America. These had begun to grow alarmingly a couple of years earlier and were continuing to do so, as Peter Keen had predicted and as Dick Outhwaite was finding to his cost. Outhwaite had already closed and then been forced to reopen his 1982 account. He had issued his letter stating that he still believed 1982 would be a profitable year. In late 1986 however the whisper went out that all was not well with Outhwaite 1982.

Peter Nutting was the Surrey businessman who had been elected to Lloyd's in 1972 when the merchant bank of which he was a director bought an interest in the R.W. Sturge agency. Nutting was better connected than most external members – and some working members – to the grapevine of the market.

Nutting was an Outhwaite Name and since his election in 1972 he had done well out of Lloyd's membership. He had received cheques every year from the profits of a spread of syndicates and twice a year in the case of Posgate. He had been able to live the lifestyle of a man who was making money as well as earning it. He had paid the school fees and done so without using up capital at a time of what he described as 'spifflicating' levels of income tax. He was an amiable man with a large manor house in the pastures of Surrey. It would take more than Lloyd's to unseat the likes of Peter Nutting in this particular corner of England.

Nutting was a close friend of Brian Taylor, the managing director of his members agency. When Nutting began to hear what he termed 'bad vibrations' about Outhwaite 1982, Taylor confirmed that he too had heard rumours. Outhwaite was looking at big losses. But Taylor had not said anything about this to the members agents whose Names supported Outhwaite's syndicate 317/661.

'We don't know anything for sure,' Taylor told Nutting.

Nutting had been a director of his own members agency and had the interests of himself and the other members keenly to heart.

'What are you saying to the members?' Nutting asked him.

'It's very difficult to say anything,' Taylor replied, 'if you don't know anything for sure.'

'Look,' Nutting told him, 'what you are telling me is that next July there could be a big cash call. If I had just had a little windfall I might be in the process of doing something with it, completely oblivious of the fact that in July you are going to come and hit me for a large sum of money. Can't you give people any sort of warning?'

Taylor thought about this.

'Well, yes and no,' he said, 'bad for the market, that sort of thing.'

Nutting understood his friend's fears. This was the traditional view of the man in the market. But who would it be bad for, if not for the Names? Nutting heard no more from the members agent for a while. But he kept on hearing the bad vibrations about Outhwaite 1982.

Her Majesty the Queen opened the new headquarters of Lloyd's at Number 1, Lime Street. Lloyd's as ever had the royal seal of approval.

For Sir Peter Green it was the realisation of the 'world-class building' he had first seen in model form nearly ten years earlier.

For Peter Miller it was a building untouched by scandal and with its Adam Committee Room intact.

For the Queen it was 'without doubt a landmark, both in terms of the skyline of the City and in the history of Lloyd's.'

The Royal Institute of British Architecture said it was 'a tour de force of structural ingenuity, constructural quality and a design of almost medieval richness of form.'

'Early urinal or late lavatorial?' asked former Chairman of Lloyd's, Paul Dixey.

'Lloyd's is a very high quality building but it fails to provide basic human requirements,' said Sheena Wilson of Building US Studies, a firm which specialised in investigating user complaints. 'It is totally inhumane. That design approach is guaranteed to induce a condition of mild clinical psychosis.'

In they came . . . the brokers and underwriters and corporation staff and Committee and Council and the members dining in the Captain's Room. *Is Lloyd's fit for the Queen?* wrote John Moore, the bane of Lime Street. But Moore's was not the voice that reflected the new bullish mood.

Members on Henry Chester's marine syndicate 762 saw a return of £8,629 for every £10,000 of business they had underwritten that year. The best non-marine syndicate, Nevitt 503, only made them £3,929 for a £10,000 line, but this was still real money made on assets theoretically pledged but in reality earning interest elsewhere. Nobody wanted to hear about the losses of marine 514 – £4,333 for every £10,000 underwritten – let alone the holocaust – £12,597 lost per £10,000 line – that had befallen Oakeley Vaughan 551.

In six weeks' time, on 1 January 1987, the new members would start underwriting. Michael Colvin MP in Westminster, Nichola

1. The first picture of the Committee of Lloyd's only appeared in 1960

2. 'Not a gentleman' – but ten years after his expulsion Ian 'Goldfinger' Posgate was hailed as a prophet and the gentlemen of Lloyd's were scoundrels

3. 'What began in a coffee house will end in a percolator' – One, Lime Street, London EC3, designed by Richard Rogers

4. Edward St George, eminence grise and link between Lloyd's, the British Royal Family and the Bahamas

5 and 6. Peter Dixon (left) and Peter Cameron-Webb, the men who got away with the biggest fraud in the history of Lloyd's

7. The Chairman of
Lloyd's during the early
1980s, Sir Peter Green

8. Ian Hay Davison,
Lloyd's first Chief
Executive. His exposure
of corrupt accountancy
practices made him the
most unpopular man in
Lloyd's and ultimately
led to his departure

9. 'It seemed like a good
idea at the time' – but
Richard Outhwaite may
have cost his members
over £1 billion

10. 'We do not hound
people to bankruptcy'
Dr Mary Archer

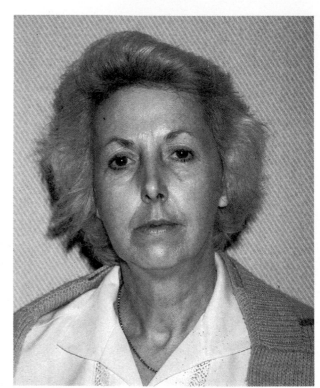

11. 'No, they just bleed you to death, drop by drop' – Betty Atkins

12. Piper Alpha. What began as a $700 million insurance loss became a $16 billion game of 'pass the parcel'

13. 'Lloyd's used to be a bastion of respectability – now we have discovered certain aspects of it stink' – Tom Benyon

14. 'There is no crisis' – the Chairman of Lloyd's, David Coleridge, with his wife

15. Dale Schreiber, the New York lawyer who went gunning for Lloyd's under the RICO statutes, normally reserved for mobsters and drug-traffickers

16. 'I'm the best in the market' — 'Big Bill' Brown became one of Britain's highest-paid men through broking risks to syndicates on the doomed 'LMX spiral'

Colvin in Hampshire, Princess Michael of Kent in Kensington Palace, John Francome in Berkshire, David Stirling in Dumfriesshire, Dr Pakozdi in Ontario and nearly 3,000 others were all in their different ways saying the same thing.

No matter that the last Budget had eroded some of those fabled tax breaks. Those were for the super-rich and like the British Empire the days of the dominance of the super-rich at Lloyd's were gone for ever. But for those with reasonably high earnings, modest fortunes or simply a bit of land that could be used as collateral, making your money make even more money was still a good thing and the new building at 1, Lime Street was still the best, the only way to do it. In this brave spirit did the new members enter the new building and the new era.

Sir Patrick Neill reported as instructed and as expected. He made seventy specific recommendations for reform and the Council of Lloyd's immediately accepted them all in principle as the Committee had accepted the Fisher Report; the alternative was external regulation of the market.

Neill was critical of three areas — agents charged too much for doing too little, the standard agency agreement was inadequate, and parallel or 'baby' syndicates had to go. The last of these were immediately outlawed, although of course this did not put an end to the existence of preferential syndicates for working members and other insiders.

The Council accepted that they had to give proportionally more seats to external members. Peter Miller said he saw this move as 'evolutionary rather than revolutionary.'

There was relief on the Council and in the market at what Sir Patrick Neill did not do; he did not fundamentally question self-regulation, he did not recommend the separation of managing agents who ran the syndicates and members agents and he did not insist that members agents should share both the profits and the losses of their members (one agent said this would be 'very complicated' and would lead to higher agents' charges).

Above all, there was relief that Sir Patrick Neill did not propose that Lloyd's should come under the control of the Securities and Investments Board.

Peter Miller's old colleague and adversary Ian Hay Davison was cautiously optimistic. He said the changes were 'a major step forward and reflected the fact that 82% of Lloyd's members were now external Names.'

But Miller was exultant. He already had a Chief Executive in Alan Lord who made remarks like: 'There is no friction between the Chairman and myself – we work as equals.' Now he had an externally-appointed commission's seal of approval.

'There is now firm evidence,' Miller could quote from the Neill Report, 'that there exists in the Lloyd's community a strong determination to ensure high standards of conduct in the market.'

In his letter to members, Miller quoted further: 'We know of no profession or equivalent organisation which has accomplished such a major programme of reform in such a short time.'

If Miller was pleased with the Neill Report, so were the market and the Government. To those critics of the Government who said Lloyd's should come under the Financial Services Act, the Neill Report proved that this need not be so. To those in the market who said Lloyd's should not come under the Financial Services Act, the Neill Report proved that this was the correct view. To those outside Government and the market the Neill Report gave the strong impression that both Lloyd's and the Government were trying their hardest to sort out the matter of self-regulation once and for all.

Yet less than five years later the words Cromer, Fisher and Neill would be uttered in the same bitter breath. The market would be in disarray and among thousands of members the idea of self-regulation would have been discredited. Why and how did this latest well-meaning attempt at best make so little difference and at worst fail to prevent things from going horribly wrong?

Peter Nutting was no longer the only person hearing vibrations about Outhwaite 1982. In the early months of 1987 the Outhwaite members learned by letter that Outhwaite was 'questioning the basis on which certain of these policies were placed.' Shortly afterwards they also learned that the syndicate was facing a 25% cash call; £2,500 for every £10,000 of business a member underwrote.

The Outhwaite members were not pleased of course to receive these letters but in many cases they were in a position to absorb the loss. Peter Nutting, Eddie Kulukundis, Susan Hampshire and Robin Kingsley were all wealthy people with close market connections. Charles and Edward St George were also unlikely to be driven to the wall by this setback to their fortunes.

But members like Lord Alexander, Edward Molesworth and Wilfred Sherman were already under heavy pressure from their losses through Oakeley Vaughan. Lord Alexander was not only on Oakeley Vaughan and Outhwaite 1982 but also on the troubled Warrilow 553. Virginia Wade was not only on Outhwaite 1982 and Warrilow 553 but also on Spicer and White 'nodding donkey' 895.

Then there were Betty Atkins and Sylvia Hatton.

The two former secretaries made working members had never been on a wide spread of syndicates but each had a £20,000 line on Outhwaite 317/662. Mrs Atkins wanted to work part-time and in accordance with the rules had therefore resigned as a working member of Lloyd's. She lived with her elderly mother. Mrs Hatton had been made redundant after the retirement of their employer Dick Rowbotham and lived with her ailing husband. Neither woman could afford a loss of any description.

But both of them had the open year on Outhwaite 1982. The rules were clear; members with open years could not resign altogether until those open years were closed and an end brought to their liabilities. The two secretaries were neither able to stay in nor get out. How lucky it was then that their former employer had undertaken, as they understood it, to indemnify them in the unlikely event of a loss; especially as that unlikely event had come true.

Fortunately however they did not have to confront Mr Rowbotham with the embarrassing request for help. They had never received much from Lloyd's membership but their reserves contained enough to cover the cash call and they had stop loss. In the case of Mrs Atkins the 25% cash call of £4,849 was absorbed in this way; she could never have found the money otherwise.

Mrs Atkins and Mrs Hatton were very relieved at this as they did not want to go cap in hand to their former employer however much they had earned his generosity. In common with everyone else on the syndicate they also hoped that what Mr Outhwaite had said in one of his many and increasingly complex letters would come true – and profitability would return to the 1982 account of syndicate 317/661.

The 25% cash call on Outhwaite 1982 seemed less serious at the time than the 48% loss on the 1984 year of Warrilow 553. The colourful former underwriter had left a poisoned chalice for his members.

Lord Kimball, the foxhunting peer on the Council of Lloyd's, was a Warrilow member.

Kimball would be philosophical. 'It's swings and roundabouts,' he declared. 'Sometimes you win, sometimes you lose. You always pay your bookmaker. Underwriting is the same. You pay up and shut up.'

'I don't even know what share I've got,' Kimball added, and flew back from London to one of his substantial country estates.

Tom Benyon disagreed. To him there was a difference between bookmaking and underwriting. At least with a bookmaker you could choose the horse on which you wanted him to place your bet.

Unlike Lord Kimball, and the Outhwaite Names who still lived in hope, Benyon decided to form the Warrilow Action group.

His hope was that he and other Warrilow members would be able to secure legal redress for bad underwriting. His targets were the managing agents of the Warrilow syndicates and the potential redress that existed in their Errors and Omissions policies.

Litigation at Lloyd's was a long and expensive road with no certainty of profit except for the lawyers along the way. The idea of an action group for members of an individual syndicate was still a rare one but Benyon was a rare character. An old boy of Wellington School, Somerset, his contemporaries there had included the flamboyant television cook Keith Floyd and the equally colourful former Tory MP and Lloyd's member Jeffrey Archer. Benyon's political and business career were also eventful but there was steel under the exterior of the man.

This was just as well because Lloyd's did not give Benyon an easy ride. He had been altogether too independent-minded a Chairman of the Association of Lloyd's Members for their liking.

Benyon's problem was that he did not know how many Warrilow Names there were around the world; incredibly, even after Cromer, Fisher and Neill, this was still not the kind of information it was believed within Lloyd's should be available to the members who put up the underwriting capital. The various members agents involved refused to mail his letters to other Warrilow members and Lloyd's refused to give him their addresses so that he could mail them himself. But Benyon was never more dangerous than when confronted with what he saw as an obstinate and complacent establishment.

Eventually he located a retired schoolmaster in Sussex who had spent several years compiling an unofficial list of the names and addresses of Lloyd's members. The schoolmaster managed to do this by taking the members' names listed in the annual Lloyd's Blue Books and cross-referrring them against the names (and the addresses and telephone numbers) of alumni of Oxford, Cambridge, Sandhurst and the like. The cross-reference had proved to be especially fertile; it had given him 9,000 names and addresses.

Benyon purchased a copy of the list from the schoolmaster for 40 pence a name out of his own pocket. Thus it was that Lord Alexander in London, Virginia Wade in Sussex, John Clementson in Hertfordshire, Hugh Bourn in Lincolnshire, Desmond O'Neill on the Bay of Tralee, John Pearson in Malta, Michael Oakes in the Bahamas, Robert Zildjian in Bermuda and many other distressed and ashamed Warrilow Names around the world learned of each other's existence. Whether or not they wanted to join the litigation was up to them; but at least they had the chance to decide on the basis of information that had hitherto been withheld.

In this way the Warrilow Action Group was born. It was the first such group since the Sasse Names had banded together nearly a decade earlier and formed what had become the Association of Lloyd's Members. But in the next few years there were to be many others.

Lloyd's announced its first set of results since the move to 1, Lime Street. The underwriting year 1984 suffered less from the Cameron-Webb factor and as Peter Miller had predicted rates had risen and there was a record £279 million profit. £138 million of this was from actual underwriting.

As well as the influx of new Names many existing members had increased the amount of business they were underwriting. Many members agents, and in particular Robin Kingsley of Kingsley Underwriting Agencies and Lime Street, were encouraging their members to do this on Feltrim, Gooda Walker and the other rapidly-growing Excess of Loss syndicates.

Some Lime Street names like Dr John Mathias in Boston and Robert Zildjian in Bermuda were happy to do so. But others began to question the type as well as the amount of business they were underwriting.

Michael Oakes, the retired quantity surveyor introduced to Lloyd's over a Wimbledon tennis court, quit after concluding that the risks outweighed the benefits of membership. John Pearson, the retired company pensioner living in Malta, had made modest returns for a few years but had taken a battering from Warrilow 553. Pearson was also on the Feltrim and Gooda Walker syndicates but he did not subscribe to the bullish attitude of Robin Kingsley and his managing director Robert Hallam.

Pearson met Hallam in London after their latest trip to North America. In an angry exchange he told him that had he known he would never have agreed to underwrite stop loss syndicates such as Gooda Walker 387. Pearson resigned his membership but it was too late. He would return to his wife and rented basement flat in Malta pursued by uncertainty about the three years it would take to leave Lloyd's and by open years already going back to 1980.

Others were simply hoping to trade out of what was becoming a worrying position. Desmond O'Neill on the Bay of Tralee had, as he had feared, been forced to borrow to fund his latest losses of £7,000. Robert Zildjian in Bermuda had second thoughts and requested the papers in order to resign. Several of his syndicates, it seemed to him, were acting irresponsibly and amateurishly. The excess clauses on his stop loss policies were rising so rapidly that Zildjian correctly concluded that the market itself was saying the rate of losses was rising.

The reassurances and bright predictions of Lime Street were overwhelming and Zildjian decided to continue underwriting. Zildjian was in the music business in America and not in insurance; he left all the decisions up to the men in London.

The traditional 'Lloyd's men' would have held up these examples as proof that members should never be allowed to 'interfere' in agents' and underwriters' business. As Frank 'the Bank' Barber had said, any member who did so could take his or her business elsewhere.

Barber made handsome capital appreciation from his members even when he wrote at a loss for his non-marine syndicate 990. Barber's members included Mr and Mrs Peter Miller, both the current Deputy Chairmen of Lloyd's, a number of former Deputy

Chairmen, several senior figures from Sedgwick, Willis Faber and Bowring, the biggest brokers at Lloyd's, and the lead underwriters of other blue-chip syndicates of which Frank 'the Bank' was a member. As Christopher Thomas-Everard had discovered such syndicates had long waiting lists – so long that it was not worth waiting.

There was never a waiting list, it seemed, to be placed on the Excess of Loss syndicates like Feltrim and Gooda Walker. Yet these syndicates were eminently desirable according to agents like Stancomb and Kenington and Robin Kingsley. So, were Frank 'the Bank' Barber and Mr and Mrs Peter Miller, and the current Deputy Chairmen of Lloyd's, and the men from Sedgwick, Willis Faber and Bowring all clamouring to be placed on these syndicates? It seemed not. Yet at the same time agents like Kingsley and others were encouraging their members to increase their lines on the very same syndicates.

What did this mean? At the time all this meant was that a few external members were beginning to have misgivings about the kind of business done by certain underwriters, in spite of the assurances of their agents. But what did this mean to the underwriters themselves who went in to do battle in the 250-foot glass-topped Room in the building that was to take Lloyd's into the 21st century?

Ed Cowen had joined as a junior broker in the 1958 building and was doing well as active underwriter for the non-marine syndicate 529. Cowen held that the better members agencies could be identified by the fact that they could place their members wherever they wanted. There were four or five top agencies and as long as he had the support of at least two of them he felt he had peer approval. He was thinking of Willis Faber, Barings, Merrett, Sturge, and Sedgwick.

Cowen held the same view of the brokers. When they came to his box Cowen wanted to know about their board, their accounting, their statistics. If Cowen did not like what he heard he would not do business with them.

Cowen did not do business with the brokers of LMX or London Market Excess of Loss risks; the risks that were reinsured ad infinitum around the London market. These risks not only went round and round like a bicycle wheel, they also went up and up like a spiral. To Cowen it seemed wrong that one broker should have to travel halfway round the world and give presentations for a cut of 2½%, while another could take a 10% cut simply travelling a distance of 20 feet.

Cowen was a self-made man from Essex and he was not a snob, but he knew the barrow boy brokers who encouraged certain underwriters to play golf and drink at the bar. Cowen did not respect those brokers or those underwriters. He did not accept the underwriters' explanations that they wrote LMX business because the broker bullied them and if they did not agree they would not have their own reinsurances placed in turn. Cowen thought these brokers and underwriters distorted the market. There was plenty of money to be made without succumbing to that kind of thing.

Cowen felt the same about the members agencies who supported these syndicates. The main interest of many seemed to be where Cowen was sending his children to school. Cowen had worked in North America and Canada and he did not think where he sent his children to school was relevant to the workings of a dynamic international insurance market. He made major distinctions in his mind between the agents who placed their members on syndicates like Feltrim and Gooda Walker and the kinds of agents with whom he wanted to do business. Cowen believed it was a matter of fundamental principle. The job of the underwriter was to put the assured in touch with the capital providers. If he did so and made a 2% return, that was fine. But how could an underwriter make a 20% return and still reserve properly against future claims? It did not make sense. Yet all the time the number of members of the spiral syndicates was going up and up and so were the capacities of those syndicates. In the end they were all going to blow up. This was why Ed Cowen and non-marine syndicate 529 did not want to be seen to be supported by the likes of Gooda Walker. He did not want them – or their members – on his stamp at all.

The PCW members received a second settlement; too little for some and too late for others. But the Names were relieved of all liability and Lloyd's would meet any further losses.

In order to achieve the latter Lloyd's had to set up what was virtually a separate Central Fund simply to deal with the losses incurred by Cameron-Webb. The fund was to be called Lioncover. But where was Lloyd's to find all the money in question?

The answer lay among other places in the reserves of the old PCW syndicates. There were a large number of these syndicates and after the gallant but abortive attempt to maintain them by Richard Beckett, most of them had gone into run-off, which meant that henceforth they did no more business but existed merely to pay out the losses incurred by the underwriters.

Most, but not all.

Patrick Feltrim Fagan, the new underwriter for syndicates 540 and 847, was well aware of the fact that his syndicates had an indirect PCW connection through the defunct WMD agencies of which he had once been a minor part. But syndicates 540 and 847 had not gone into run-off and there was no suggestion that they should do so.

Fagan had registered Feltrim Underwriting Agencies after the usual Rota Committee scrutiny. He had begun active under-writing. He had those £24 million of reserves which as far as members agents were concerned was a point in his favour. He was all the more disturbed to learn that Lloyd's now proposed to take those reserves away as part of the PCW Lioncover settlement.

Fagan was officially told the news at a meeting in late 1986. His premium trust fund of £23,883,000 was to be taken by Lloyd's for syndicate 9001/Lioncover along with his 1983 liabilities.

The notes of the meeting read: 'When pressed, he [Mr Prior

of the Lloyd's legal department] did say that the Council itself had approved the inclusion of the 1983 year of 540/542 in the PCW Settlement.'

The notes went on: 'But this was highly confidential and could not be disclosed to anyone, and that until the details of the settlement went public, nothing was actually set in stone.'

Fagan was understandably upset to learn that the Council of Lloyd's had reached this decision. This was not least because he had already written 50% of his 1987 business and committed himself to reinsurance contracts. The removal of his trust fund would totally destroy the delicate balance of his finances.

Fagan protested but it was no use. He tried to point out that he would be entering 1987 in a severely weakened position. On 13 March 1987 the news was confirmed at a private meeting between himself, Prior of the legal department and Peter Miller. Furthermore the second PCW settlement had not yet been announced and therefore Fagan was still unable to tell anyone what was happening.

What did happen next was to lead to misunderstanding, misplaced faith and ultimately to catastrophe.

The misunderstanding lay in the impression given to members by their agents: 'PCW had a number of good underwriters and therefore a lot of good insurance business. Mr Fagan, with a smaller stamp, will be able to pick and choose the best of this from the broker wishing to renew. He will not have to cut his rates to attract business as other new syndicates would. His ratio of reserves is one of the highest in Lloyd's.'

This was what one agent typically had said. By June 1987 the Feltrim syndicate accounts had been published and so had the information about the missing reserves. But instead of being presented up front it was buried in the small print and went unnoticed, both by members and apparently by the agents who charged so much to look after their interests.

Shortly afterwards the same agent who had written the above

wrote of Feltrim 540 and 542: 'These are Excess of Loss Syndicates. The 1983 account was kept open due to the problems with reinsurances effected with the PCW syndicates. 1984 was profitable ... the 1985 account is developing satisfactorily ... the Underwriter is optimistic.'

The misplaced faith lay in the fact that members continued to be placed on Feltrim 540 and 542 after Lloyd's had removed the £24 million and left Fagan with a mere £4 million in reserves to cover three years' liabilities. This was not even enough to buy adequate reinsurance, let alone meet any claims. But the agents appeared not to have read the small print and so encouraged new and existing members to go on underwriting.

But the misunderstanding and misplaced faith were nothing compared to the catastrophe now in the making.

For not only had Patrick Feltrim Fagan gone on underwriting without sufficient reserves; although the accounts of the syndicates merely stated that they were in 'marine and incidental non-marine reinsurance', they were in fact writing Excess of Loss business in its riskiest form. Feltrim 540 and 542 were not only Excess of Loss syndicates; they were at the very top of the LMX spiral.

Christopher Thomas-Everard, the sheep farmer with the £25,000 line on Feltrim 540, had continued to make modest profits from his spread of syndicates. He had no complaints about this or about his members agent and had even encouraged his daughter Lucilla at 21 years and one month to become Lloyd's youngest member.

But he still entertained nagging doubts about the ease with which he had been placed on Feltrim 540 and the ease with which he had been taken off Mander 552.

Early in February 1988 he wrote what turned out to be a prophetic letter to the Lloyd's Regulatory Services Group:

'Since the reduction of preferred underwriting on baby syndicates, one notices that certain syndicates are now only

available to working Members and their families. These are
the consistently profitable ones.

'This matter is more serious than merely being aware
of a "commercial reality" (as Lloyd's had described it to
Thomas-Everard on the telephone). There would appear to
be a danger that, as this advantage to privileged Members
increases, there will be a polarisation between good
syndicates, with a high proportion of insider Members,
receiving the best insurance business on the one hand, and
on the other, the much less profitable syndicates being left
for the external Names only.

'I do not know,' Thomas-Everard went on, 'the ratio
between the total Means provided by insider Members to
that provided by external Members but it appears to be
about 3% to 97%. I suspect the ratio of profit is very
different. **The potential for a scandal awaits.**

'The problem is greater when, as now, there are too
many Members for the available insurance business. As an
external Member dies or retires, he is replaced on the good
syndicates by a working Member with inside pull.

'Under the proposed Members Agents Information
Reports, Lloyd's and the Members Agents could be vulnerable
to a charge of offering misleading information. As drafted,
the Reports will imply that potential new Members of an
agent would sooner or later be able to join the profitable
syndicates as well as the less profitable ones on that agent's
list. Yet, if the best syndicates are rationed to insider
Members only, such implications would be a deceit.

'To help Lloyd's avoid accusations of deception,' Thomas-
Everard concluded, 'I submit that you need to differentiate
in the Information Reports between the results achieved by
ordinary external Members and the results available only to
favoured insiders . . .'

Needless to say, this remarkable and prophetic letter received an unremarkable and unenlightened reply.

Peter Miller had forecast record profits for the 1985 underwriting year on the strength of a continued rise in insurance rates. Miller had been knighted and succeeded as Chairman by the underwriter and former Deputy Chairman Murray Lawrence.

Interest rates had gone down however and costs had gone up, which led to a more cautious forecast. Meanwhile there was no cause for optimism for the members of the Oakeley Vaughan syndicates, Warrilow 553 and Aragorn 384.

The Oakeley Vaughan syndicates were being run off by Additional Underwriting Agencies (6) and huge cash calls were being made on the Names to repay the claims settled by the Central Fund. The loss spread over the Oakeley Vaughan syndicates was a staggering 285%; £28,500 to be paid for every £10,000 line. For the Oakeley Vaughan Names whose stop loss was running out and who would not or could not be bailed out by the St George brothers, this was a nightmare which deepened every time an AUA(6) envelope came through the letterbox.

For the Warrilow Names too the nightmare seemed to have no end. The combination of overwriting and inadequate reinsurance meant that they were now facing a loss on the 1985 account of 171%; £17,100 to be paid for every £10,000 of business underwritten. The number of Names began to grow on Tom Benyon's action group.

Aragorn 384 was also a casualty of Warrilow; a non-marine syndicate whose underwriter was banned from underwriting.

For Lord Alexander, who was on Oakeley Vaughan, Warrilow and Aragorn, the sunny times he had spent in the Bahamas had turned into the darkest period of his life. An honourable and far from wealthy man, he was now having to come to terms with the fact that unlike his illustrious father who had won so many battles he was in danger of going down in history as the man who lost everything down to his last pair of cufflinks; and, to his eternal shame, through his own greed and gullibility.

Lord Alexander would receive encouragement from the most unlikely source, although he did not yet know this. Meanwhile, on top of his other losses, he had to face the collapse of the one syndicate he had hoped would bail him out: the mounting horror that was Outhwaite 1982.

Peter Nutting had paid up and shut up, as Lord Kimball might have said of another troubled syndicate. But Nutting had not heard the last of it.

It was Wednesday in Royal Ascot Week. Nutting was talking to his solicitor.

'What's all this about Outhwaite?' he said.

'Oh my God, Peter,' his solicitor said, 'you're not on that syndicate, are you?'

Nutting quietly confirmed that he was.

'Well,' said the solicitor, 'I've been doing quite a bit of work on it and it's a nightmare.'

Nutting began to experience a sinking feeling.

'Are you coming to the meeting?' the solicitor said. 'It's at the Baltic Exchange. There's going to be an action group.'

'Bloody inconvenient,' Nutting replied, as casually as he could, 'we're going to Ascot. I'm supposed to be staying with friends that night. I'm going to be very unpopular . . . I'll try to come.'

Nutting went to the meeting at the Baltic Exchange of members of the Outhwaite syndicate 317/661. Various people spoke and then a small man stood up without announcing his name and suggested that they were all making a lot of fuss about nothing – Lloyd's would sort everything out.

'Who is that funny little chap?' people whispered. 'What's your name, sir?' they cried; and they gave him even shorter shrift when they heard what he was saying.

Sir Peter Miller was not amused.

The background to the Baltic Exchange meeting was Part 1 of the Freshfields solicitors report. This had been commissioned by

Outhwaite members and concluded that there was a substantial case against Outhwaite for breach of duty. Although the remit of the lawyers had been necessarily narrow this was taken as a broad hint that the Outhwaite members had a case.

Nutting had ended up in the chair at a second meeting and suggested that if they were going to form an action group they should do so in a businesslike manner. He suggested they ask people to pay £250 and 4% of their underwriting each towards what would be substantial legal costs. Within a fairly short time they would have £250,000.

But there were members of Lloyd's who could not even afford £250.

East Greenwich, London, 1988

East Greenwich is not a smart part of London but it was where Betty Atkins had lived for many years. She shared her small house with her elderly mother.

Betty Atkins and her friend Sylvia Hatton from the Rowbotham agency had received copies of the correspondence detailing the worsening position of Outhwaite 317/661 for the underwriting year 1982. As working Names elected through their former employer they had deeply regretted the fact that things seemed to have taken a turn for the worse.

They had hoped not to have to embarrass Mr Rowbotham, especially now that he had retired and the company had been taken over:

'Dear Mrs Atkins,' wrote C.I. de Rougemont & Company Ltd. who had taken over the Rowbotham agency:

I am writing further to my letter of the 12th May when I informed you that the R.H.M. Outhwaite marine Syndicate 317/661 would produce a substantial overall loss in respect of the 1982 Underwriting Account.

You will see from the enclosed letter, which Mr Outhwaite has sent to his direct Names, that the overall loss is approximately 207% of allocated premium income . . .

A schedule summarising your underwriting position at 31st December 1987 is enclosed from which you will note that the cash call will be approximately £7,400. When the exact figures are known we will write to you again . . .

'Dear Betty,

I should be glad if you would send me your cheque for £7,010.72 made payable to 'C.I. de Rougemont & Co. Limited' as soon as possible . . .

At this stage Betty Atkins sat down and wrote a letter. She did not quite know how to make sense of the thoughts and fears that were reeling through her mind. She must concentrate. She was so frightened that all she could remember was her secretarial training:

The Chairman
The Rowbotham Group
9, St. Clare Street
Minories
London EC3

Dear Sir

As you may know I was an employee of the Rowbotham Group from 1954 to 1983 and after completion of 25 years service, as a token of appreciation, I, together with Mrs Sylvia Hatton, was made an Underwriting Member of Lloyd's. Rowbothams supplied the necessary Bank Guarantee and at their decision we were put on the following Syndicates commencing 1st January, 1980.

No.   317/661   R.H.M. Outhwaite

254	L.H. Marchant
463	G.B. McKay Forbes

I resigned from 317 with effect from 31.12.85 and from Underwriting Membership with effect from 31.12.86. My plan being to complete the necessary three year period to close the underwriting before giving up fulltime work.

As you will know 317 has made considerable losses on the 1982 account and Names may be asked to fund money which could be in excess of the Stop Loss Insurance Policies effected by Rowbothams on behalf of Mrs Hatton and myself.

While I am aware there have been various changes within the Rowbotham organisation since my departure, both Mrs Hatton and I were assured when put up for Membership of Lloyd's that such a situation as this would be met by that Company as it was appreciated that we would not be in a position to meet such an eventuality.

I should be obliged if you would consider this letter and let me have your advices.

> Yours faithfully,
> Betty Atkins.

Mrs Atkins read and reread the letter and carefully sealed the envelope. She posted it and immediately felt better; everything was going to be all right.

The next three weeks were difficult, but she reminded herself that there was probably a lot of paperwork involved. People had to be contacted and agreements confirmed. Soon, she told herself, she could relax.

The reply came on 21 July 1988:

Dear Mrs Atkins

Thank you for your letter of 1st June 1988.
I was very concerned to hear of the predicament in

which you now find yourself in relation to your membership of Lloyd's.

I have made enquiries as to the circumstances in which the Company assisted your membership, but I am afraid there is nothing to suggest any sort of commitment to indemnify you against losses incurred as a result of that membership. Indeed, it would be highly unusual if any such arrangement did exist.

Regrettably, whilst I have every sympathy for you on a personal level, I am unable to make any sort of commitment so far as the companies are concerned . . .

Later, Betty Atkins would reread this letter and be physically sick. She could not believe that the assurances she and Sylvia Hatton had been given could be denied in this way. She could not believe that these assurances would not be honoured. She did not immediately join the Outhwaite action group for the very reason that she still believed the matter would be sorted out. But Betty Atkins and her friend Sylvia Hatton had already entered an unimaginable nightmare; and it had only just begun.

* * *

Clive Francis had done well out of changing agencies to the Kingsley subsidiary, Sudbrook, run by Robert Hallam. But Francis was taking no chances after being left with nine open years by his previous agent. He subscribed to the *Digest of Lloyd's News* and employed one of Chatset's founders, John Rew, to look over his syndicates on a consultancy basis.

Francis felt he was on rather a lot of Excess of Loss syndicates: Feltrim 540, 52 and 847, and the Gooda Walker range.

Lunch with his agent was always a splendid affair with wonderful food and exquisite wines. Francis felt almost apologetic about raising the subject of business; but he was alarmed at the number of Excess of Loss syndicates on which they had placed him.

'My dear boy,' Robert Hallam replied jovially, 'first of all, your share of these syndicates is not disproportionate. Secondly, Excess of Loss is the professional end of the market.'

'What about the other end of the market?' said Francis.

'Oh,' Hallam was quick to reply, 'they're very professional too . . .'

Francis had raised his overall line from £350,000 to £1.3 million. On the one hand this meant that an 8% profit overall would make him over £100,000. On the other hand, a similar loss would wipe out his previous gains and leave him with a big problem even after stop loss and rebates from the taxman. In the event it was the second scenario that came true.

None of this mattered as long as the kind of catastrophe against which the underwriters insured and reinsured did not actually happen. As Dominique Osborne was reminded at the party Lime Street had held at the offices of Gooda Walker, how often did two jumbo jets collide over New York? How often did California disappear into the San Andreas Fault?

The obvious answer was almost never. But these were deliberately extreme examples given in all likelihood to allay the fears of an underwriting member. In fact a more representative example was the kind of risk that had been insured and reinsured within Lloyd's for centuries. Such a risk did not necessarily turn into a claim, either. But when it did, like the catastrophe itself, it was on a terrifying scale.

The North Sea, 6 July 1988

There had been a lot of activity on the Piper Alpha platform for weeks; midsummer was the maintenance period and new construction work was taking place as well as the usual oil and gas production. Piper Alpha was old and badly-equipped and the men who lived and worked here were cynical about the cost-cutting and penny-pinching that kept it that way.

The men from the day shift were in the cinema watching the horror film *Carrie* when the surge of the gas flare suddenly struck. A few minutes later, at 21.58, a high-pitched scream was heard in the mechanics workshop. There was a massive and violent explosion. The first blast destroyed Piper Alpha's communications systems and the controls for the fire pumps, none of which was set on automatic at the time.

The men ran from the cinema leaving *Carrie* for a real-life horror of their own. Twenty minutes later, under the rig, eleven and a half miles of eighteen-inch-diameter gas pipeline began releasing hydrocarbon gas at a pressure of 1,800 p.s.i. A fireball exploded so intensely that it lit up the sky for miles around. At 20.52 the remaining gas pipelines connected to Piper Alpha erupted in an even bigger fireball. Millions of cubic feet of gas in pressurised steel tubes fed an already unstoppable fire. To observers on other rigs all that was now visible were flames shooting out of the sea.

167 men died that night and it was a miracle that as many as 67 survived. The families of the dead and the survivors were left to count the human cost. Occidental Petroleum, the owners and operators, were left to count the financial damage. For this terrible eventuality they had made suitable provision. Like many oil rigs and gas platforms around the world Piper Alpha was insured at Lloyd's.

The story of how the world's worst oil industry disaster turned from a perfectly acceptable catastrophe claim into a disaster for Lloyd's would remain a secret until this book was published. Piper Alpha was a disaster that need never have happened, either in the North Sea or at 1, Lime Street. Like Piper Alpha, Lloyd's lacked the management controls and above all the necessary safety equipment.

The way it should have worked was simple. The oil company's broker placed $700 million cover for the platform with twenty leading underwriters each of whom wrote $35 million of cover for $1 million premium each. The broker received a 3% commission on the deal.

Twenty more underwriters then reinsured 50% above the first $17.5 million for $300,000 each, or $6 million in total. The broker received 10%.

At this stage reinsurance had taken place and any further reinsurance might be expected to have taken place outside the Lloyd's market. Munich Re, Swiss Re and Allianz AG were all specialists in this field. But this was not the case.

Twenty more underwriters reinsured a package of the above risks for $9 million in total – the brokers again received 10%. Ten more underwriters then followed suit for $4 million in total – the broker took his 10%.

Five more underwriters then reinsured the package for $9 million – the broker received his 10%.

Finally, the last layer of underwriters reinsured the overall catastrophe risk for $9 million – and of course the broker received his 10%.

The fact that the reinsurance at no point went outside the Lloyd's market to, say, Munich Re, was bad enough; this meant there was no 'fire door' to limit the potential losses of those in the chain. What was worse was the fact that the last two sets of underwriters reinsured themselves with the two sets of underwriters who preceded them in the chain; thus in the event of a claim they would end up paying their own reinsurance claims.

Everything was fine, as long as the catastrophe reinsured so many times did not actually turn into a claim. This was particularly the case with the underwriters and syndicates at the end of the chain. If there was a claim, and the music stopped, then so would the parcel; and, in the case of Piper Alpha, the parcel would stop in the hands of the syndicates like Gooda Walker, Devonshire and Rose Thomson Young; and, fatally, in the hands of Patrick Feltrim Fagan and his already under-reserved syndicates 540 and 542.

*   *   *

Two weeks after Piper Alpha blew up and this sequence of
events started, Oakeley Vaughan became the first underwriting
agency in the history of Lloyd's to be forced into liquidation by
its aggrieved members. In spite of the willingness of the St George
brothers quietly to pay out money in return for the promise that
the members would not resort to law, legal action was being taken
by Lord Alexander and a number of the members in question.

The travails of Lord Alexander and the Oakeley Vaughan
members were read about with interest in some unlikely places.

Freeport, Grand Bahama, 1988

John Hinchliffe, the Port Director who had taken such an
interest in the Cameron-Webb yacht *Nirene*, had seen his relationship deteriorate with Edward St George, his boss at the Grand
Bahama Port Authority.

He fell out with St George when he refused to help give the
Prime Minister's sister-in-law an executive position for which he
believed she lacked the necessary qualifications. The final straw
came when he tried to do something about the behaviour of
Freeport taxi drivers, many of whom were notorious for their
rudeness to tourists and some for their drug habits.

Hinchliffe, who had been commended for his services in the
cause of a multi-racial community by the Bahamian Red Cross,
was accused of 'racism' by his antagonists. He retorted that he
was personally responsible for safety measures at what was a
private harbour; and he felt in this he did not have St George's
full support. Pindling himself would end up pleading with the
taxi drivers to improve their behaviour.

Hinchliffe had seen the harbour business expand under his
care and was pleased at the rise in tourists and commercial traffic
for which he was due considerable credit. But the expatriate paradise to which he had brought his wife and children was turning

into a garden where the serpent ruled. Freeport was increasingly bedevilled by crime and drugs and Hinchliffe had taken to doing what many Bahamians did: he slept with a pump action shotgun under his bed for security.

One of Hinchliffe's last acts as Port Director was to follow up an enquiry from American anti-narcotic contacts. He located the vessel *Lucy J* in the marina of the Xanadu Hotel, then owned by the Grand Bahama Port Authority. He passed on the information to the Americans and the following day the vessel was seized by a DEA boarding party. The boarding party found 1,307 kilograms of cocaine.

At this time Hinchcliffe and St George had a further disagreement over the dismissal of their security contractor. The Port Director was ejected from his office. On 2 July he and his family left the Bahamas for good. His successor would commute weekly from Miami.

Hinchliffe left behind the text of an interview with Athena Damianos, a reporter from the *Tribune* in Nassau, which was published on the front page of the paper on 13 July 1988.

Three days later, speaking from London, St George responded.

'I'm rather sorry for Hinchcliffe,' he told the *Tribune*. 'He had a very bad accident in Freeport. Mr Hinchliffe was an extremely good Port Director,' St George went on. 'He will be missed by the company, but since his unfortunate accident I've felt that he's found it difficult to accept instructions from the management of the company.'

St George added that Captain Hinchliffe's remarks that his loyalty was to Sir Jack Hayward, co-Chairman of the Port Authority, were 'obviously asinine because Jack hired him on behalf of the company of which I am Chairman.'

St George disagreed that Hinchliffe had acted reasonably over the matter of the Prime Minister's sister-in-law. 'Really,' he said, 'I think it explains itself. Obviously the man couldn't carry out instructions . . .'

But Captain Hinchliffe received numerous letters after his resignation, including one from John Blashford-Snell, whom he had assisted in Operation Raleigh, a commendation from the First Sea Lord and a fulsome tribute from the American Ambassador for his stand against drugs and his personal efforts that went 'far beyond your official duties.' Sir Jack Hayward was surprised and disappointed however when Hinchliffe received no word of thanks from the British High Commission in the Bahamas.

Hinchliffe and his family returned to Britain and their cottage in Lincolnshire. He worked in the Falkland Islands for a while, and then became harbourmaster of Padstow in Cornwall. He also maintained his keen interest in the unfinished saga of Oakeley Vaughan.

* * *

At 1, Lime Street the new Chairman Murray Lawrence announced the results of the 1985 underwriting year. Overall profits had fallen from £279 million to £211 million although there was a slight rise in the underwriting profits. The tax breaks that traditionally made Lloyd's so attractive had been whittled down by the last Budget.

Once underwriting losses could have been offset against tax, which meant that a 60% taxpayer would never have to pay more than 40% of his or her Lloyd's losses. But the top rate of income tax had now fallen to 40% and so had the top rate of tax relief. Nor was tax relief allowed any longer on pure underwriting losses, but only on net losses after investment income had been taken into account.

The result was that a record 1,064 of the 33,532 members had decided to quit. Many of these were not big Names and they could no longer afford to take big losses. Many other members, especially those on the Excess of Loss syndicates, took another long hard look at their exposure and were in many cases reassured even more heartily by their members agents.

The members agents could also point out that, although over 1,000 people were leaving, there were even more people waiting to come in. This was in spite of the fact that from 1990 Lloyd's had decided to increase the minimum assets showable from £100,000 to £250,000: an attempt to deter short-term investors and increase its underwriting capacity. However the falling purchasing power of money and the multifarious ways of obtaining bank guarantees meant that in reality there was little likelihood of deterring borderline cases. Nor would existing members have to resign if they could not put up the extra money.

Members agents communicated these and other matters in various ways to their members. One matter they did not communicate, however, was the contents of a letter circulating within the Lloyd's market.

This explosive and prophetic letter came into the hands of this author, and its dull prose belies the extraordinary events which were already happening within the reinsurance market. It would turn out to be of importance to the members of the syndicates concerned beyond all proportion to the attention it appears to have received at the time.

LLOYD'S UNDERWRITING AGENTS' ASSOCIATION

Room 617
Lloyd's
Lime Street
London EC3M 7DQ

8th November 1988

TO ALL MANAGING AND COMBINED AGENCIES

Dear Chairman/Senior Partner

Market Losses

Your Committee is concerned that two recent catastrophe losses, the October storm and Piper Alpha, seem to have been offloaded on to the reinsurance market and then to be disappearing. As we are dealing with the largest Non-Marine and Marine physical damage losses the insurance world has ever seen, we would expect Lloyd's underwriters to be paying rather more than what appear to be a few fairly modest retentions.

Your Committee feels that we need to go beyond the rather comforting letters which Managing Agents have sent out on Piper Alpha. The attached questionnaire is designed, after considerable market consultation, to find out where these two losses, and Alicia [the recent hurricane], are finally going to rest so that your Members Agents get the information which they need for themselves and their Names.

The author of the letter was Robin Gilkes, Chairman of the Lloyd's Underwriting Agents' Association. Gilkes asked agents to fill in the attached questionnaire for each of their managed syndicates and send it to members agents 'as soon as possible.'

Gilkes added that syndicates not involved in the Piper Alpha and other losses, or in the reinsurance market at all, should send a 'nil return.' He acknowledged that some managing agents might not want to fill in the questionnaire but concluded that 'there really is no option, given the system within which we operate.'

Why was the Gilkes letter so important? First, it clearly acknowledged the presence of a phenomenon other insiders already knew existed; instead of reinsuring and making proper reserves, underwriters had passed the parcel that was Piper Alpha around in a reinsurance spiral in which the principal motives were the broker's commission and underwriter's premium.

Second, it acknowledged the possibility that such a phenomenon was a 'churned' market and was only safe as long as claims were not made on the catastrophe risks in question.

Third, it showed there was serious concern at this practice

within the Lloyd's market at high official levels; a fact that Lloyd's would still be denying four years later.

The Gilkes letter did not lead to any public action by Lloyd's; four years later it would be alleged that some parties had too much of a vested interest in continuing to unload their catastrophe risk reinsurances on to the syndicates in the spiral.

Nobody said a word. Lloyd's held its 300th anniversary ball in the Temple Gardens by the Thames and in they came . . . In Abidjan on the Ivory Coast of Africa the American lawyer and diplomat Andrew Grossman was elected through the members agent J.H. Davies.

Grossman and his wife had their base in Chelsea and the brother of a friend had suggested they could make the property work more effectively: 'There's something I want to talk to you about . . .'

Grossman made two trips to London. He had heard of PCW. 'Oh, no,' he was told, 'you will only be on low risk syndicates.'

'What about Outhwaite?' Grossman asked.

'It could never happen again,' he was told, 'and in any case that is certainly not the kind of underwriting you would be doing.'

Grossman was duly elected and placed on a spread of syndicates with a total line of £220,000: these included Sturge 206, Gresham 321, Octavian 843, Rose Thomson Young 255, and Feltrim 540, 542 and 847.

In Hamilton, Ontario, Jacki Levin and her husband were elected together through Robin Kingsley's Lime Street Agency. Like Dr Pakozdi the Levins were introduced to Lime Street by the retired dentist Dr Neil Webster. They were both busy professionals with four children, and membership of Lloyd's as it was presented appealed to them as a good passive investment. The only independent advice they took concerned the letters of credit they obtained for £70,000 each, via a collateral mortgage on their family home, from the Toronto branch of Citibank Canada.

They knew nothing about insurance or how Lloyd's worked

but they knew they were joining an organisation with a sterling reputation 300 years old. They also knew many other professional people like themselves who felt the same way and had joined through Lime Street Agencies. There were eleven married couples like them and one family with a widowed mother and two adult children.

Thus it was that the Levins and their friends and neighbours in this exclusive club came to London and went through the Rota interview after being coached as to what to say by Robert Hallam. They had a wonderful lunch and stared in awe at the Adam Room's 100-foot polished mahogany table and chandeliers and paintings and moulded ceiling. They were placed on a spread of syndicates including Feltrim 540, 542 and Gooda Walker, including the stop-loss syndicate 387, broked to by Kingsley Carritt. Then they went back to Hamilton, Ontario.

In Wimbledon, London, Denise Knights also joined through Robin Kingsley's Lime Street Underwriting Agency.

Mrs Knights was a divorcee with little income but she was 55 years old and owned her house. As a friend remarked, and another person to whom she was introduced who was an Allied Dunbar financial 'consultant', it was easy enough to obtain a £100,000 bank guarantee. With £140,000 of assets, as Lime Street pointed out, she could underwrite business of up to £350,000 a year and thus ensure a better income in her old age.

But there was one further obstacle before Mrs Knights could become a member. This was the £10,000 joining cost including the £3,200 membership fee and the stop loss policy. Mrs Knights could not afford this.

No problem, the Allied Dunbar consultant assured her. She could take out a second mortgage to pay this, backed by an endowment policy.

Mrs Knights took this advice. Everything she owned in the world was now at risk if she suffered major losses at Lloyd's. She began underwriting through the Lime Street Agency and was placed on a risk-spreading portfolio of syndicates again including Feltrim and Gooda Walker.

In they came ... but elsewhere in certain quarters the whisper was out. One well-heeled old Etonian thinking of joining was taken aside by an underwriter friend in the market. 'I wouldn't bother joining just now, old boy,' he was told, and the friend added, 'If God hadn't wished them to be fleeced, he wouldn't have made them sheep.'

Stephen Garland was a Lime Street working member whose Anglo-Italian family had been associated with Lloyd's worldwide agency network for generations. Garland was not an old Etonian but he too smelled burning in the air. His agent told him things were going to be 'even better' in the near future. But Garland had made up his mind. He watched these people come in, and walked the other way.

One last event took place at the end of 1988. On 22 December the Serious Fraud Office at last announced that warrants had been issued for the arrest of Peter Dixon and Peter Cameron-Webb.

Cameron-Webb had been sighted in London on at least one occasion since his disappearance by a member of the Council of Lloyd's who saw Cameron-Webb entering his daughter's Sloane Square flat. The timing of the warrant was not of course intended to bring about his arrest, but to dissuade him from making further such visits to Britain.

Ian Posgate was facing criminal charges at the time, arising out of the Howden affair, of which he was acquitted. Posgate was amused to have his suspicions confirmed by the police handling his own case. Cameron-Webb knew too much and there was never any intention of bringing him back to Britain.

The Serious Fraud Office and the Director of Public Prosecutions were apparently not taking any chances, which was why they authorised the issue of the arrest warrant when they did. This was just two days before Christmas and eight days before the end of the year – and after the expiry of the Statute of Limitations under which extradition and prosecution would have been possible. For Cameron-Webb and Dixon at least it would be a happy new year.

EIGHT

NIGHTMARE
ON LIME STREET

The damage done by Piper Alpha and other catastrophe risks that had turned into claims and disappeared into the spiral would eventually filter through, of course; but nobody yet knew where they would land or to what extent they would explode on impact.

When they did know, some old-fashioned optimists would point out that the spiral syndicates were only a relatively small proportion of the market. This was true. What was also true, however, was that, by the end of 1988, 83 syndicates had been forced to leave open the 1985 underwriting year; this was 20% of all the syndicates operating in The Room. Furthermore, none of them claimed, as poor Dick Outhwaite had done of 1982, that the story would eventually have a happy ending.

The total number of open years was even higher when you took into account those left by the syndicates that had ceased trading altogether. These were the blackest of black holes in Lloyd's firmament; their dull numbers belied their once-proud parentage and precious lives like the name tags on a corpse in a mortuary drawer.

Here was a real antique: Tim Sasse's non-marine 762, the casualty of the computer leases, the Den-Har binder and the torched tenements.

Here were the Oakeley Vaughan syndicates, preserved in formaldehyde, yet still draining the lifeblood from their members.

Aviation 168 had ceased over half a decade ago on 31 December

1983, and was running off outstanding claims for 1982 and 1983 at an address simply given in *Lloyd's Syndicate List* as 'Liveried Staff subsidiary post room – Upper Basement.'

Marine 420 had ceased even longer ago on 31 December 1982, and was running off the 1982 year under Terence Pepper on box 204.

Non-marine 423 had ceased at 31 December 1983 and again was running off three consecutive years, 1981, 1982 and 1983, somewhere in the Upper Basement.

Non-marine 551, the worst of all, had ceased at 31 December 1983 and was still running off 1982 and 1983.

Aviation 862 had also ceased at 31 December 1983 and was running off four consecutive years, 1981 to 1984, in the Upper Basement of the new building where nobody ever went unless they lost their way.

Here was Spicer and White's 'nodding donkey' marine 895, eventually the subject of an action group and a small out-of-court settlement.

Here on box 237 was Cyril Warrilow's non-marine 553, ceased at 31 December 1987 and running off four chronically overwritten years from 1984 to 1987.

Here were Posgate and Denby's marine 700 and non-marine 701, frozen in time at 31 December 1982 and running off the claims from the 1982 year under John Charman, the regular underwriter of syndicate 488.

Here were the ultimate unmentionables which had ceased trading seven years earlier: the syndicates once run by Peter Cameron-Webb. Non-marine 157, 918 and 940; the marine syndicates 810 and 869; and the baby syndicates 893, 954 and 986.

This was Lloyd's chamber of horrors in the opening days of 1989. Among the exhibits was a little-known Outhwaite failure, non-marine 518, ceased at the end of 1985 and running off that same year. But although the fates had called many to the chamber of horrors of open years, where once there had been none, the long-tail furies had chosen to reserve their full wrath for the 1982 members of Outhwaite 317/661.

The one thousand six hundred Outhwaite members were for the most part an affluent crowd and they intended to stay that way. No matter that in some cases they would retrieve more than half their losses from the taxman. They were accustomed to seeing their money work twice over and they could not accept that what had happened to them was the downside of several years of easy winnings.

The Outhwaite members were looking at average cash calls of £47,000 each on an open year which was set to stay with them for the rest of their lives. Three hundred of them were working members and in many cases in relatively junior positions; they did not have the wealth to bear these losses. To add to their distress they and all the other Outhwaite Names were receiving a stream of contradictory messages about what to do.

Some were being advised to stay in Lloyd's and try to 'trade out' of their losses in what Lloyd's itself regarded as the correct spirit. Others were being advised that if they did not sue they would receive discreet 'help' with the cash calls. Others were advised not to sue on the grounds that it would jeopardise any ultimate settlement.

There were doubts as to who should sue whom, and for what; although the Council of Lloyd's was supposed to regulate the market it was immune to suit under the 1982 Lloyd's Act. A more appropriate target for those seeking financial redress was the Errors and Omissions insurance policies held by Outhwaite and the other 81 agencies involved.

The Council of Lloyd's had little time for the complaints of the active underwriter or his members. 'Outhwaite knew what he was doing,' declared Deputy Chairman David Coleridge. 'If we helped him, we'd have to help every other underwriter.'

The Chairman of Lloyd's, Murray Lawrence, who in his capacity as underwriter had laid off his own asbestosis risks with Outhwaite, was of the same opinion, and in his capacity as Chairman said so in a letter to members. Later, this letter would come back to haunt the 600 members who heeded the implicit advice it contained not to sue.

Nearly 1,000 others had paid £250 to join the Outhwaite 1982 Association led by Peter Nutting. The fighting fund of £¼ million purchased the financial and legal firepower without which Nutting knew they did not have a prayer. Nutting had been receiving a stream of telephone calls from anxious members and he had accumulated twenty ring-binders of correspondence which he and his secretary had answered. His own stop loss policy was no longer taking the strain of the cash calls and he was having to liquidate other assets to meet the bill. But with its fighting fund the Association was able to hire Touche Ross to handle the accounting and engage the law firm of Richards Butler.

Edward Molesworth, the former Outhwaite employee and director of Oakeley Vaughan, took on the Association's routine office work. Like Lord Alexander, Molesworth had the misfortune to be on the Oakeley Vaughan syndicates and on Outhwaite 1982. The Richards Butler legal team acquired the services of Anthony Boswood QC, a quietly-spoken and unassuming barrister with a reputation for lethal effectiveness when cross-examining people in the witness box.

Presiding over everything from the converted outbuildings of his Surrey manor house Nutting had turned what started as a distraction on the way to Ascot into a well-funded upper middle-class citizens action group. Like all successful action groups, whatever their persuasion, its strength lay in the fact that self-interest was at the heart of the motives of every single one of its members.

The publication of the first part of the Freshfields report into Outhwaite had suggested there was a case to be answered; this had inspired the meeting at the Baltic Exchange attended by Sir Peter Miller. Lloyd's had then commissioned Stuart Boyd QC at their own expense to report to the members as to whether or not Freshfields had correctly addressed the issues. Boyd duly reported and while he too commented on the narrowness of the brief he broadly hinted that every Name on the syndicate would do well to take legal advice.

Lloyd's were surprised and disappointed at Boyd's conclusions. Nutting was delighted.

The Outhwaite Association commissioned a report drawing on the Boyd and Freshfields conclusions and sent it to all their members. Nutting hired a PR man to give the Association credibility. His aim was simple: to show they meant business and embarrass Lloyd's into making a settlement, as they had done in the case of Cameron-Webb.

Nutting had the members and the resources and the professional help. Now he needed Lloyd's to change its mind. In his meetings with David Coleridge and Murray Lawrence he was disappointed to find that Lloyd's had no intention of so doing.

Nutting had some regard for Coleridge, whom he had known for many years. But, when Coleridge and Lawrence suggested he shut his mouth and stop whingeing, Nutting was outraged. He consulted Anthony Boswood QC and the two men considered trying to obtain an injunction to prevent Lloyd's from meeting the claims by drawing down on the Outhwaite members' deposits: the funds held at Lloyd's without which members could not go on underwriting.

Boswood concluded that such an exercise would be a costly and time-consuming failure. He felt the best thing to do was put Outhwaite on the stand and let Boswood and his expert witnesses shoot him to pieces. Three years later another lawyer in another case concerning Lloyd's members, Michael Freeman, would consider trying to obtain the same injunction against Lloyd's and amidst a considerable amount of controversy would decide to proceed.

By August 1989 the Outhwaite Association had counsel's opinion that they had a strong enough case. The verdict of Anthony

Boswood QC and Michael Hart QC was that the conduct of Dick Outhwaite, on whose syndicate his members had clamoured to be placed, 'fell far below the standard of skill and competence reasonably expected of him in the conduct of the syndicate's affairs.'

By this time the Outhwaite losses had passed £300 million and were the biggest in Lloyd's history. The 1,600 members who had so far paid the cash calls were now looking at combined losses of over £1 billion: an unprecedented figure not just for one syndicate but for the entire 400 syndicates of Lloyd's.

Who were the Outhwaite members and who among them were in the Association and thinking of suing? Eddie Kulukundis and his wife Susan Hampshire had lost heavily by being placed on Outhwaite through the Thomas Miller agency, but were not going to sue. The former MP Sir John Langford-Holt had been in Lloyd's twenty years and had survived Hurricane Betsy; he too was going to take the rough with the smooth.

The former Prime Minister Edward Heath was in favour of suing and had paid in his £250 to the fighting fund. So had Lord Alexander and Edward Molesworth; this was a chance to mitigate not only the Outhwaite cash calls but the horrific losses they were continuing to suffer each year from Oakeley Vaughan. So had the golfer Tony Jacklin and the former tennis champion Virginia Wade. Jacklin had stopped underwriting and vowed to keep what money he had left in the bank.

So had Lady Middleton, who had fought back over Sasse and helped found the Association of Lloyd's Members. Her agent did not approve of her suing and told her so; her reaction had been to resign from Lloyd's. But like everyone else she was still left with the problem of Outhwaite 1982.

Rupert Hambro too had resigned but was left with the open year of 1982, his very first year of underwriting. Hambro could have afforded to stay in Lloyd's but he did not like the signals he was receiving from the market. The tax breaks were diminishing, the American claims were rising and many more people were leaving Lloyd's than were coming in. Hambro had been told after Piper Alpha that insurance rates would rise and the market would be a brighter and bouncier place. This had not happened as far as Hambro could see.

Hambro was on the board of the *Daily Telegraph*. He remembered a remark by the editor, Max Hastings: 'Rupert, I never joined Lloyd's, because all the stupidest boys I was at school with seemed to go into it . . . and that worried me.'

When 'Goldfinger' Posgate was closed down, Geoffrey Rickman, like many other Posgate Names, had been encouraged to join Dick Outhwaite and his syndicate 317/661.

Rickman had done reasonably well out of Lloyd's since 1978. He had one open year on syndicate 701 but the tax breaks had been good to him and the cheques had come flowing in. He had raised his underwriting from £80,000 to £150,000. He did not have stop loss because he felt he could carry any losses. He had every reason to stay but he did not.

Later, he could give a whole stream of reasons. The profits were too dependent on investment income instead of actual underwriting. He knew too little about the market. He sensed the market knew too little about some of the risks it was insuring and reinsuring. The tax breaks were diminishing but he himself was not earning any more from conventional income, which he would have had to do if he was to continue to benefit from them on the scale he had done in the past. He also thought the practice of syndicates reinsuring with each other could destabilise the market in the event of a major risk turning into a claim.

Later, Geoffrey Rickman could quote all these arguments in his defence. But these were not the reasons at the time. 'Why did I get out?' he said. 'The whole thing was getting too big for little chaps in the country with peaked caps and brogues.'

Nothing more than sheer gut feeling; this was how Rickman resigned and so escaped the black hole that was Outhwaite 1982.

The Outhwaite 1982 Association held another meeting, at the

Central Hall, Westminster. This shrine of sober and industrious Methodism was crammed with hundreds of people for whom the wages of greed were sleepless nights and letters bringing calls for cash.

Outhwaite, unlike many troubled syndicates, had over 300 working members, many of whom were in dire straits as a result. But it was hard for some observers to feel sorry for any of them when they read and heard the stories of Names who were now complaining.

Howard Harper, a surgeon from Tunbridge Wells, complained that he was faced with selling one of his houses to cover his Lloyd's losses. Harper talked as if he had been mugged in an unprovoked attack rather than lost on a risky investment.

'They are hitting me for about £51,000 now and coming back for another helping the same size next year,' he told the *Mail on Sunday*. 'Two years after that there will be another helping.'

Harper went on: 'My average profits from Lloyd's were about £20,000 in a good year and less in bad ones . . .'

Harper had been a member since 1978 and had therefore done well in a comparatively short time. He may or may not have ploughed those profits back into his reserves. He may or may not have taken out stop loss insurance. Either way, £20,000 profit earned on assets that were already accumulating interest somewhere else was not just 'a good year'; this was money for old rope.

Yet, precisely because this was so, it was so easy to forget this, and to describe anything less as 'a bad year.' A profit from Lloyd's, however big or small, was a unique bonus; and it had a unique downside, regardless of whether or not there was fault on the part of the active underwriter.

Meetings of wealthy Lloyd's members who had suddenly lost money could be an unedifying sight. This at least was how it seemed to Betty Atkins and Sylvia Hatton in that summer of 1989.

Central Hall, Westminster, 1989

The two former secretaries arrived early for the meeting and had time to spare. It was a sunny afternoon. They walked past Westminster Abbey and the throng of tourists, across Parliament Square, to Westminster Bridge. Mrs Atkins suggested they jump off it.

Over a year had passed since they had received the letters confirming that there was no documentary evidence of the undertaking made to them by their former employers. Nor had their former employers been able to reassure them in person. Meanwhile the cash calls from Lloyd's and the anguish of the two women had steadily mounted.

Mrs Hatton was close to breaking; her husband had died two months earlier, the stress of their circumstances having in part contributed to his death. Mrs Atkins was still living with her elderly mother for whom she had to care while shielding her from the news that seemed to become more and more terrible with every letter. By night Mrs Atkins lay awake in bed unable to sleep for worrying. By day she went to work as if nothing had happened, until the realisation of her plight returned as it did whenever there was room in her mind.

Her hair had gone white and she looked older than her age. More than once she began crossing the road on her way home and stopped midway in the face of the oncoming traffic, unable to convince herself for a moment that it was worth carrying on.

Both women had steadfastly refused to join the Outhwaite 1982 Association. They still believed their problems would be solved by those in whom they had placed their trust. In a series of letters it became clear that, far from this being the case, their problems were rapidly worsening. Lloyd's wanted the money and it wanted the money now.

By this time the amount had risen from £7,000 to £42,000.

Deputy Chairman

David Coleridge

16 September 1988

Dear Mrs Atkins

I would firstly apologise for the delay in responding to you but, as I am sure you will realise, given the amount of time that has elapsed since the Rowbotham Group sponsored your Membership of Lloyd's and the change in the structure of the Group that has taken place during that period, enquiries have taken longer than I first anticipated.

I have noted the comments regarding the assurances that you claim were made to Mrs Hatton and yourself by your former employers regarding your liability to any losses that may arise from your Membership of Lloyd's. I have been in contact with Mr Peter Dennis and have corresponded with Mr Richard Rowbotham, Mr Sidney Bloch and, through him, Mr Stuart Speller. However, none of these gentlemen can recall any such assurances being made to yourselves . . .

Moreover, the relevant files have been reviewed and no evidence of the assurances you refer to can be traced. I trust that you will therefore appreciate I am unable to comment on this aspect. Further, even if such evidence did exist, the position is complicated by the fact that the Rowbotham broking house and underwriting agency have changed completely, both in terms of ownership and structure in the period . . .

By October 1989 the amount of money Mrs Atkins owed was £68,000. By November it was £78,000. Their former employers at Rowbotham & Sons continued to insist that they could not recall assurances made in 1979. In 1982 Rowbotham & Sons had become Rowbotham de Rougemont Ltd and on 31 December 1985 Rowbotham de Rougemont had been sold to C.I. de Rougemont & Co. C.I. de Rougemont and Co. continued to insist that no assurances could be honoured which had been made before 1 April 1985: six years after the two secretaries had been elected as working members.

At this stage Betty Atkins and Sylvia Hatton had decided that the only option left apart from suicide was to join the Outhwaite 1982 Association.

They had arrived early for the meeting and walked to Westminster Bridge. They stared down into the muddy waters of the Thames. Then they walked back across Parliament Square, to the Methodist Central Hall.

Inside, a lot of people were asking Peter Nutting and the Committee questions like: 'How will this affect my tax position?'

Betty Atkins and Sylvia Hatton sat down and wondered if they had come to the right meeting. Everybody else looked very well-heeled. Nobody else looked very worried.

There were microphones positioned around the auditorium. Mrs Hatton said to Mrs Atkins that she thought they ought to ask a question. Mrs Hatton had been widowed eight weeks earlier. Mrs Atkins said she would ask the question for them.

She queued up behind a man whom she recognised as a Name through the Rowbotham agency. Apart from Sylvia he was the only person there whom she knew. The man spoke and then it was the turn of Mrs Atkins. She was shaking and everyone was looking curiously at her. She went on speaking and asking questions. People began to sit up and take notice.

'I don't care about income tax. What I want to know is, things are so bad for me and Sylvia, is there any reason why we shouldn't just have jumped off that bloody bridge?'

Betty Atkins went back to her seat and sat down. She was still shaking. But she felt better than she had done before she spoke out.

So did Lord Alexander in another place.

The House of Lords, Westminster, 1989

Lord Alexander had seen the honourable values of his upbringing shattered and his trust miserably betrayed as a result of his Lloyd's membership. All his syndicates, Oakeley Vaughan, Warrilow, Aragorn and Outhwaite, had collapsed either through negligence, misfortune or calamity that had befallen those in whom he had placed his trust. Apart from the prospect of financial ruin and the stress placed upon himself and his family, he felt badly humiliated as a businessman. The money Charles St George had paid him had proved hopelessly inadequate and his stop loss policies had proved likewise. As his losses had risen the income had fallen with which he had once naively thought he could pay them off; and with this had fallen his ability to claw back some of those losses from the taxman.

Before long he would have paid out over £100,000. Nobody could second-guess the final figure but it would be far greater; it would gobble up all his remaining assets and possessions, pursue him to his grave and haunt his children after he was gone. Lord Alexander felt sick to his bones that he could leave such an inheritance.

Every time an Additional Underwriting Agencics (6) envelope came through the letterbox of their house on Wandsworth Common his wife Davina had a panic attack. What particularly galled Lord Alexander was the fact that among the employees of AUA(6) whose job it was to ask him for money to pay for losses incurred by Oakeley Vaughan was Mark St George, whose signature had been on the letter of 1981 that had given Lord Alexander and others the impression that all was well with the now-liquidated agency. It was enough to break the stoutest heart.

But, unlike some distressed Names who pranced around forming action groups and protesting too much, Lord Alexander had kept silent. Meanwhile the cash calls had continued to come in as the claims were run off and the interest was piling up on his outstanding debt. Soon he would be unable to supply any more borrowing guarantees and he would be suspended from underwriting. At this point he realised that silence was no longer an option; as well as joining the Oakeley Vaughan legal action, he decided to speak out.

He tabled a question in the House of Lords, asking what the Government proposed to do about cleaning up Lloyd's of London.

The day before the debate Lord Alexander was approached by Lord Kimball, a fellow Warrilow Name and the foxhunting peer who had been instrumental in the passage of the Lloyd's Act. Kimball asked him if he would like to put his thoughts about Oakeley Vaughan to Lloyd's Chief Executive, Alan Lord.

Lord Alexander confirmed that he would. In Lord's office he was a little taken aback to see that a clerk was taking notes of their meeting. However, he proceeded to tell Lord in no uncertain terms what he thought of Lloyd's attempts at self-regulation.

He was aware that the problems with Oakeley Vaughan had begun before the Lloyd's Act; but pointed out that Lloyd's appeared to have covered them up in order to avoid jeopardising the passage of the act through Parliament. Lord Alexander added that there were many aggrieved Names such as himself, but very few who could put down questions in the House of Lords.

He felt better after the interview. But he received only an anodyne reply which in spite of the presence of a stenographer bore only a passing resemblance to the meeting he had attended.

In the House of Lords during the debate in question he received just as unsatisfactory an answer.

'Is the Government,' Lord Alexander asked, 'planning a further investigation into Lloyd's, in the light of a Lloyd's report into the Oakeley Vaughan syndicate on which Names lost substantial sums of money in the early 1980s?'

Lord Young of Graffham replied.

'There is no question,' said Lord Young, 'of any further Government enquiries into self-regulation in the Lloyd's market.'

'Lloyd's,' he went on, 'has almost completed full implementation of recommendations contained in the Neill committee of enquiry in 1986, and further investigations will therefore not be necessary.'

This filled Lord Alexander with frustration; but within a few days his questions produced two further answers in the form of letters from unexpected quarters.

One was pleasant and one was less so. The latter was from Chethams, a firm of London solicitors:

Dear Lord Alexander

We are Solicitors to Edward St George who took over the winding down of Oakeley Vaughan (Underwriting) Limited in 1985 to help sort out the problems of the earlier years at the request of Lloyd's. As you, a former director of the company, are well aware, Edward St George had no involvement directly or indirectly with the management of the Oakeley Vaughan syndicates.

On 24th October 1985 you executed a Release and Undertaking. It appears that notwithstanding this, according to our information, at the meeting of creditors of the company you purported to claim as a creditor and vote at that meeting of creditors.

We are further instructed that you sought to institute proceedings involving the corporation of Lloyd's in your capacity as a Name in respect of the Oakeley Vaughan syndicates.

Our Client was particularly disturbed to be informed that recently you had suggested proceedings against him personally in the United States of America on some illusory pretext as 'he had plenty of money' even though our Client was in no way involved in the unfortunate affairs of the company other than as a Name.

In fact, it is understood you are planning to take advantage of the cloak of privilege in the House of Lords to make an attack on Oakeley Vaughan there. Our Client considers that your actions constitute an unpleasant attempt to extort money from him without merit.

We have to inform you our Client considers that in view of your Release and Undertaking your conduct is dishonourable and the matter ought to be brought to the attention of the committee of Lloyd's for full investigation.

We are however instructed by our Client that he accepts that it is possible you may have overlooked the Undertaking which you in fact gave – a copy of which is enclosed. If therefore on reflection you wish to apologise for speaking as you have and retract and resile from all actions and proceedings, our Client is quite prepared to accept this and not pursue matters further or otherwise.

Lord Alexander's reaction to this letter was one of outrage that the language of honour and chivalry should be invoked to accuse him of extortion. No such legal action was forthcoming from St George. Lord Alexander persisted in his own legal action as one of the fifty members suing Lloyd's for redress over the mismanagement of the Oakeley Vaughan affair.

But it was not only in the British courts that the St Georges were feeling the heat. In Houston, Texas, attorneys for Jay C. Hirsch, the Oakeley Vaughan member introduced to Lloyd's by Wilfred Sherman, were attempting to bring proceedings against Oakeley Vaughan and Lloyd's under the RICO Act – Racketeer Influenced Corrupt Organisation – the statute normally used to prosecute the Mafia and Colombian cocaine traffickers.

The proceedings would be referred to the Texas Supreme Court and would still be on the table of the US Supreme Court two years later in 1991. This was not the last time the RICO Act was invoked against the gentlemen of Lloyd's.

The second letter to Lord Alexander was from a far less likely quarter: the former Port Director of Freeport:

Dear Sir

Re. Oakeley Vaughan

I read with growing interest that your enquiry to Lord Young in the House of Lords (Lloyd's List 18.7.89) was apparently dismissed rather lightly, particularly when one considers the serious nature of your question. The Howden case is going through the courts and one is left to wonder if there are many similarities with Oakeley Vaughan.

I have read the Chester Report and I think I detect a certain 'modus operandi' . . . I can well understand the anger of the 50 or so Names now seeking redress.

I hope that you and others will continue to give the Oakeley Vaughan crowd a thoroughly good airing.

Yours faithfully

John Hinchliffe

Lord Alexander was intrigued by this letter and invited Hinchliffe to his London offices. The former Freeport Port Director and the peer who owned land on the Bahamian island of Exuma discovered they had a common interest in the affairs of Oakeley Vaughan.

Lord Alexander was particularly interested to learn of the keen attention that had been paid to this matter by Captain Hinchliffe while the latter was in the Bahamas. Captain Hinchliffe was particularly interested to learn that Edward St George had been a director of Oakeley Vaughan (Underwriting) Ltd and for at least sixteen years a director and major shareholder of Oakeley Vaughan & Company Ltd.

This last fact, confirmed by a search at Companies House in London, seemed somewhat at odds with the statement in the letter from St George's solicitors to Lord Alexander that their client had 'no involvement either directly or indirectly with the management of the Oakeley Vaughan syndicates.' The syndicates had been an integral part of the Oakeley Vaughan broking, underwriting and members agency business of which Oakeley Vaughan & Company Ltd was the broking and holding company, and one of the roles of a director was to keep an eye on the management of a company and have sight of the annual accounts.

A search at Companies House also confirmed that Edward St George had only retired or resigned as a director of Oakeley Vaughan & Company Ltd at some point between 31 March 1988 and 31 March 1989.

Lord Alexander and Captain Hinchliffe agreed it might be worth their whiles to keep in touch. Perhaps the questions Lord Alexander had asked in the House of Lords had done some good after all.

* * *

Over a year had passed since the disaster which had taken the lives of 167 men in the North Sea. The Piper Alpha claim, as the Gilkes letter had predicted, had disappeared into the reinsurance spiral.

Down the line it had passed, from the lead underwriters to the primary insurers, to the secondary reinsurers and into the third and fourth layers of the reinsurance market. Here it began to spin back and forth between reinsurers and so it started to 'spiral.'

Round and round it went, and up and up, and, long after the men from Occidental Petroleum had congratulated the men from Lloyd's on how quickly the claims had been settled, the Piper Alpha parcel was still spinning round and round and up and up the spiral. Each time it landed on the desk of an underwriter that underwriter paid off his share and in turn called up his reinsurer. Each underwriter knew of course that this series of dull claim forms in reality spelled doom for any underwriter who did not in turn have his reinsurance in place; this was the only way to keep the parcel moving. Whenever the parcel stopped, heaven help the underwriter who did not have the reinsurance in place to start it moving again.

It is not difficult to imagine the feelings of Patrick Feltrim Fagan, once the Piper Alpha parcel had come smoking and hissing into his hands at the box where he underwrote for syndicate 540/542. Fagan knew the problem and equally he knew the solution. But therein lay his undoing. Where is my reinsurance? *Where is my reinsurance?*

Fagan had some reinsurance; but to his horror he discovered he did not have enough to cover the damage that would be done when the parcel he was holding blew up in his face. This was not least because most of his reserves had been taken away as part of the PCW settlement, about which he had protested so vigorously and been told to keep his mouth shut for his pains.

The Piper Alpha parcel had stopped moving and he did not have the reinsurance in place to start it off again. Patrick Feltrim Fagan had a problem. A big problem. He also had another problem. He had to tell somebody; and soon.

A big catastrophe claim at Lloyd's was like a tidal wave far out at sea; it began with only a barely perceptible growth in the height and speed of the waves that splashed on the beach. The bathers continued to paddle among them unaware that it was already too late.

The first ripples came to the members via their agents, in letters that acknowledged the existence, but played down the magnitude of the tidal wave to come.

29 September 1989

Dear Member

We are writing to inform you that we have recently been advised by Feltrim, the managing agent of syndicate 540/542, that the Piper Alpha disaster is likely to produce a loss of approximately 66% on line for the syndicate's 1988 account, and that it may be necessary for a cash call to be made next May or June to cover at least part of the loss. This news obviously caused us to consider our continuing involvement with this syndicate extremely carefully.

This letter went on:

We had a meeting with the underwriter, Patrick Fagan, and his management last week, as a result of which we advise you to remain on the syndicate for the time being for the following reasons:
1. The Piper Alpha disaster was the biggest loss in monetary terms ever to affect the Marine market, and it is reasonable to expect syndicates writing a similar account to Fagan's to produce losses in these circumstances. Many of them will.
2. If Fagan's loss is 66%, it will not be the worst, as far as we can tell at the moment.

The letter added that Fagan had 'reacted sensibly to the loss' by, among other things, purchasing more reinsurance. The members agent was satisfied with Fagan's explanation of how in its current trading position the syndicate 'would in all probability be able to withstand a loss similar to Piper Alpha.'

The members agent stated in the letter that they were 'favourably impressed' by the management of the Feltrim syndicates. They added that rates were rising in the Marine Excess of Loss market. 'Excess of Loss syndicates of this type,' they concluded, 'can be expected to make above average profits in most years . . .' however, 'they are exposed to losses when major catastrophes occur.'

'You may well therefore wish to discuss,' the agent told his members, 'with the director who handles your affairs, how a line on this syndicate fits in with your other participations.'

This letter was typical of the many sent out by agents to members around the world, playing down the reasons why those members should come off the Feltrim syndicates. One reason not given, of course, was that the membership of Feltrim 540 had nearly doubled from 1987 to 1989, rising from 996 to 1,669 people. 94% of these were external members and only 6% actually worked in the market.

The agents who had recently placed their members on Feltrim would have looked extremely silly if they now wrote to those same members and advised them to come off the syndicate. This would not have been a good example of the expertise for which their members paid them their salaries. Indeed, there was a further disincentive for their doing so, in that any decrease in the membership of Feltrim at this critical stage would inevitably have resulted in an increase in the average losses of the remaining members; and the members agents would again get the blame. If anything, the Feltrim syndicate needed more and not fewer members; and some agents proceeded to place their new members there for this very reason.

However, contrary to the impression given by Feltrim to one members agent that there was no withdrawal of support, fifteen agents did quietly withdraw their members from Feltrim at this time.

Meanwhile the rest of the agents wrote their reassuring letters and mailed them out to their members in London and Somerset and New York State and Ontario. The members stayed on the syndicate and Patrick Feltrim Fagan went on underwriting. The waves splashed on the beach just that little bit higher and faster. But the sun was still shining and the children still played in the sand. And all the time that tidal wave grew and grew, far out to sea.

The Princess Royal was made an honorary member of Lloyd's and collected a cheque for £10,000 for a London children's hospital of whose appeal she was patron. One joke circulated to the effect that, even if she had been a working member, in the present climate she would have had to have been on an extraordinarily good range of syndicates to come away with that kind of money.

The smaller working members too were suffering from disasters such as Outhwaite 1982 and the catastrophe claims that were slowly eating their way through the market. Many of these working members did not have the resources to meet even the smaller cash calls to which they were exposed by their modest premium limits.

Some working Names were helped by their employers in this respect. Others were writing smaller lines but still resigned, unwilling to live with even the modest exposure they had been given through membership of their agencies' syndicates. Working membership of Lloyd's had long been seen as a barometer of confidence in the market; and that barometer was falling.

For members who wanted to resign and had open years there were standard procedures to enable them to cover their outstanding liabilities. For elderly members, the importance of protecting their surviving spouses was paramount.

The standard procedure was for the member to take out an estate protection policy. In this way the deceased member's deposit was released by Lloyd's to his or her estate and the surviving spouse did not have the trauma of bereavement compounded by cash calls from their late husband or wife's open years.

For a male member approaching death and the woman who was to be his widow, this was of some comfort as their life together drew to a close. But for the wife of one such member whose life was coming to an end late in 1989 the trauma of widowhood was to be nothing compared with the seemingly indissoluble knot her husband had tied with Lloyd's of London.

Duffield, Derbyshire, 1989

Clive Bemrose had never achieved the ambition he had recorded in his diary on joining Lloyd's in the early 1950s: 'If Lloyd's does bring in several thousand pounds per annum in a few years, I shall feel very tempted to give up business and devote myself to home, scouting, magistrates, gardening . . .'

Bemrose had not failed in his ambition through any fault of his own, but because he was a temperamentally energetic man. In his seventies he learned to play the violin and passed Geology 'O' Level. He was awarded the OBE for his services to the Boy Scout movement. He patronised an orphanage. He was High Sheriff of Derbyshire. When he wanted to know more about India, he did not buy a handsome coffee-table book, like most people of his means and age; he boarded an aeroplane and went to see for himself.

Bemrose had done modestly well as a small Name at Lloyd's and survived the 0.37.5 pence settlement and the shock to his trust that came with his losses over Cameron-Webb. He was a man of enthusiasms and was not inclined to resign because of what he regarded as one atypical setback. But on his five syndicates he had two open years: the 1983 account of Merrett 421 and Holloway 604; the latter was a casualty of the long tail furies.

As he grew older he grew more muddled and his wife Enid was forced to deal with his correspondence. Enid Bemrose was seventeen years younger than her husband but she was not a young woman and after reading his correspondence she shared his mounting concern that after his death she and not Lloyd's should have the benefit of his deposit.

Mrs Bemrose knew about estate protection policies and was relieved to learn that her ailing husband had one. The correspondence she dealt with included chapter and verse on how after his death the policy would enable his deposit to be released to her and would free her from any liability. The policy was renewable annually on 1 January and after that there was a 90-day carry-over period during which time the new premium could still be paid without prejudice to the member.

Enid Bemrose re-read all this correspondence from time to time to check that the policy was up to date. She also read *The Times*; and in particular an article about possible inadequacies of stop loss and estate protection policies. She picked up the telephone and dialled her husband's members agent.

'Have no concern!' the agent told her. He seemed angry even to be doubted on this matter.

Mrs Bemrose had spent thirty years as a magistrate. 'Am I to believe *The Times*?' she said. 'Or am I to believe you?'

Her agent became irritated. 'You obviously don't understand,' he said. 'I will write you a letter so that you do.'

The letter never arrived. Mrs Bemrose was worried. Since her husband's original agent had retired little things had gone wrong which had not gone wrong before.

They had had a letter containing a cash call for £64,000 which turned out to be a clerical error. They had had a letter thanking them for £1,400 which they had not sent. They were small mistakes but they added up and Clive Bemrose's blood pressure began to rise whenever another envelope from the agency came through the letter box.

It was late 1989 and her husband had only a short time to live. Mrs Bemrose forgot about everything else and tried to concentrate on the short time they had left together. After forty-three years of marriage, the memory would soon be all she had; at least she knew she had no financial worries.

*   *   *

That same week the news was announced that Piper Alpha had claimed its first victim on the spiral: Gooda Walker 298.

In fact Gooda Walker 298 was just the first of many such victims to be announced and Piper Alpha was just one of a clutch of catastrophe risks reinsured by Gooda Walker 298 and others. Hurricane Alicia, the unnamed British Hurricane, the Exxon Valdez spillage, Hurricane Hugo and the Californian earthquake were all catastrophe risks that had turned into catastrophic claims; but Piper Alpha was the biggest so far and it was getting bigger all the time.

Gooda Walker announced that syndicate 298 would have to cease trading for 1990. Fifteen hundred members had been taken off it by their agents and the syndicate's underwriting capacity had fallen from £44.7 million to £6 million. There were no longer enough members to fund the underwriting; their problem would be how to fund the losses.

None of the agents or their members yet knew when the Gooda Walker Names would have to start paying up or how big the cash calls would be. Nor did they know at the time that Gooda Walker 298 had an astonishing *13,500* insurance contracts which included liability for Piper Alpha. The agents tried to make reassuring noises and the members tried to believe them. Gooda Walker 387, a smaller syndicate underwriting stop loss business, would also remain open with staggering losses of up to 1,000% or £100,000 lost for every £10,000 line.

Derek Walker, the underwriter who never flew his small private aircraft too high or too far, would run off four consecutive years of syndicate 387 while continuing to underwrite for Gooda Walker syndicate 290. Walker had a smaller exposure to Piper Alpha than Gooda Walker 298's underwriter Kenneth Boden, but he had three times the exposure to Hurricane Hugo. Because of this, Walker's turn, like Patrick Feltrim Fagan's, would not be long in coming and his members too would be washed away when the tidal wave hit the beach.

What of the men who had broked and rebroked these catastrophe risks with the market? Sedgwick, one of the biggest brokers, were prominent in this and other areas. But the man whom everybody talked about, and who never talked to the press, was 'Big Bill' Brown: the broking equivalent of 'Goldfinger' of his time.

Brown was Chairman of Walsham Brothers, a broking firm owned by him and his family. Walsham's accounts for 1989 showed a turnover of £36.6 million and pre-tax profits of £20.4 million.

Brown's father had spotted a gap in the reinsurance market during the Second World War and his son had astutely exploited this market over the last decade. However many times Bill Brown broked a reinsurance risk, he took his cut, and Patrick Feltrim Fagan, Derek Walker, Kenneth Boden and all the other LMX underwriters took theirs. Even when that catastrophe risk turned into a catastrophic claim this did not unduly worry Brown; after all he was a broker and did not share the losses of the syndicates in question.

Brown was a working member of Lloyd's and had been since 1958. He was not on Feltrim or Gooda Walker but he was a member of Cotesworth Berry 536 and other blue-chip syndicates well away from the spiral.

The reinsurance game involved the broker travelling only a few yards instead of round the world and yet it had turned into a goldmine. Bill Brown was a multi-millionaire and his salary of £8.1 million led him to be one of the highest-paid men in Britain. His collection of classic cars and horses grew in size. He had a Rolls-Royce Corniche (BB7) and a Mercedes (BILLY) and a Ferrari and a Porsche Turbo. He could be seen most days drinking Buck's Fizz at the Howard Hotel or that other well-known Lloyd's watering-hole, the City Flogger.

Brown stories abounded within the market. After one particularly splendid lunch he and his brother strolled past a BMW showroom. His brother expressed a liking for a new model. 'I'll get you that,' Brown told him, 'you paid for lunch.'

Brown broked to many of the leading underwriters like Alec Sharp of 839 who earned £1½ million a year after salary and profit commission, and Roy Hill of syndicate 2: men who made handsome profits for themselves and their syndicate members. But he also broked and repeatedly rebroked to Patrick Feltrim Fagan and Derek Walker and his critics claimed he fuelled the spiral by 'churning' high risk business or keeping it going to the detriment of the market and simply to make an extra 10%. He was criticised for encouraging underwriters to 'pass the parcel' and for removing the incentive for underwriters to make better reserves for possible catastrophe claims; something that had already rung alarm bells in the Gilkes letter.

Yet Brown was apparently doing nothing to contravene the rules that existed under self-regulation. He never spoke to the press but he spoke to other great players, past and present.

'Ian,' he told Ian Posgate, 'if Lloyd's insisted I only charge 1% brokerage, I'd do it. I'm the best in the market.'

Posgate had to agree. Brown was simply working the system. If the system was wrong it was up to the regulatory authorities to do something about it. Meanwhile, every time a reinsurance parcel landed in an underwriter's hands, the chances were that it had been broked by Bill Brown and Walsham Brothers. For the underwriter who had not placed his reinsurance properly (again through Walsham Brothers) the parcel would stop moving and the time bomb would blow up in his and his members' faces.

For the members of Gooda Walker and Feltrim it was an anxious time as they read and re-read those letters from their agents. But for 'Big Bill' Brown that year it was business – and Christmas – as usual.

The New Year of 1990 started with some underwriters reducing their catastrophe risk exposure and others pulling out of the market altogether. There was a desperate scramble by brokers inside and outside Lloyd's to secure what little spare reinsurance cover there was available. Some reinsurance rates shot up from 10% to 100% and this threw the whole spiral into an even greater frenzy. Even Bill Brown was confronted with the possibility of a pay cut.

Attempts were made in vain to change the terms of these reinsurances so that underwriters would retain more of the coverage rather than spin it round and round the spiral. The trouble was that if any more catastrophes on the scale of 1989 took place in 1990 the spiral market would come under severe strain. When storms battered Britain and mainland Europe in the early months of 1990 these fears seemed to be coming true. While nobody on the outside seemed to know what was going on, observers on the inside began gleefully to paint the ultimate scenario.

If the Big One – a Tokyo earthquake or a hurricane in New York – also happened, the whole spiral market would go through the ceiling of its sorely-pressed reinsurance cover. It would explode, turning from a self-perpetuating galaxy of gamblers into a gargantuan black hole.

On the one hand, was this not the very heart, nay soul, of self-regulation; a part of the market dying and being born again? On the other hand, as a few were quick to point out, there were the external members to consider: the people whose assets made possible this and every other kind of broking and underwriting.

For the external members had no idea of the existence of the 'spiral' or the Gilkes letter or the tidal wave of catastrophe claims which threatened to engulf the syndicates on which they were underwriting. They knew little about the complexities of the international insurance business or the real extent of the deep structural differences between the other players in that business and Lloyd's of London. They had not the faintest idea that these phenomena were not permitted to exist elsewhere.

For, unlike Lloyd's, the other big European reinsurers like Allianz and Munich Re did not permit the existence of a 'spiral' because they did not permit the endless reinsurance of catastrophe risks within the same market. There was no Monsieur Guillaume LeBrun or Herr Wilhelm Braun endlessly broking catastrophe risks round the reinsurance markets of Paris and Frankfurt. After a year of catastrophes like 1989 the worst that could happen to Allianz, or Munich Re, or Swiss Re, was that they made a bigger provision for reserves and still paid a dividend to their shareholders.

True, those shareholders had not enjoyed an annual tax-free return of 10%–15% throughout the late 1970s and early 1980s. But the Germans and Swiss would have retorted that there was something seriously wrong with an insurance institution where such profits had been possible. Reinsurance was about building up reserves and not about handing out quick profits; and the losses suffered by members of Lloyd's during the early 1990s would in no way be suffered by the shareholders in Allianz and Munich Re during the years in question.

But, unlike the shareholder in Munich Re or Allianz, for a member of Lloyd's on a syndicate like Gooda Walker, or, as it would shortly turn out, on Feltrim, Rose Thomson Young, Devonshire and a whole raft of others, there was a further and infinitely greater downside to their investment. If the January storms had not taken the roofs from over their heads, the 1988 losses at Lloyd's surely would do it for them; after all, they had unlimited liability.

And, as for Lloyd's itself, were there also not dark conclusions to be drawn? Allianz and Munich Re had massive reserves in the form of conventional shareholdings and conventional solvency. Lloyd's too claimed to have massive reserves including in the form of the assets of its members. But typically those assets were fluctuating entities like equities and property and the solvency of around 50% of the members of Lloyd's had been achieved through bank guarantees. The crash of 1987 had wiped billions off the value of the assets that underpinned those guarantees, yet most of those members were still underwriting as much as ever. Furthermore, so-called 'independent financial advisors' – many of them members of Lloyd's on commission from members agencies – were still offering to help would-be members or existing members with solvency problems to obtain guarantees secured on their pensions and houses.

What was going to happen to those members – and to Lloyd's

– when the full scale of the 1988 and 1989 losses became known?

The answer was that Lloyd's was going to lose members and some members were going to lose everything. The mainland European reinsurers would take advantage of this and put up their premium rates. Lloyd's, having lost members, would lose capacity to do business and lose out to the competition.

Later, everybody would find somebody else rather than themselves to blame. This was the way of the world. At the time, if these questions had been asked, the answers would have been simple. But nobody wanted to know.

Gooda Walker 387 joined the chamber of horrors of ceased syndicates with open years being run off somewhere in the building.

Possibly as a result of the January storms, the great glass roof of the new building at 1, Lime Street itself began to leak, and mops and buckets were placed on the marble floor of The Room. On another occasion one of the marbles used to count votes by the Council fell off the great mahogany table; and there was a stunned silence as it refused to lie where it was but rolled to the side of the Committee Room.

In Derbyshire, Enid Bemrose was at least consoled by the fact that she still had a roof over her head. Now she was to find it could still come crashing down without warning.

The Widow's Tale

Clive Bemrose died on 3 January 1990. On 4 January his son Christopher telephoned his late father's members agency.

Christopher Bemrose informed the members agency that his father had died and asked them to confirm that he was covered by estate protection policy.

The agency's reply was swift and uncompromising.

'Your mother has no need for concern,' they told him, 'the

estate is covered by the estate protection policy. The deposit will be paid over in a matter of weeks. There may be some delay on the special reserve but other than that it will all be handed over.'

Mrs Bemrose was sitting next to her son as he made the call. She was relieved to hear the good news. On the day her husband died there had been but one bright thought in her mind. She had finished with Lloyd's.

Three weeks passed and the Bemroses did not hear anything more from the agency. Mrs Bemrose was going through her late husband's papers when she came across the estate protection policy. She noted that it expired on 31 December 1989.

They did not usually ask for the renewal premium until February or March; that was the ninety-day carry-over period.

Mrs Bemrose telephoned her accountant. He advised her to telephone the members agency.

The agent answered the telephone. Mrs Bemrose repeated to him what she had said to her accountant.

'I presume this is all right?' she said.

'Oh, no,' he replied, 'your husband was not covered by estate protection policy after 31 December 1989. I am afraid we will be unable to release the deposits.'

Mrs Bemrose spoke to him for quite a long time because she was unable to grasp the meaning of what he was saying.

'Do you mean, not for two or three years?' she asked him.

'Certainly ten years,' he replied.

The deposit amounted to £140,000. Mrs Bemrose had an old age pension and a small amount of capital. Now the meaning of what he was saying sank in. Her son knew nothing of this and she did not want to burden him with it. But she knew. She had lost everything.

'I tell you what,' the agent said brightly, 'why don't you come and have lunch?'

* * *

The Outhwaite 1982 Association began the largest law suit Lloyd's had ever seen. The writ alleged negligence against Dick Outhwaite and the 80 or so agencies who had introduced members to his syndicate 317/661.

If the writ succeeded, the Errors and Omissions syndicates like Malcolm Cox's syndicate 990, Stephen Merrett's syndicate 418 and Brian Smith's syndicate 45, which insured against claims such as this, would have to pay up large amounts of money.

These were blue-chip syndicates on which people would beg, borrow or steal to be placed by their members agencies, usually to no effect. Cox's 990 – formerly the preserve of Frank 'the Bank' Barber – had 1,051 Names, 33% of whom were working members and who underwrote 40% of the syndicate's capacity. Merrett's 418 had 5,683 members, 11% of whom were working Names and who provided 11% of its capacity. Smith's 45 had 649 members, a hefty 33% of whom were working Names and who provided 37% of the syndicate's capacity. Merrett himself wrote a £290,000 line on his syndicate 418 and Smith wrote a cool £500,000 line on his syndicate 45; doubtless they all reinsured elsewhere and possibly outside Lloyd's.

Outhwaite's syndicate 317 by contrast had seen its membership fall from 3,545 in 1986 to 2,611 in 1990. The proportion of working members had fallen from 13% to just over 8%. For Dick Outhwaite, once Roy Merrett's joint heir-apparent and Stephen Merrett's great rival, the barometer had definitely fallen and would go on doing so.

Peter Nutting regretted bringing the legal action but he had tried and failed to explore every other avenue in order to secure redress.

'The Chairman of Lloyd's, Mr Murray Lawrence, and the authorities at Lloyd's have been totally uncompromising,' he declared, 'we have been told to pay up and shut up.'

Nutting was equally uncompromising about what he saw were their grounds for complaint.

'Mr Outhwaite,' he said, 'insured 40 other insurers against

their US liabilities relating to asbestosis and pollution. He was a marine underwriter.

'He wrote a huge book of business and it was quite clear that, if one of these contracts went wrong, they would all go wrong, because asbestosis was common to all of them. They were all the same risk. He wrote 18 unlimited liability policies and he had no reinsurance.'

Outhwaite may not have attended the Leeds Castle meeting to consider the long tail asbestos peril, but the information gathered by the asbestosis working party was common knowledge in the market.

'It was reported in *Lloyds List*,' Nutting went on, 'but Mr Outhwaite, by his own admission in the Freshfields report, said he had no special knowledge or understanding of asbestosis problems.'

Outhwaite replied through his solicitor that he was confident of victory. Outhwaite was a selfmade Yorkshireman and he was unrepentant in spite of his shrinking membership. His opening defence document would state bluntly that members 'ought to know that the underwriting of insurance business at Lloyd's exposes them to the risk of unlimited liability.' They should also know that, 'because of the relationship between premium and risk, the greater the opportunity of profit, the greater the risk of loss.'

For his 1982 members that loss had risen to £45,247 for every £10,000 line they had on the syndicate; lines of £20,000 were commonplace.

One hundred and seventy two Spicer and White 'nodding donkey' victims of syndicate 895 at last received a belated partial settlement averaging 20% of their losses over the years 1980 to 1982. The losses had been caused by the chronic overwriting which the brokers had so eagerly exploited. There was a £40,000 loss for a £20,000 line on the 1982 year alone. £10,000 back of that was less than the members had hoped, but it was the best they could get.

The Oakeley Vaughan members in litigation were interested to note that Charles St George had made an out of court settlement with David Becker. Becker was suing him over what he claimed was a breach of the undertaking to indemnify him that St George had made in 1984.

St George had wined and dined Becker, an architect, who claimed he had wanted to become a member of Lloyd's 'more for the cachet than the cash.' This may have signified a misplaced hope on Becker's part, but it also signified a misplaced hope on the part of Charles St George. Becker and many of the other distressed Oakeley Vaughan members to whom he and his brother Edward had since paid money may have been greedy and gullible in the first place, but they were not necessarily fall guys who were going to go away. Becker's losses were over £120,000. Surprise, surprise: suddenly the priorities were reversed and cash was more important than cachet after all.

Every time members of Lloyd's had taken legal action they had eventually won some sort of settlement. The cases of Sasse, Brooks and Dooley, Spicer and White 895 and others had all ended either directly or indirectly in defeat for Lloyd's and victory of some kind for the members. Some legal actions were more expensive than others and some victories were more moral than financial, but they were victories all the same. These messages were received and understood by Peter Nutting. Yet Lloyd's had continued to play down the idea of litigation in the case of both Outhwaite and Oakeley Vaughan.

If Lloyd's felt it could not afford Outhwaite losing, this was perhaps understandable. Likewise some of the members felt they could not afford the legal action it would take to win. The view of many on the Council of Lloyd's was that a verdict against an underwriter of Dick Outhwaite's stature, even if he successfully denied the charge of negligence, would do immeasurable harm to the market if not the man. Whether or not such a verdict would suggest a change was needed in the way that market operated was quite another matter.

But for Lloyd's to fight the Oakeley Vaughan litigants as if they were the victims of an error of judgement on the part of an otherwise highly successful and respected underwriter was little short of madness. Yet Lloyd's persisted in doing so.

Oliver Carruthers of the *Digest of Lloyd's News* had noted while attending the Becker hearing in Court 36 of the Royal Courts of Justice: 'The Oakeley Vaughan fiasco is not yet over, and it is sleazier and nastier than any of the other problems facing Names . . .'

Meanwhile the 1987 losses were beginning to make themselves known to a generation of Lloyd's members for many of whom the Outhwaite and Oakeley Vaughan affairs were other people's problems.

There was no dramatic announcement or press furore and the whole thing was played down in time-honoured manner. The letters went out suggesting that there might at some point in time be cash calls but that there was no cause for alarm. The first some members knew of the losses from their agents was over a good lunch.

Giles Curtis had done modestly well over the years. But he had noticed that while his profits had remained the same his underwriting had risen substantially, thus increasing his exposure to risk for no apparent extra return. He had never taken out stop loss insurance because he felt the premiums were too high.

Early in 1990 he was entertaining a director of his members agency at a smart restaurant in Covent Garden.

The agent was retiring. He watched happily as Curtis ordered the finest food and wine to thank him for services rendered over the years.

The agent then turned his attention from the menu.

'First,' he said, 'the bad news . . .'

Curtis did not take long to compute that for a man of his relatively modest means there were going to be no more expensive lunches for the foreseeable future.

Later, when the 1988 and 1989 figures had come in and the

losses exceeded everything he had made over the years, he would remember the first lunch he and his agent ever had together. Had it really been free?

Out they went ... the letters to members around the world bearing the bad news. Bridget Milling, now Milling-Smith, the young widow with two children who had gone into Lloyd's in 1979 through an independent financial advisor connected to the Cox and Bell agency, had made £8,000 in her first year. She had made a loss every year thereafter; this year her cash calls would total £75,000 on asbestosis syndicates hit by the long tail furies.

She had remarried, a rural GP, and they had a child with cerebral palsy. Her husband struggled to pay the cash calls while she struggled to find work and fretted about the future of her child.

Marjorie Walsh, the older widow who had joined in the same year, also had large losses on spiral syndicates and her members agent Laurance Philipps had merged with another company. After two hip operations and one for cancer Mrs Walsh was resigning with a number of open years as all she had to show for Lloyd's membership.

Denise Knights, who had joined in 1988 after her Lloyd's deposit had been paid for by a second mortgage on the advice of an independent financial advisor, had been placed on a risk-spreading portfolio of syndicates including Feltrim and Gooda Walker. Mrs Knights had had no time to build up reserves and was unable to meet a cash call for £22,500 from the Lime Street Agency; further calls followed and she would soon owe an estimated £100,000 for losses and advance cash calls on 1989 and 1990.

The Lime Street Agency members were to pay long and hard for the risk-spreading portfolio of syndicates which had blown up in the faces of the underwriters, and eventually in the face of the agent who had placed them there. Robin Kingsley and his colleagues at Fleur de Lys House in Houndsditch were still making positive noises, and controversy would later rage as to how aware they were of the problem at the time.

Cash calls from Lime Street for Feltrim and Gooda Walker meant Dominique Osborne and her husband had to pay up £26,000 each that year; but this was a fraction of the horror in store. Kingsley's brother-in-law Martin de Laszlo was a travel agent who had arranged Kingsley's American and Canadian selling trips. He had seen Kingsley's tastes in airline seats grow from year to year from Club Class to First Class to Concorde. De Laszlo, his father, his wife Mary and his cousin Damon were now facing huge cash calls from losses of syndicates on the spiral.

Clive Francis, also a Lime Street member, cursed the day he had ever believed the men who had told him that Excess of Loss was 'the professional end of the market.' Francis would face cash calls of a staggering £700,000 on Feltrim and Gooda Walker for 1988, 1989 and 1990 and like Bridget Milling-Smith had the further misfortune to be on Pulbrook 334.

Francis, unlike many others, would never forgive himself for 'the mixture of greed and flattery' through which he had allowed himself to be landed like a fat spring salmon on the shore of Lloyd's. Among the many who would rush to take legal action and blame everyone but themselves, Francis's would be one of the few voices always to remind people that however distressed they were they had all entered Lloyd's of their own free will.

Other members agencies which had placed large numbers of their members on spiral syndicates were sending the same bad tidings. Michael Colvin MP's wife Nichola had been placed on Gooda Walker and Feltrim by her agent, Stancomb and Kenington. This was the agency which looked after the interests of Hugh Bourn, the Lincolnshire farmer.

Bourn and his family had believed David Kenington when he had come to lunch at their house and undertaken to place Mrs Bourn on 'low risk' syndicates. Quite possibly Kenington had believed it too. Kenington was now unwell and his partner Bill Stancomb took over dealing with the Bourns and other members.

This included sending the Bourns letters asking for £130,000 to pay cash calls on the 1987 year.

Hugh Bourn took a deep breath and paid up. Stancomb, as his partner had done, came up to Lincolnshire.

'This time next year' he told them, 'I can promise you will all receive cheques.'

They shook hands all round.

Out they went . . . the letters bearing the bad tidings to Britain, and Ireland, and America, and Canada, and Africa, and Australia and New Zealand.

On the Bay of Tralee Desmond O'Neill had a cash call of £35,000 and this time the retired engineer had to borrow every penny to pay it. O'Neill was a Lime Street Agency member and the letters that had begun 'Dear Desmond' were now less friendly; on one this had been scratched out and 'Dear Mr O'Neill' put in its place. O'Neill was on Warrilow 553, Gooda Walker 290, 298 and 387; in the last case he had been underwriting other people's stop loss policies, on which the claims were piling up, when he had not even felt able to afford to take out such a policy for himself.

In Boston, Massachusetts, Dr John Mathias had a £25,000 line on Feltrim 847 after being told stop loss was not necessary because the market 'had turned around.' Dr Mathias would face losses of £250,000 on 1988 and 1989 but would try to stay underwriting and trade his way out.

'Remember,' he told this author, 'Lloyd's is a club and, in order to protect yourself, you have to stay a member.'

In the pretty little town of Tuxedo Park, New York State, Dale Jenkins was the Lime Street Name who had noted the comment Kingsley had made when he was elected: 'A syndicate is only as good as its reinsurance.'

Jenkins had a £15,000 line on Feltrim 847 among other spiral syndicates and now he was finding out how good that reinsurance had been.

Jenkins would take the opposite view to Dr Mathias and come to the conclusion that in order to protect himself against the club he was going to hire some serious legal firepower.

In Hamilton, Ontario, Dr George Pakozdi made a small profit on the 1987 year. But Dr Pakozdi was worried; the original profit had been £25,000 but was reduced to £5,000 because of cash calls for 1988. When Robin Kingsley and Robert Hallam came on their annual visit to Hamilton in March 1990 Dr Pakozdi initiated a long conversation.

What was his exposure to Excess of Loss syndicates? he asked. Dr Pakozdi had been reading the newspapers and specifically wanted to know about the concentration of risk from Hurricane Hugo; also the possible risk of earthquake exposure in California and Tokyo.

Kingsley assured him that Hurricane Hugo would result in losses but that these would not be catastrophic due to the spread of his syndicates. He assured Dr Pakozdi that he monitored each syndicate and its exposure and factored all the information into each member's portfolio.

Dr Pakozdi was reassured to hear this. Kingsley and Hallam flew back to London.

Three months later the Canadian Association of Lloyd's Members sponsored John Peel, an early associate of Chatset and *Lloyd's League Tables*, to come to Toronto. Many members had of course interpreted the *League Tables* to mean that the rapidly growing spiral syndicates were a good bet – but Peel took one look at Pakozdi's spread of syndicates and advised him to change it immediately. He said he was drastically over-exposed to Feltrim and Gooda Walker.

Dr Pakozdi tried to change but it was too late; he was on those syndicates for 1991.

Jacki Levin and her husband, who along with so many friends in Hamilton, Burlington and Bracebridge had joined through Lime Street, had not yet had time to build up reserves and now they were getting the first warning that there were going to be cash calls on Gooda Walker 298: £21,000 for Jacki and £6,000 for her husband.

In a panic they telephoned Robin Kingsley.

'Oh,' he told them, 'it's just a cash flow problem. The year hasn't closed yet, and 1988's profitable syndicates haven't yet given you your profits. This particular syndicate is a little short of cash; that's all. It will all come back next June.'

Many of the Levins' friends had the same anxious conversation and they too paid their losses.

In Abidjan, on the Ivory Coast of Africa, Andrew Grossman, the American lawyer and diplomat, was having trouble obtaining up-to-date news from his members agent; the agent insisted on sending all the mail by boat.

Grossman's portfolio of syndicates included Feltrim 540/2 and 847, Gresham 321, Octavian 853 (which underwrote stop loss, something Grossman did not have personally) and 255 Rose Thomson Young, like Feltrim and Gresham a casualty of the spiral.

Grossman paid his cash calls and brooded. Although he was still a relatively young man he had hoped to retire shortly. This would no longer be possible. Grossman did not like this. Something was wrong.

Australia accounted for only 2 per cent of Lloyd's membership, but nearly half the 600 Australian Names were on syndicates on the spiral. Dr Gavan Griffith had risen to be Solicitor-General on the National Circuit. As a lawyer he was unimpressed the more he learned about Lloyd's and the Gooda Walker syndicates of which he had the misfortune to be a member. 'If Messrs "X" and "Y" were to come to Australia,' he wrote of the directors of another troubled Lloyd's agency, 'I would call in the Fraud Squad.'

'The problems are obvious enough,' he told this author. 'What may be questioned is the capacity of the Council of Lloyd's and the underwriters to accept that the party is over.'

In Taupo, New Zealand, Elizabeth Harker had a £25,000

line on Feltrim 847 among other syndicates in the risk-spreading portfolio arranged and monitored for her by Lime Street Agencies. Mrs Harker was beginning to regret the introduction through her husband's old friend Wing Commander Gus Holden to Robin Kingsley. London – and the expectations she had entertained on election – suddenly seemed a long way away.

Out they went . . . these and other letters to people around the world who suddenly realised how far away they were from the institution which had dropped a bombshell into their lives.

A few, a very few, were able to explain to themselves and their families the weird and terrible chain of events through which the deaths of 167 men on a North Sea gas platform and the pollution from a supertanker in Alaska several years earlier could now threaten them with the loss of their homes and property.

Most were unable to comprehend how such a chain of events could have happened and found their analytical faculties blurred by shock and guilt. Doctors began having heart attacks and professors began having to take their children out of school. Houses went up for sale for no discernible reason as far as the neighbours were concerned. Why, they had always seemed like such a happy family.

One or two around the world had already decided to fight back. Even for the stoutest of hearts the odds were heavily stacked against them. For an elderly woman recently widowed they seemed almost insuperable; until she overcame her feelings of guilt and told her son, and her son told her they were not going to leave it there.

The Widow's Tale #2

Enid Bemrose had not accepted her late husband's agent's cheery invitation to lunch. Given that her life had just collapsed around her she did not feel in the mood.

She eventually received the news in writing: 'I confirm as you are aware that your late husband was not enrolled under the 1990 Estate Protection Plan . . .'

Mrs Bemrose had not of course been aware of this until it was too late. Looking through the files of correspondence she became aware of another letter from the agency, sent on 18 November 1988, over a year before her husband's death: 'Cover is available under a separate scheme for those Names who have resigned their membership but who have been left with a run-off at 31 December 1987. This does not yet concern you . . .'

What had happened was this. Hitherto the policy had been automatically renewed and the premium collected from Clive Bemrose at some point within the 90-day carry-over period. Now the terms of Clive Bemrose's eligibility for Estate Protection Plan, as this letter correctly stated, had changed.

The broker in question had advised the members agency that henceforth their Estate Protection Policy would not be available to members with open years. Clive Bemrose had open years. A further letter from the members agency also correctly stated that because Clive Bemrose was resigning he would have to pay the Estate Protection Premium himself. But he had not been notified by the agency that he would have to pay that premium before the end of the year: 'This does not yet concern you . . .'

But this had concerned her; and now it was too late.

Mrs Bemrose eventually plucked up the strength to ask the agent what else could be done. The agent thought about this and offered her reinsurance. He said this would release the deposit. But it would cost between £5,000 and £10,000.

Mrs Bemrose leaped at the chance.

Three weeks passed. She watched for every post and jumped at every telephone call. Nothing. Eventually she telephoned the agency.

'Sorry,' they said, 'what about £20,000?'

Mrs Bemrose again leaped at the chance.

More time passed. They did not write or call. She telephoned again.

'Sorry,' they said, '£20,000 is not enough.'

Eventually it rose to £150,000 – more than the value of the deposit. For the first time in her life Mrs Bemrose wanted to be dead; and could understand why people killed themselves in order to achieve this.

Christopher Bemrose was appalled when he returned from abroad and discovered the state of his mother.

His mother had also spoken to her cousin, a local business-man and Lloyd's member who carried considerable weight in the financial community. He too was outraged. He played golf with the Chairman of Lloyd's, Murray Lawrence, and advised Mrs Bemrose to write to Lawrence. Lawrence wrote back to her saying he was 'deeply grieved.' He also advised her to contact the newly-formed Lloyd's Members' Hardship Committee.

Mrs Bemrose had never heard of the Members' Hardship Committee. But there were other distressed members who had heard and who as a result were becoming more and more dis-tressed every day.

* * *

It was an inspired decision by somebody to give the position of chair and frontwoman of the Lloyd's Members' Hardship Committee to Dr Mary Archer.

Dr Archer had already inspired a judge to utter the immortal words, 'Has she elegance? Has she fragrance?', in the summing up of the libel case that threatened to destroy her husband Jeffrey's career. She and her husband had been members of Lloyd's since the 1970s and had increased their underwriting to £1 million; she described this as a 'nice round sum.'

But by the looking-glass standards of Lime Street and the moneyed middle classes Dr Archer had also known hardship.

She had seen her husband lose his seat as an MP and his assets in a speculative share investment. After he was revealed to have paid £2,000 to a prostitute she had endured the full horror of the prurient tabloid press.

Dr Archer had survived all these gruesome hardships and emerged smelling of roses. She sat on the committees of the great and the good, many of whom shared the sentiments of the judge. She was elected to the Council of Lloyd's.

After the scale of the Outhwaite losses became known the threat to members' – and Lloyd's – liquidity was perceived to be so great that special measures had to be taken. There was no point in Lloyd's waiting for distressed members to become insolvent when it was already having to meet some of the claims for which they were liable from its Central Fund. As the solvency of those members deteriorated that pressure on the Central Fund increased; and so did the need for a means to limit the damage.

The needs of Lloyd's, and not the needs of the members, were the priority behind the invention of the Members Hardship Committee. But no one could deny that it might also serve good public relations purposes at a time when the worsening losses were bringing a worsening press to Lime Street.

Dr Archer was the perfect person for the job. She enthused about the Lloyd's 'buccaneering and entrepreneurial style' with such conviction that it was impossible to believe she had ever heard of Cameron-Webb or the Grobfather or the Gang of Four or Oakeley Vaughan or Warrilow or the nodding donkey or the spiral. Possibly she had not. Possibly, given that these were matters which the Council of Lloyd's did not wish discussed publicly, she too did not care to comment.

But she cared; and there was a Members' Hardship Committee questionnaire to prove it. What is your employment? and your spouse's employment? How much do you earn? and your spouse? What are your assets? and your spouse's? How much is your spouse worth? How much is your house worth? Do you own other properties? How about your spouse? Furniture, jewellery, works of art? What is the surrender value of your life insurance policies? and your spouse's?

What is your household expenditure? How much is your poll tax? Your gas bill? Electricity? Telephone? What do you eat? Do you have a cleaner? You do? How much do you pay them? You have a car?

If you have disposed of any assets within the previous five years, we would like to know. You have? What is the description of those assets? The date of disposal? The value of those assets at the date of that disposal? The proceeds of that disposal?

Why *did* you dispose of those assets when you did . . . ?

Dr Archer and her Members' Hardship Committee cared so much that they wanted to know all these things.

For a distressed member such as Bridget Milling-Smith or Denise Knights or Betty Atkins or Sylvia Hatton, filling in a Members' Hardship Committee application form was like being interrogated immediately after the death of a spouse. You loved him? How much did you love him? Did he love you? How much did he love you exactly? Were there any other people involved? Did that love diminish as you grew older, or did it accrue interest . . . sorry . . . grow in strength? Are there any special circumstances which you feel should be taken into account when your application is considered?

Yes . . . please leave me alone.

But Mrs Milling-Smith and Mrs Knights and Mrs Atkins and Mrs Hatton and others were all encouraged to fill out these forms because they were reminded that if they did not do so there was a very real likelihood that their bank guarantees would be called in or seizure be made on their assets and they would be driven to bankruptcy. In return for accepting the terms of the Hardship Committee they would be absolved of their liabilities and allowed to live in their houses until they died. The houses would then revert to Lloyd's.

Unless, of course, those houses were deemed too big for their purposes; in which case the terms of the Hardship Committee stated that they would have to be sold and the distressed member would have to purchase a more modest property suited to his or her reduced status.

The same went for any investment income a distressed member still had after the battering he or she had taken from losses brought about by membership of this 'buccaneering and entrepreneurial' institution. If this income was deemed to be beyond a member's basic needs, then it too would have to be liquidated and only a modest sum of capital allowed to remain in his or her possession. The terms of a successful Hardship Committee application were less favourable than those of American bankruptcy law.

There was a further condition to the successful Hardship Application. The member in question had to undertake not to divulge the terms of the settlement; the strong impression being given that, if they did, those terms were forfeited.

One distressed member took one look at the questionnaire and threw up. Another described it as 'the ultimate oubliette'; the aim was to lock you up and throw away the key. Many applicants completed the forms, re-read them, tore them up and tried to blot out the reality of the situation from their minds. They would tell the Hardship Committee they had posted the forms and play for time. Many others would simply delay filling them in for as long as possible.

They included Mrs Bemrose, Mrs Milling-Smith, Mrs Knights, and Mrs Atkins. Mrs Bemrose did not see why she should forfeit her house when through no fault of her own she had already forfeited most of her husband's estate. Mrs Milling-Smith did not see why she should hand over her house to Lloyd's when resources would be needed to care for her severely handicapped child after her own death. Mrs Knights did not see why she should lose everything because she had taken the advice of an independent financial adviser. Mrs Atkins did not see why she should be required to declare the meagre assets of her elderly mother and expose them both to the risk of being removed to a two-bedroom flat.

But for Mrs Hatton there was nowhere else to go. In the absence of any sign from her former employer or the company's new owners that they would honour the undertaking once made to her, under stress from the mounting cash calls, and unable to cope since her husband's death, Sylvia Hatton went through the process of the Hardship Committee.

She was prohibited from talking about the terms of the settlement even to her friend Betty Atkins. In return for being released from her liabilities, Sylvia Hatton, the secretary who had been made a working member of Lloyd's and placed on Outhwaite 317/661 as a long-service award, took the vow of silence and entered the ultimate oubliette.

The Outhwaite 1982 losses were running at around 200% or minus £20,000 for every £10,000 line; this was a cash call for just one year, and the cash calls for Outhwaite went on and on, year after year, and would do so for years to come.

Several marine syndicates, battered by Piper Alpha and by their participation in the spiral, were already making advance cash calls for the 1988 year, in spite of the fact that another nine months would normally have passed before they fell due.

Rose Thomson Young 255 wanted 70% or £7,000 per £10,000 line. Gooda Walker 298 wanted 30%. Feltrim 540 wanted 75%. The letters went out to the members around the world; all of whom would eventually contemplate legal action against the managers of the syndicates in question.

In the United States an Ohio State Court granted a preliminary injunction to three members of the Stone family from Cincinnati. The Stones were among the many American members of Oakeley Vaughan.

Wilfred Sherman, the Penarth sporting man who had introduced the Stones and others to Lloyd's in the late 1970s, had already been subpoenaed to appear at the Jay C. Hirsch hearing against Lloyd's in Texas. Sherman was visited in Marbella by members of the Stones' Columbus law firm.

In London Lloyd's issued a statement.

'We do not consider,' it declared, 'that this affects the ultimate security of the establishment or of US Names generally.'

The issue of Lloyd's reputation to American policyholders was of far greater importance than the complaints of a few members who had the bad luck to become involved with Oakeley Vaughan. The link between the two however was that the members supplied Lloyd's solvency, on which rested its fabled ability to meet claims. This was precisely why, elsewhere in the United States, the Chairman of Lloyd's himself was taking no chances.

The Hyatt Regency Hotel, Chicago, 17 September 1990

Murray Lawrence was the first Chairman of Lloyd's to be invited to address the Annual Convention of the Independent Insurance Agents of America. After a few insurance jokes about the Mayflower and the Boston Tea Party he came straight to the point.

'Let me begin by saying something about Lloyd's latest global results which, since we operate a triennial accounting system, relate to the 1987 account. These showed an overall profit of just under one billion dollars [£509 million] which, when taken with the record return of just over one billion dollars [£607 million] for the previous year, represent the high point of the present cycle.

'Since then,' Lawrence went on, 'the picture has deteriorated and although the 1989 account, at this stage, appears not unreasonable . . .'

The 1988 account would be announced nine months later in June 1991.

'. . . not unreasonable, it seems likely that 1989 will mark the first overall loss for more than twenty years and 1990 has not made a promising start.

'This is hardly surprising, perhaps,' Lawrence added, 'bearing in mind such disasters as the San Francisco earthquake, Hurricane Hugo and the European windstorms.'

Lawrence did not of course mention the fears that the spiral market would collapse if there were any more such catastrophes. He was adamant that Lloyd's would not lower its rates and he felt sure the market would soon start to harden.

'It is hard to soar with eagles,' he told them, 'when you fly with turkeys.'

Lawrence was at pains to show that the American policy-holders who provided so much of Lloyd's business need have no fear when it came to Lloyd's ability to keep its house in order.

'Of course,' he told them, 'the term U.S. general liability business covers a massive spectrum from the most difficult risks – which have been the cause of most of the problems – to the more straightforward types of cover. While the market is still extremely wary of writing the former, except with the most stringent safeguards.'

Was Lawrence thinking of the American asbestosis business he himself had laid off with Dick Outhwaite in 1982?

'. . . the most stringent safeguards, some of the latter can be and indeed are currently being underwritten at Lloyd's.

'One previous area of concern, however, that has responded even more readily to treatment is that of regulation. Following the passing of Lloyd's private Act of Parliament in 1982 we have put in place a first-class self-regulation system. As one who has been privileged to serve on the Council of Lloyd's both as Deputy Chairman and Chairman throughout that period, I am delighted to say that this difficult and time consuming although essential operation has now been successfully completed.

'The significance of this,' Lawrence went on, 'from a commercial point of view is that the Council of Lloyd's, the

Society's governing body, can now turn its attention more towards facilitating the business of the market, the aim being to foster its entrepreneurial flair.

'At the same time we have been at pains to counter the adverse publicity which some loss-making syndicates have been attracting not only in Britain but throughout the world. The Council, while sympathising wholeheartedly with the Names concerned and assisting them in numerous ways, has no alternative but to require that all underwriting obligations, legitimately incurred, must be fully met. That, in essence, is what the principle of unlimited liability, to which all members of Lloyd's unreservedly subscribe, really means . . .

'Whatever damage these disputes, which are now in many cases resolved, may have done to the good name of Lloyd's, it must be stressed that in no instance have they adversely affected the policyholder outside Lloyd's, nor, as it happens, the capacity of the market, since, during the last two years, some 1,260 new Names have been elected and no less than 9,000 have increased their participation so that our capacity and, therefore, our ability to accept business has actually increased despite the fact that resignations during that period may have appeared to suggest otherwise. Even more encouraging are the current esti-mates for 1991 which show the figures for those leaving Lloyd's to be appreciably less than last year and for those intending to raise their limits, up by nearly 50 per cent.'

These words received applause in Chicago that night, but they would come back to haunt Lawrence in less than a year's time, when the scale of the 'not unreasonable' 1988 losses became known and Lloyd's and its members entered the worst cash crisis in their history.

To what extent was Murray Lawrence, an affable and well-liked man, aware of the misgivings already circulating secretly and at high levels in London? One measure of his awareness was the degree to which he and his advisors felt impelled to defend

Lloyd's to such an extent in front of such an important audience. Another was the extent to which Lloyd's was trying to keep the lid on its troubles at home.

* * *

Murray Lawrence's reassuring words that no dispute within the market would adversely affect the policyholder outside Lloyd's were not strictly true.

Pulbrook 334 was an old-established syndicate that had been badly hit by the long tail asbestos losses. But 283 of its 581 members were claiming that this disaster need never have happened to them. In 1981 the syndicate, like its sister Pulbrook 90, had reinsured itself with Merrett 418.

In February 1990, Stephen Merrett, son of the legendary Roy Merrett and active underwriter of 418, had invoked a legal precedent set some years earlier and successfully petitioned for the contracts with 334 and 90 to be made void. This had saved Merrett and his members on 418 a great deal of money. The asbestosis claims subsequently came in to the tune of £60 million, and instead of having them met by Merrett 418 the members of Pulbrook 90 and 334 faced losses on average of over £100,000 each.

Among them were Bridget Milling-Smith and Clive Francis, the Lime Street Name and chairman of the Pulbrook 334 1985 Association who was now facing losses of £700,000.

In June 1990 the Association held its first meeting in the Old Library at Lloyd's in Lime Street. Stephen Merrett was present.

'Mr Merrett,' Francis told him, 'we have tried conciliation. We have to say we are gravely disappointed in you.'

Amid much cheering and clapping Merrett stalked out of the meeting.

Francis, the former RAF pilot and property tycoon, was now faced with having to move out of his own property. His complaint on behalf of himself and his 282 members was that they had not been told that the legal basis on which the reinsurance had been placed had changed. They maintained that they should have been told and that had they been told they might have been able to take appropriate action to renew their protection.

What particularly galled Francis and many of his members was that Stephen Merrett, the owner and active underwriter of Merrett 418, who had repudiated the policy, was also the proprietor of Pulbrook Underwriting, the agency against whom they had raised their complaint. Not only that, but Merrett controlled the Errors and Omissions market and was a member of the Council of Lloyd's, its regulatory body. Merrett also sat on the Suspension Committee, to which many of those appealing to be allowed to go on underwriting were Pulbrook 334 and 90 members.

To Francis the presence of Merrett in all these different capacities illustrated the lunacy of Lloyd's attempts at self-regulation. Nor was he the only person who felt this way.

Lloyd's, London, 15 November 1990

James Sinclair was Managing Director of the members agency arm of the Lloyd's giant Willis Faber. One of his responsibilities was for the distressed members on Pulbrook 90 and 334. Sinclair was sufficiently concerned about the situation to write a private letter to Bob Hewes, Head of Regulatory Services at Lloyd's.

Sinclair summed up the feelings of members who were being pushed towards bankruptcy by the sudden repudiation of a reinsurance policy which had been in place for many years. 'Collectively,' he wrote, 'they think Lloyd's stinks.'

'The various Action Groups,' Sinclair told Hewes, 'are becoming more and more alarmed about what they see as the Lloyd's Society's non-compliance to contract and breakdown of Market discipline.

'Many Members ask us: "How can I be sure my other Syndicates will not suddenly have a failure of a Lloyd's contract?" or "How can I have any confidence in the system following my 334 experience?" The sad answer, our unhappy Names have concluded, is the way the society is carrying on you cannot have any confidence in Lloyd's – Policies, Regulatory Control or Agents.

'I really wonder what will become of us all a few years down the line? A senior Stewart Wrightson Name, Lord Weidenfeld, is putting together a major article in the USA *Forbes* Magazine, well researched and centring on, so I understand, the failure of Lloyd's contracts and other distasteful aspects of the community's tactics in bouncing liability around the Market. He sees it as a wonderful example of Lloyd's trashing up the value of its contracts.

'Culminating in the bad underwriting years 1988/89 plus the realisation Lloyd's contracts can and do fail, I guess Names will herd out of the Market as confidence plummets.

'Lloyd's will have a very high price to pay for the clottish Underwriting Policy of a few of our greedy Underwriters . . . And it will all happen in the next 24 months.'

This was the message of the head of the agency arm of a major player in the market to the head of the regulatory arm of that market's self-appointed governors and watchdogs.

Bob Hewes replied: 'We do not feel comfortable about what has happened and there is a great deal of genuine sympathy for members who have clearly been taken by surprise.'

But, he went on: 'Given that this is a dispute between the agent and the Names, there is no procedural way in which Lloyd's can intervene to propose a result.'

Sinclair's warning would prove prophetic in that it disproved the notion that no dispute within Lloyd's would adversely affect the policyholder outside the market; especially in the United States of America.

In a letter to Clive Francis, one Pulbrook 334 member made
this strikingly clear.

> When I agreed to participate on Syndicate 334 I did
> so having been assured categorically that the Syndicate
> had reinsured out its past asbestos/pollution liabilities with
> Syndicate 418.
> My family has been in the insurance brokers business
> since 1917. We all felt that a policy at Lloyd's was the finest
> security available. Certainly, at Lloyd's, the underwriting
> society, where the motto is 'utmost good faith', surely as
> between market people insuring or reinsuring with each other,
> in no situation would one underwriter repudiate a claim
> from another. A claim arose. The policy was repudiated.
> Now even following its repudiation, all concerned deny all
> responsibility for the loss to us Names. In these circumstances
> ... I can think only to quote Cuthbert Heath from a 1931
> issue of 'Syren & Shipping' where that gentleman, regarded
> as the 'father' of non-marine business at Lloyd's, stated:
> '. . . there is one thing which is still with us and shines as
> brightly as ever. It is the honourable feeling that, privileged
> as we are among traders in that our contracts are those of
> "uberimmae fidei", our good faith must also be the supreme
> law of our existence. I feel quite certain that underwriters
> generally are still as determined as ever to do what is fair
> rather than to insist on legal rights.'
> In view of all the circumstances where the failure of a
> Lloyd's policy has caused loss to the Names on Syndicate
> 334, coupled by Lloyd's current lack of leadership both
> administrative and underwriting, I can no longer feel that
> Lloyd's will always pay its policy obligations in the fair
> manner, as so cogently expressed by Cuthbert Heath in
> 1931.
> Therefore, since learning of the problem with the Syndicate
> 334 reinsurance I have advised all my business associates to

select underwriters other than Lloyd's, wherever possible to
do so, and I shall continue so advising others unless the 334
matter is settled in a manner which lives up to the dictum
of Cuthbert Heath.

The author of this letter was a prominent New Orleans insurance
agent. Five months earlier, he too had attended the Convention
of Independent Insurance Agents of America.

* * *

Other distressed American members were becoming active. Were
they merely bad losers or could they prove that there was some
legal remedy to their losses?

One man thought he could, and set about doing so with
all possible speed.

The Sophisticated American

Andrew Grossman was the lawyer and diplomat whose agent
had sent the mail by boat from Lime Street to Abidjan. Grossman
had paid out a fortune in cash calls on the spiral syndicates and
now he wanted an explanation.

Grossman moved around a lot in his job and was now working
in San Francisco. The postal service was better here; especially the
inland mail:

Enforcement Division
Securities and Exchange Commission
Washington DC

Dear Sir

I am enclosing a copy of a letter I have just sent to
the Council of Lloyd's, Lime Street, London EC3, England.

In view of the recent notoriety that has surrounded the bankrupting of members ('Names') of Lloyd's in recent years, and the likelihood of a new wave of such tragedies befalling Americans now that they are being actively recruited, **I would like to know if the SEC has addressed the issue of whether membership in Lloyd's is a security or an investment under the Securities and Exchange Act . . .**

Please let me know whether the SEC has ever addressed this matter. If not, or if it has done so in the past without taking action, the severe losses of hundreds of American members justify a new look at the issue. The Council of Lloyd's vociferously denies being subject to the jurisdiction of U.S. courts but I understand that this claim cannot hold insofar as Lloyd's is recruiting and doing business in the United States and among U.S. citizens and residents.

Grossman had discovered a possible means by which it might be proved that Lloyd's members agencies had breached the U.S. securities laws.

SEC Form 'D' was a device by which foreigners could solicit investment business in the U.S.A. without having to go through the usual channels. The conditions were that the investors were not solicited in a 'hot' or hard sell manner and that a certain proportion had to be 'sophisticated' investors with $1 million or more to invest. If the members agencies recruited too many below the $1 million threshold, then Lloyd's might be in breach of the U.S. securities laws.

Some forty Lloyd's members agencies had filed Forms 'D' at 1 January 1989 as advised by Leboeuf Lamb Leiby & McCrae, Lloyd's New York City lawyers.

Leboeuf Lamb's Sheila Marshall was an indefatigable guardian of Lloyd's interests in the U.S.A. She once followed Tom Benyon around the country as he made what he thought were provocative speeches to American Lloyd's members (at the end of the tour she told him that she agreed with nearly everything he said).

Grossman's contention was that SEC Form 'D' was fertile ground for a legal case against those members agencies and against Lloyd's. The letters he received seemed to bear this out:

United States Securities and Exchange Commission
Office of the General Counsel

Dear Mr Grossman

. . .Thank you for bringing this matter to our attention. The Commission and its staff appreciate the willingness of investors to alert the Commission to possible violations of the federal securities laws . . .

Followed by:

Dear Mr Grossman

Re: In the Matter of Lloyd's of London Syndications

The staff of the Securities and Exchange Committee is conducting the informal investigation captioned above. In connection therewith, the Division of Enforcement requests that you voluntarily provide us with certain documents and information . . .

These included computer disks, documents and details of every aspect of Lloyd's membership through the opening contact and election to suspension, insolvency and the Hardship Committee.

Grossman was happy to oblige. So were many others. In time the SEC would accumulate sufficient data about this mysterious institution to draw certain provisional conclusions.

'It is the Division's position,' wrote Mary T. Beach, Senior Associate Director of the SEC to Congressman Don J. Pease of the United States House of Representatives, 'that the solicitation of participations involves the sale of a security, with the issuer of that security being the particular members agent involved.

Accordingly, such U.S. sales would be subject to all of the provisions of the Securities Act and the Exchange Act, including the
anti-fraud provisions . . .'

This did not necessarily mean that the members agents in
question were in breach of any of those provisions – it depended
on whether or not they had stuck to the advice given them by
Leboeuf Lamb. But, if they had not, they would incur the wrath
of the SEC.

'There is no existing precedent as to whether Lloyd's participations are securities,' the letter went on, 'but, as was pointed
out above, the Division of Corporate Finance believes they are
securities and as such are subject to the provisions of the Federal
securities laws in the same manner and to the same extent as more
conventional securities.

'Subject to certain limitations and conditions,' it concluded,
'the provisions of the Federal securities laws generally are as
applicable to the sales of foreign securities (including participations in Lloyd's) in the United States as they are to the sales of
domestic securities.'

These and other letters followed enquiries initiated by Andrew
Grossman as a result of cash calls received while he was in Abidjan
and letters written while he was in San Francisco.

By the date of this last letter he was in Geneva. Grossman
moved around a lot in his job and sometimes it was hard for
the SEC – as well as Lloyd's and his members agency – to keep
up with him. Grossman may not have been worth $1 million but
he most certainly was a sophisticated investor.

*   *   *

The advance calls for cash to meet losses on the underwriting
year 1988 had frightened many of the Lime Street members in
Hamilton, Ontario, although Robin Kingsley had reassured them
over the telephone.

Jacki Levin and her husband had only joined two years earlier and the scale of their losses meant that their family home was at risk. In late 1990 her husband flew to London.

Kingsley entertained him to a splendid lunch near Fleur de Lys House, the Lime Street Agency headquarters in Houndsditch. 'Mr Levin,' he said, 'everything is going to be fine.'

Levin looked at him. Kingsley really seemed to believe this. Still anxious, but unable to disprove the assertions of his members agent, Levin flew back to Canada.

Kingsley, meanwhile, was still advising members against taking out stop loss policies on the grounds that the market had 'turned around.'

At about this time Enid Bemrose also paid a visit to her late husband's members agency, a few hundred yards to the north of Kingsley, in Fenchurch Street. She still did not feel like lunch, but it was time for her to make her feelings known.

The Widow's Tale #3

The Members' Hardship Committee had asked Mrs Bemrose to fill in the questionnaire and return it with a certificate of probate. There was no need, they said, for an accountant's certification. Mrs Bemrose had objected to having to pay further accountant's fees which this would have necessitated.

Mrs Bemrose had filled in the form and sent it off with the information required. The Hardship Committee had sent back another form asking for an accountant's certification.

Mrs Bemrose deliberately telephoned them before she had calmed down. She was incensed. The Hardship Committee telephoned her with the information that she should sell her house. It was not a large house and she did not see why she should do so. She was understandably upset at the prospect.

Mary Archer also wrote her a letter saying she would look into the matter. Mrs Bemrose never heard from her again.

Christopher Bemrose also wrote a number of letters. One of them was to his late father's agency: 'The onus always appears to be on my mother or my father to seek explanational clarification. Surely as my father's agent you have an obligation to provide full and frank explanations and not rely on her to question every angle . . .'

Mrs Bemrose had lasted a long time; now she began to crack up. She started to take tranquillisers. Her son and her cousin began seriously to fear for her wellbeing. They arranged to accompany her to London.

At their first meeting the representatives of the members agency were uncompromising.

One of them said: 'I do regret this happening, particularly at the end of my career.'

Mrs Bemrose regretted this too. To every question about releasing her husband's deposit to his estate they had the same reply: 'We can't discuss that.'

The two men took her home in a state of deep distress. Some months later they decided to try again. They came back to London.

Her late husband's agent had retired. The new agent said he had discussed the matter with their legal department and there was nothing they could do.

Suddenly the effect of the tranquillisers lifted. Mrs Bemrose hit the roof.

'After forty-three years of marriage,' she said, 'I have so far spent eleven months of bereavement trying to obtain any accurate and reliable information about my husband's Lloyd's-related financial affairs. On all sides I have met with the minimum of facts reluctantly given – and then contradicted.

'My health has been eroded,' she went on. 'Anxiety, uncertainty, fear and confusion have been with me every day for nearly a year.'

Mrs Bemrose ran through the long list of broken promises.

'You assured me,' she said, 'that the estate protection policy would release the deposit when my husband died. But you knew as early as 1988 that there were doubts about the future of estate protection policy. I was never told that the policy would not release the money until well after he died – and then only because I telephoned you.

'Eleven months,' she said, 'of bewilderment, uncertainty and misleading advice and information. Looking back at the last ten years, have you really acted for and in the interest of the Name?'

It seemed that this was the first time the new agent understood her case. He asked why she had not told anyone of her problems.

She explained how her many efforts had met with no success; eight letters had been ignored, long telephone calls had led nowhere.

She then left, never to return.

* * *

Murray Lawrence came home from his journeys abroad and announced his retirement as Chairman of Lloyd's.

There was speculation as to whether or not his decision was related to the Outhwaite affair. Lawrence had been closely involved in this both as an active underwriter and as a member of the asbestos committee. Lawrence and Alan Lord denied this was so, but neither would elaborate. 'You have to do what is best,' was all Lawrence would say, 'and it is time for a change.'

One of Lawrence's last acts as Chairman was to make a telephone call to Hong Kong. David Rowland was Chairman of Sedgwick, one of Lloyd's largest brokers. Lawrence wanted Rowland, a man of considerable intelligence, to head an enquiry into ways of making Lloyd's more competitive in the 1990s: a subject he had hinted at in his speech in Chicago.

Rowland accepted the invitation.

Just over a year later, the real reasons for commissioning the Rowland Task Force Report would have been lost amidst a welter of recrimination and litigation unprecedented in Lloyd's 300-year history. But at the time there was no doubt either to Lawrence or Rowland about the Task Force's first priority. This was to find a way to build a better market for Lloyd's and its policyholders; not rewrite the constitution for the external members who supplied most of the market's capital.

For were the rights of those members not already in safe hands after the 1982 Lloyd's Act and the 1987 Neill Report?

Lawrence had said in Chicago: 'Following the passing of Lloyd's private Act of Parliament in 1982 we have put in place a first class self-regulatory system. As one who has been privileged to serve on the Council of Lloyd's both as Deputy Chairman and Chairman throughout that period I am delighted to say that this difficult and time-consuming although essential operation has now been successfully completed.'

Lawrence had gone on to say: 'The significance of this, from a commercial point of view, is that the Council of Lloyd's, the Society's governing body, can now turn its attention more towards facilitating the business of the market, the aim being to foster its entrepreneurial flair.'

Lawrence's successor as Chairman of Lloyd's was David Coleridge. Coleridge would soon find out how well that self-regulatory system worked. As Chairman of Sturge Holdings plc he already knew how entrepreneurial the market could be.

NINE

FOR WHOM
THE BELL TOLLS

1991 sowed the seeds of Lloyd's biggest-ever solvency crisis, and the year began with a crisis of solvency for many members.

Lord Alexander had paid out over £100,000 over the years for losses on Oakeley Vaughan and other syndicates. He had nineteen open years. He had been suspended from underwriting. He had paid a further price for being prepared to stand up and speak out in the House of Lords. Lord Alexander had been identified in the press as a man in financial trouble and a member of the Council of Lloyd's had branded him a 'troublemaker.'

The latest indignity was that the litigation by Oakeley Vaughan members against Lloyd's had not prevented Lloyd's from pressing the Oakeley Vaughan members to meet the latest cash calls; even though the cash calls were the grounds for the litigation.

Lloyd's of London

Dear Sir

Syndicate Nos 551 and 553
You should be aware that as you have appealed to the Members' Hardship Committee regarding the necessary deposit drawdown, the Council of Lloyd's has received a formal request from your underwriting agents, Additional Underwriting Agencies (No 6) . . .

This kind of letter gave his wife another panic attack.

> In the light of the above, we hereby give notice that
> you are required to pay the sum of £47,111.33 to the
> Society within 30 days . . .

These were cash calls for losses on Oakeley Vaughan 551 and
Warrilow 553. The following day he received more.

Lloyd's of London

Dear Sir

Syndicate Nos 317 and 384
> In the light of the above, we hereby give you notice
> that you are required to pay the sum of £66,656.47 to
> the Society within 30 days . . .

These were cash calls for losses on Outhwaite 317 and Aragorn
384. Within two days Lord Alexander received cash calls of
£113,767.80 for four syndicates, three of which were already
subject to legal proceedings and the fourth of which would also
be disputed. Yet Lloyd's still seemed to think that he should pay
now and sue later.

Lord Alexander was not going to pay until the litigation
had proved who was right and who was wrong. He went to
see a non-underwriting member of the Council of Lloyd's, the
Chairman of Lloyd's Bank, Sir Jeremy Morse.

Sir Jeremy Morse was unable to offer much constructive
advice. 'I would never take on any unlimited liability,' Morse
told him.

'But, Sir Jeremy,' came the reply, 'it's the fact that people
like you are on the Council that is supposed to give people like
me confidence!'

Wilfred Sherman also bitterly regretted the day he ever came
into contact with Lloyd's and Oakeley Vaughan. He had on his

conscience the heart attacks and deaths of several members in America and Australia whom he had helped bring to Lloyd's. Those people may have been greedy and gullible but they were dead before their time.

When he was not being subpoenaed to appear at court hearings in Texas or being visited by American lawyers at home near Marbella, the cash calls forced the elderly Welshman to spend his retirement working harder than ever.

Sherman was eighty years old in January 1991. As a lifelong racing man he was gratified by the headline in the *Sporting Life* which read: 'Wilfred Sherman: 80 not out.'

He was still chuckling when the telephone rang. Charles St George was also wishing him a happy birthday.

Sherman replied politely and replaced the receiver. He sat down unable to speak. After all that Oakeley Vaughan had done to Sherman's life Charles St George could still act as if it had been no more than an unsuccessful flutter at the races.

The official view of the Chairman and Council of Lloyd's continued to be that these problems either did not exist or would somehow go away. After all the warnings, and the Chester Report, and the spiral disaster, and the Gilkes letter and the letter from James Sinclair to Bob Hewes, they still could not or would not see that the immunity of the Council to suit and the withholding of information by members agencies would only fuel the fire that was burning.

'It is not the task of the Council of Lloyd's,' wrote Murray Lawrence in *The Times*, 'to intervene in the commercial aspects of Lloyd's where these related to the transaction of insurance business in the market or in the agreements which exist between names and their Agents. Its task is to regulate the conduct of Lloyd's within the framework of the 1982 Lloyd's Act.'

Yet the Lloyd's Act of 1982 stated as follows: 'Powers of the council and of the committee. Paragraph 6 (1). The council shall have the management and superintendence of the affairs of the society and the power to regulate and direct the business of insurance at Lloyd's . . .'

Was there a fine distinction nobody knew about except the occupants of the Adam Room on the twelfth floor at 1, Lime Street? If so was it not time to share this secret knowledge with the underwriting members whose capital made the transaction of that insurance business possible?

Afterwards everybody would find somebody else to blame. At the time nobody seemed to know.

Out they went . . . the letters such as those received by Lord Alexander, to the members around the world. In Tuxedo Park, New York State, Dale Jenkins had paid out £200,000 in Feltrim and Gooda Walker losses and the pretty house in the countryside was up for sale. Jenkins and John Roby, another American member and former FBI agent, and eighty others, had come to the same conclusion as Andrew Grossman. They were not going to pay any more.

In Hamilton, Ontario, three months after Robin Kingsley had told them everything would be fine, the Levins received a cash call for £14,000 for Feltrim and Gooda Walker. Two weeks later they received another.

This time they telephoned their friends and came to the same conclusions: 'We don't believe anything they say any more . . . and we don't pay.'

The Levins and their friends Dr Pakozdi and Dr Webster, the retired dentist who had introduced them to Lime Street Agencies in the first place, formed an action group. As Tom Benyon had found in England, it was difficult to obtain information; the Lime Street Agency would not give them the addresses of other members.

The Hamilton, Burlington and Bracebridge members were law-abiding citizens who paid their bills on time. But something smelled wrong here; this did not seem like a legitimate debt. They were nervous about the step they were taking, but they found that the more members to whom they spoke, the more they believed that what they were proposing to do was right. They were going to take legal advice; and in the meantime they were not going to pay any more cash calls.

'The British are crazy,' Jacki Levin told a friend, 'they are divided when they should be saying all together, "We're not going to pay up!" We took it in blind faith,' she said, 'we were joining an organisation with a sterling reputation three hundred years old. We weren't joining a members agency; on my membership card it says Lloyd's of London and not Lime Street Agencies.'

Dr Pakozdi put it even more bluntly:

'We are not cry babies. We pay up for legitimate losses as honourable business people. But we will not be fleeced for the benefit of people on the inside.'

'You have a very high standard of fraud in your country,' Dr Pakozdi told this author. 'Basically you have to steal the crown jewels and get caught before you call it by that name. But if the people at Lloyd's behaved like this in the USA they would be in the penitentiary with Boesky and Milliken.

'When it suits them, they are Lloyd's; like when they want your money. When it doesn't suit them – like when you have the effrontery to want to know something – they pass the buck – to the agents, the underwriters, anyone.'

Out they went . . . the letters to members in Britain and North America and Canada and Australia and New Zealand. But this time the matter-of-fact and impersonal approach in many cases only succeeded in provoking a highly personal reaction. How could they ask us for these huge sums? Where did they – and not we – go wrong?

Rightly or wrongly, the climate of doubt was fuelled by a sudden increase in legal activity that spring and early summer. The Oakeley Vaughan case came to court and the first ever litigation against the Corporation of Lloyd's looked set to be a long haul, with Lloyd's fighting the distressed members every inch of the way. But the revelations of false accounting and backhanders and concealed reports made lurid headlines in the press and were read with interest by other distressed members.

The Outhwaite case had not yet reached court but the news spread fast that the Department of Trade and Industry and the Serious Fraud Office were looking into the affair of the asbestosis contracts. (They concluded that there were no grounds for action, which only heated the climate further and fuelled rumours of a high-level cover-up.) The Warrilow and Pulbrook members were also taking advice about litigation. The number of members action groups no longer willing to contain their grievances within the quasi-autonomous Association of Lloyd's Members was rising fast.

Dominique Osborne and her husband were the Lime Street Agency members who had paid out considerable losses in spite of reducing the number of syndicates they had in common. Their losses this year made last year look like an expensive restaurant tip: £384,000 for him and £434,000 for her and rising. They had open year cash calls on Feltrim and Gooda Walker. After stop loss and reserves, Dominique Osborne's bill was still £220,831.41.

She received a statement with the figure in brackets to show that it was a minus. In the small print it pointed out that stop loss did not pay cash calls in advance and if she wanted to save interest she would be well-advised to send them a cheque.

John Osborne was determined to resign and put the whole business behind him but his wife was not so sure. She decided to wait until Lloyd's came round with bolt-cutters and padlocks; meanwhile they were not going to pay.

Dominique Osborne noticed that the worst-hit spiral syndicates such as Feltrim and Gooda Walker seemed to have a larger number of names from Lime Street than from any other members agency. Was this a coincidence or did it denote either by negligence or worse a policy that enriched the agent at the members' expense?

It was as hard to obtain information about Lime Street Agencies as it was for any member to obtain information about their agents. Mrs Osborne persisted in her quest. She obtained a list of names and addresses through the Association of Lloyd's Members. She learned of the existence of the Lime Street members in America and Canada. She spoke to the Levins and Dr Pakozdi. She learned that over thirty of the Canadian members expected to be made bankrupt.

She learned of hard-pressed pensioners in the Bahamas and Malta. She learned of a woman in the Midlands whose husband was incapacitated in a car crash and who did not even know where to look for the papers that revealed he was a Lime Street Agency member of Lloyd's. She learned of the existence of others like her who had thought their losses were unique and that they had no one but themselves to blame.

She went to see her solicitors.

'Our advice' they said, 'is not to waste your time looking into this matter. Lloyd's is in a mess. Just pay up and put it down to bitter experience.'

Mrs Osborne however became convinced that something was lacking in the way she and others had been treated by their members agency. She obtained copies of Lime Street Underwriting Agencies accounts from Companies House. She obtained estate agent's details offering for sale Robin Kingsley's house on Ham Common.

She learned that the Lime Street Agencies offices at Fleur de Lys House were rented for £40,000 a year from a trust in the name of Kingsley's daughters. She learned of the existence of his ski chalet in the French Alps. She did not know that Kingsley himself was a Name on over one hundred syndicates.

She heard that Lime Street Agencies had been thinking of selling itself and its membership for several years (according to Kingsley because the senior directors were nearing retirement). They had in fact succeeded in selling its 'goodwill' as it was known – the fees from members and potential profits over the next few years. She telephoned the purchaser, Bankside Agencies.

'May I speak to Robin Kingsley please?'

'Mr Kingsley is not available.'

'When will he be available?'

They did not know. They said they were 'surprised' that there was animosity against him. They hinted that he would be coming into the office infrequently in future as a consultant, and that the remit of his consultancy was unclear.

Mrs Osborne told them she had been informed by Lloyd's that Kingsley was responsible for Lime Street Agencies members until 31 December 1991. She put down the receiver.

Twenty minutes later her telephone rang.

'Can I help you?' said Kingsley.

'Yes,' said Mrs Osborne, 'a lot of people would like to talk to you. They would like you to explain why things have gone wrong.'

'Oh,' he said.

'May I give them your home telephone number?' she asked.

Kingsley was reluctant that she should do so. He maintained that all the Lime Street members had been made aware by personal letter or newsletter of the series of catastrophe claims such as Hurricane Hugo and Piper Alpha that had hit the market.

He felt 'the correct procedure' was for members who wanted to talk to somebody to do so either with their existing agent who was in possession of the relevant statistics and computer data, or with their new agent at Bankside. Kingsley did not think it was 'helpful' for members to telephone and speak to him at home, where he did not have the statistics and computer data in question.

Mrs Osborne listened politely and the conversation came to an end. She resolved to pursue her enquiries into Lime Street Agencies even more vigorously in future.

The Lime Street Agencies directors had negotiated the sale of the goodwill to Bankside for a relatively modest sum. This was because the number of Lime Street Names had fallen from 516 in 1988 to 358 by January 1991. A year later only 105 would still be underwriting through Bankside; 44 had gone to other agents and the rest would have been wiped out.

A members agency whose members had been wiped out to such an extent was not worth very much and the highest price they could secure from Bankside was £197,000 plus a retention for litigation. In May 1991, a Lime Street non-executive director was asked by the other directors to apportion some of the profit commission between them. The basis for this was the fact that this was the agency's last trading year and it was a reflection of the work each director had contributed to the company.

Robin Kingsley was given £100,000; his financial director said he had drawn no salary from Lime Street for the eight years from 1976 to 1984. Richard Gethin-Jones was offered £100,000, Patrick Corbett £150,000 and Robert Hallam £50,000.

The total of £400,000 was less than the average loss of their members which then stood at £535,000. But Lime Street Agencies had not yet received any writs from those members although those writs would very shortly be forthcoming and the agency would be forced into liquidation. The four men meanwhile were acting within their rights as directors of the company.

Then they went their separate ways and would not meet there again.

The defiant reactions of members around the world and the growing crisis of confidence in Lloyd's at home were not the anticipated effects of the 1982 Lloyd's Act and the 1987 Neill Report. Nor was it helpful that Chatset and *Lloyd's League Tables* had just declared that according to their independent calculations the 1988 losses, due in June 1991, would exceed £150 million. At 1, Lime Street the Chairman and Council decided something had to be done.

Alan Lord, the Chief Executive, announced the latest device to allay members' anxieties. Lloyd's would institute a loss review of any of its 354 syndicates which announced a loss of more than 150% of its underwriting capacity.

The reviews would not be published but they would be available to members through their agencies. Nor would they apportion blame. Lord also announced new measures to encourage conciliation rather than litigation and promised disclosure of underwriters' salaries.

More than one member discerned a thinly-disguised attempt to persuade members not to pursue their complaints through the courts. What earthly good would a loss review do for the likes of Oakeley Vaughan? Another member likened this to a murderer being allowed to take a sociology degree and then sending his answers to his victim's family. This did not mean he was not a killer, and if he was ever released he might kill again, but at least he would know why he had done what he did.

The new Chairman, David Coleridge, also prepared his counter-attack.

'There is no crisis,' he declared; and went on to say that the American asbestosis claims were 'an absolute rip-off.'

'I had a letter from a member of the aristocracy the other day,' Coleridge went on, 'who said, "I suggest you tell the Americans that enough's enough, we're really going to draw a line and start again. It really isn't fair, old boy."'

Well, this was a start. But what about the fact that the members of the aristocracy, and other Names, had been making money for years out of the premiums on long tail business before they turned into claims? Or the fact that Lloyd's depended on America for over half its business, as his predecessor Murray Lawrence had pointed out only nine months earlier?

The celebrated *Times* columnist Bernard Levin criticised Lloyd's and revealed that he had been told by an 'inside source': 'Everyone in Lloyd's is in despair . . . the place is fundamentally bust, and unless it changes it won't exist in five years.'

Coleridge again leaped to the counter-attack. Levin was trading in 'second-hand, regurgitated inaccuracies.' He rejected Levin's claim that the 1988 losses would be £150 million; but gave the misleading impression that the true figure would be lower.

'Fortunately,' he wrote, 'the membership of Lloyd's is more intelligent than your commentator.'

For all Levin's faults, most members of Lloyd's, many of whom were *Times* readers, would have happily disputed this assertion.

'Many of them have been with us long enough to remember that in 1969, too, there were premature reports of our death and that they were followed by years of unprecedented growth and profitability . . .'

But not growth in reserves, or in the asset requirements of those members who made that profitability possible, and who had been recklessly persuaded to increase their underwriting.

'Finally,' Coleridge declared, 'Lloyd's is not "bust" fundamentally or otherwise. Even after losses, our declared assets at the end of 1990 amount to some £16 billion.'

He neglected to add that, unlike the other big European reinsurers, fifty per cent of these assets consisted of bank guarantees obtained on such volatile security as shares and property.

In *The Times* of 8 June 1991 Coleridge did little to promote the image of himself as the man who might just have dragged Lloyd's kicking and screaming into the 21st century.

His remarks were published at exactly the same time that many recently-elected members from the professional middle classes were receiving unprecedented cash calls.

Coleridge said: 'We had 30,000 members in 1988. Many of them will have lost money and they make a lot of fuss. The insurance industry worldwide is having a very tough time.'

This was true but not immediately apparent to the shareholders of big European insurance companies such as Allianz, Swiss Re or Munich Re.

Coleridge went on: 'Most of the people who are bitching and whingeing are doing it because they don't like losing. I understand that. It's human nature to only want to win. No one has been swindled and it has nothing to do with unlimited liability. It's simply pure losses.' (Coleridge later said: 'I never actually made the statement that people were "bitching and whingeing". I was asked: "Do you consider that some of the Names are whingeing?" and I said: "I think some of them probably are."')

'People have lost a percentage of their premium, and if they cannot bear a loss of 10 per cent, they shouldn't be underwriting. We have some people who have been receiving profits for 20 years. We haven't made a loss since 1967 and we've paid the members £3.6 billion over that period.'

His remarks as quoted at the time infuriated many readers both inside and outside the market. They read on with teeth sharpened and ready to bite.

How did he meet his wife? asked the interviewer.

'I probably met her at a party,' came the reply, 'that's normally how you meet girls, isn't it? As long as you had a dinner jacket and a white tie and tails you had a good time in those days. There were a lot of parties and a lot of girls around. I don't think people worked as hard then . . .'

'Nearly every member of Lloyd's who has financial problems,' Coleridge expanded, 'usually has some other problem as well. Either their business is going through a bad patch or they're getting divorced. A divorce crucifies a man with any money.'

Some members found their marriages strengthened by the adversity they were facing. Others knew they should not have joined Lloyd's but could not escape the burden of open years. To all these members, and to members whose marriages were under strain and who were taking their children out of schools, and were faced with the choice between bankruptcy and the Hardship Committee, to be lectured on business and marriage by an Old Etonian who had been born rich, married rich and become even richer was deeply offensive.

'Becoming Chairman of Sturge was easy,' Coleridge expounded, 'and becoming Chairman of Lloyd's wasn't difficult. I'm better educated than most people on the Council of Lloyd's. If you've had a privileged life, it's not very difficult.'

He said he had almost always managed to do what he wanted. He seemed unable to comprehend how others might have been unable to live their lives that way.

Coleridge wrote a letter to all members in advance of the forthcoming annual general meeting.

'The Council is keenly aware,' he said, 'of the financial hardships which many of you are facing. I wish to reassure you that I am vigorously pursuing all avenues to ensure that individually you are able to trade out successfully from the current losses.'

He said he had been in touch with the Chancellor of the Exchequer and was optimistic that he would extend the tax breaks to help them recoup their losses.

'I would not wish to belittle these difficulties,' Coleridge wrote, 'for I am only too well aware of their gravity. I have to say, however, that the recent spate of extremely negative and less than accurate stories that have appeared in the media provide an excessively alarmist rather than a realistic picture.'

Lord Alexander had already been suspended from underwriting and for him the idea of 'trading out' was an absurdity. He was in the middle of the Oakeley Vaughan hearings.

'Why can't anyone at Lloyd's stand up and admit their mistakes?' he said. 'Someone needs to take responsibility for this murky business. Suggesting that we trade out of our losses bears no relation to the real problems that Lloyd's is facing.'

The sixty or so Conservative MPs and four members of the Cabinet who were members of Lloyd's were not impressed. At a meeting which went on so long that the chairman had to be replaced because he had another engagement, Coleridge received what one MP described as 'a right roasting.'

'They were terribly rude,' said another, 'he was clearly shaken.'

The Conservative MPs were concerned at the high level of Lloyd's overheads, the competence with which syndicates were managed and the complacency of the Council. Such was their wrath that even the Labour Party Treasury spokesman Paul Boateng was moved to speak in defence of Lloyd's as a 'major international institution.'

But the complaints would only backfire when it came to the question of tax breaks to enable members to meet their losses; Britain was in a deepening recession and with three Lloyd's members on the Government Finance Bill Committee tabling the amendment, and the Treasury Whip Nicholas Baker and Economic Secretary to the Treasury John Maples also in Lloyd's, the suggestion of a Government bail-out for Lloyd's members smacked just a little too much of special pleading.

Coleridge had to announce this at the annual general meeting on 26 June 1991: 'In May I wrote to members to inform you that we were asking the Government to include members of Lloyd's in the three-year carry back of loss provisions which had been proposed for companies in this year's Finance Bill. We believe that this was a reasonable request since our competitors will benefit from the carry back. Unfortunately the Government felt unable to extend this provision to Names.'

The annual general meeting was always going to be a lively affair. The structural absurdities of the market and the contro-versies of the last few years were picked on by members who in better times would have left them well alone.

Tom Benyon had founded the Society of Names as well as the Warrilow action group and wondered whether David Coleridge, as Chairman of Lloyd's and Chairman of R. W. Sturge, the largest underwriting agency, could answer a ques-tion; and, if so, in which capacity: 'The Chairman of Sturge Holdings, whoever he might be . . . I do not want to personalise this . . . recently forecast that Sturge will maintain its dividend at last year's level for this year and also for the next two years. Can you possibly establish what proportion of this dividend will be attributable to commissions deducted by Sturge from the notional profits of Names who in fact will be writing out cheques to cover their losses for 1988 or their cash calls for 1989 and 1990?'

There was applause and laughter at this; but Coleridge would not budge from the assertion that his company was not going to reduce its dividend to shareholders even if the members of its syndicates were making losses.

'I have two questions,' asked an Oakeley Vaughan member, 'first, does the Committee or Council owe any duty of care to its members? Answer yes or no.

'Second question. Has any member of the Committee or Council been involved in defrauding members of Lloyd's in the last ten years other than Sir Peter Green who was awarded the Lloyd's gold medal? Answer yes or no.'

'Those are the two questions?' replied Coleridge.

'Yes.'

'The answer to the first,' said Coleridge, 'is of course, yes. The Council of Lloyd's does have duty of care . . .'

Twenty minutes later Coleridge interrupted his own answer to another question: 'Could I just make one statement . . . The statement made was that Sir Peter Green defrauded his Names. Sir Peter Green never defrauded any Names at all ever. I would like to make that absolutely clear . . .' (However, Sir Peter was officially censured by Lloyd's in 1987.)

Coleridge revealed the tougher side that had taken him to the chairmanship of Sturge Holdings as well as the chairmanship of Lloyd's.

To a member who had the temerity to suggest that the Council was run by insiders, he replied: 'I think your remarks are probably on a personal basis. I do not think there is much point in answering them . . .

'You do not work in Lloyd's,' he went on, 'at least I do not think you do, but I have worked in Lloyd's for 36 years. I have worked for most of that time in an underwriting agency where we depend entirely on the members for our capital. I must have said so many times, perhaps you have not listened or you have not understood my English, that without members of Lloyd's there is no Lloyd's . . .'

This tougher and more aggressive stance appealed to many of the working members present. The meeting was brought to a close by the veteran underwriter Robert Hiscox. Hiscox revealed his own uncompromising stance.

'Nobody is more surprised than I am that after twenty years of Committee-bashing I have volunteered to propose this vote of thanks to the Chairman and his Council. It is not that I have lost my critical faculties. The fact is that I believe that at the moment we have in the Chairman, David Coleridge, the best, if not the only, man to lead us in what are no less than conditions of war . . .'

These were the authentic voices of the market: xenophobic, intensely territorial, dismissive of questions that they felt could do nothing but harm to that market and the players such as themselves who had worked in it for generations.

Hiscox's fears were such that he even brought in the television personality and novelist Melvyn Bragg, a member of Lloyd's, over the heads of Lloyd's public relations department, to advise Coleridge on how to handle the media.

It was war; and the big guns were beginning to sound.

Out went the letters bearing the cash calls to members around the world, without whom, as Coleridge himself had said, there was no Lloyd's.

In Malta, the envelope came through the letterbox of the basement flat for the 73-year-old company pensioner John Pearson. Pearson had already lost ten times what he had ever made and this cash call was for another £70,000 for losses on Feltrim, Warrilow and Gooda Walker, the syndicates on which he had been placed by Lime Street Agencies.

'It is too late for me,' Pearson told this author, 'but I hope your book will help future Names to tread very carefully before joining Lloyd's.

'Being an External Name is a depressing situation,' Pearson went on, 'one is out of touch, not knowing what the next cash call will amount to. One dreads the arrival of the mail. And, when your Manager has sold his Company and departed the scene, as in my case, one has to steel one's nerves yet one more time to face the future.'

Pearson had filled out the Hardship Committee questionnaire and now thought himself lucky the flat where he and his wife lived was rented; at least Lloyd's could not take that away.

On the Bay of Tralee Desmond O'Neill was still paying off the loan he had taken out to pay his losses on 1987. His cash call for 1988 was £78,000 on Warrilow and Gooda Walker and he had neither the cash nor the means of borrowing further.

O'Neill too had filled out the questionnaire sent by the Hardship Committee. He had tried to obtain information about other Lime Street members and had no help from the agency in this. The value of the assets on which he had obtained his bank guarantee had fallen and he had resigned having gone below Lloyd's solvency requirements. His only hope was to try to find work and pray for success in the courts.

'I feel so ashamed,' he told this author, 'I took so much on trust.'

In Hampshire Michael Colvin MP was staying in Lloyd's in spite of his losses. His wife Nichola had resigned after her losses passed six figures.

'But, compared to a lot of our friends,' he told this author, 'it's not that bad. There's a lot of pain in Hampshire.'

Giles Curtis lived in Hampshire. In January he had been warned that his losses might reach £20,000. They had reached £55,000 and wiped out the proceeds of his previous years' underwriting. Curtis had to make what was probably the most dangerous decision of his life; should he get out or should he stay in?

In Hertfordshire the former oboist John Clementson was setting a record for membership of spiral syndicates hit by the tidal wave of Piper Alpha and other catastrophes.

One morning Clementson received a telephone bill for £336,

the largest he had ever incurred. This was not least because of the amount of calls he had been making to friends asking them why he should not commit suicide. That same afternoon he received a cash call for £336,000.

Clementson's agent Hubert Morris of Archdale was dead. Sometimes Clementson wished he was too. After stop loss and reserves his outstanding debts to Lloyd's were still £244,354.93.

With cash calls expected in 1991 of £190,000, next year Clementson would be wiped out. His girlfriend was supportive in this adversity but there were nights when even the bottle could not help him sleep.

'Our personal lives have been ruined,' he told this author. 'We had planned to sell our respective houses and marry. Now we cannot do that. It is a monstrous position. Any normal human plans we might have for the future are absolutely and completely shattered. We cannot live a normal life together or apart.'

In London Martin de Laszlo received cash calls of £190,000 for losses on the spiral syndicates on which he had been placed by his brother-in-law, Robin Kingsley. Relations between the two men were 'frosty.' De Laszlo intended to stay underwriting but he was already selling off possessions to do so and meet his losses, interest on which accrued before the stop loss policies came into effect.

De Laszlo posed well-meaningly for a London evening newspaper in front of his Bentley and his AC Greyhound, hoping to show that although comfortably off he was far from being a millionaire. The photograph had the opposite effect to the people on the 6.22 from Waterloo; it made him look even more like a millionaire.

In Lincolnshire the wealthy farmer Hugh Bourn and his family had seen the promise of 'cheques next year' become a cash call of first £40,000, then £70,000 and then £110,000. This had risen to £150,000 by May; then £200,000; then £300,000; by July it had reached £462,000. His members agency had been sold and an inducement made to Bourn to stay in order to facilitate the deal. Bourn declined and found another agency with whom he too hoped to remain underwriting.

Overlooking the Bristol Channel Richard Micklethwait had enormous cash calls and put up for sale the land his family had farmed for over a century. Nobody wanted to buy it. If the bank called in the guarantee secured against it, they might just let him stay on as a tenant.

Then there was Christopher Thomas-Everard.

Dulverton, Somerset, 1991

Christopher Thomas-Everard had suppressed his doubts about Excess of Loss syndicates since the reassuring letters from his members agency about Feltrim 540/2 in 1987 and 1989.

He had made a handsome profit of £37,000 on the 1986 underwriting year and although this was not solely on the basis of Excess of Loss syndicates the effect was like that of a good claret; it induced a pleasant dulling of even the most highly-developed senses. Thomas-Everard had also taken his agency's advice no longer to take out stop loss insurance; he would be better off investing the money with them.

The pleasant effect of the 1986 profit had not fully worn off when he had a £5,800 cash call on 1987.

This was followed by a cash call of £12,500 for 1988. But the figure did not stay still for long. Soon it was £68,000; then £138,000; then £160,000.

That was one morning. On the evening of the same day he received a fax in his office in the hilltop farmhouse surrounded by moor and meadow. The cash call had risen again, this time to £190,000. Shortly afterwards it rose again to £220,000.

The biggest single component of this – £78,000 – was his £25,000 line on Feltrim 540/2.

Christopher Thomas-Everard looked out of the window of his office in the farmhouse on the hill, at the land owned and farmed by his family since the time of the Domesday Book.

Now, it seemed, to this part of Somerset, Domesday had come again.

*   *   *

The total losses for 1988 had risen from being 'not unreasonable' nine months earlier, to £150 million and then to £510 million. The deadline for payment was 15 July. After this date funds at Lloyd's could be drawn on by members agents and legal action could be taken to recover the money.

However, in spite of the publicity given to the losers, some members would still receive cheques, albeit small ones, for the 1988 underwriting year. The reaction of the Committee and Council of Lloyd's was to remind the media of this fact; but the consequence was that many distressed names began asking how, in what was universally acknowledged to be a bad year, some syndicates did so much better and some did so much worse than others.

Prominent among the sceptics was Christopher Thomas-Everard, who had long harboured suspicions that an unofficial but potent hierarchy existed within Lloyd's of 'insider' and 'outsider' syndicates. He suspected this had existed since the abolition of baby syndicates in 1987. The babies had become adolescents, that was all.

Thomas-Everard was particularly struck by the fact that there seemed to be hardly any working members on syndicates such as Feltrim and Gooda Walker. These syndicates had reinsured the safer ones lower down the spiral; where he was interested to note higher proportions of working members were to be found. Too late, he had begun to suspect that this was why he had been so easily placed on the former and not on the latter; and he remembered the reassuring letters about Feltrim.

Like Dominique Osborne, Christopher Thomas-Everard decided to conduct some research in order to establish whether or not there was any basis to his suspicions; and he would produce some spectacular and controversial results.

Meanwhile in spite of the threat of legal action to recover the money, the reality was that Lloyd's did everything possible to enable members to go on underwriting. The alternative would have been to drive them out of the market and create a dangerous fall in capacity which ran counter to the expansionist strategy for Lloyd's in the 1990s.

Dire threats were issued and many distressed members paid up or went to the Hardship Committee; but an eerie silence greeted the many more who refused to pay. Only the Oakeley Vaughan members, whose unprecedented legal action was against the Corporation of Lloyd's, felt the full might of Lloyd's counter-offensive.

The Oakeley Vaughan members had pressed David Coleridge to explain his remarks at the annual general meeting that Lloyd's owed 'a duty of care' to its members. This remark appeared to run contrary to Lloyd's defence that it did not owe the Oakeley Vaughan members any such duty.

The result was worthy of Dickens' Jarndyce and Jarndyce. The duty of care question became a sub-issue and the High Court agreed to Lloyd's request that it be settled separately before the full trial.

For Lord Alexander and the band of poorly-funded Oakeley Vaughan litigants, there would be nothing but pressure and counter-pressure all the way to the bitter end. Nor did the Oakeley Vaughan members know when that end might come.

In spite of his tough and aggressive stance at the annual general meeting David Coleridge was nothing if not a courteous man, and never more so than in his communications with distressed members.

Champneys Without a Pen

Betty Atkins owed Lloyd's £137,000 for losses incurred by the syndicates on which she had been placed by her former employer. Nobody had come forward to make good the assurances given before their election as working members of Lloyd's to her and Sylvia Hatton. Mrs Hatton had gone through the Hardship process and Mrs Atkins was on her own.

She was further distressed when the Hardship Committee had expressed interest in her ailing mother's 'estate': a couple of thousand pounds in insurance policies and £445 in premium bonds. She pleaded with them to allow her to remain in the house they had occupied for many years. Mrs Atkins' mother had died mercifully unaware of the problems suffered by her daughter as a result of her membership of Lloyd's.

Betty Atkins had been in a fragile state ever since her mother's death. In desperation she had written to David Coleridge about her plight:

> 'While I know Lloyd's say they do not want to leave
> anyone without a roof over their head,' she wrote, 'in
> my case, this is the only way of doing anything at all
> about this debt. I did only ask that my mother should be
> left in what was also her home during her lifetime, which
> is now a thing of the past. I cannot bear that anyone else
> in my family should be made to be involved and must keep
> my word. This is the only way for me to pay as much as I
> can.'

Coleridge wrote back on 16 August 1991:

> Dear Mrs Atkins,
>   It is the duty of Lloyd's to ensure that all valid claims
> are met and the policyholder is paid in full. It therefore
> follows that the recovery of any monies owed to fulfil these
> obligations must be treated seriously . . .

Coleridge reminded her, as she knew all too well, that she was

in regular correspondence with the Members' Hardship Committee. He urged her to co-operate with them if she wanted to find a
solution to her problems. He repeated that he could not intervene
personally.

However, he added:

I can assure you that I am deeply sympathetic to your
situation and I believe that the Members' Hardship Comittee
may well be able to help you.

'P.S.' Coleridge added in his own hand, 'I apologise for
the biro but I am at Champneys [the famous health farm]
without a pen.'

* * *

In Ontario the Lime Street Agency members were making progress
in their inquiries in spite of the difficulty in obtaining information
and their distance from London.

Jacki Levin was treasurer of the association and they had
engaged the law firm of McCarthy Tetrault. Their aim was to
secure an interlocutory injunction, and then a permanent injunction, against their banks from paying out on their letters of credit,
and against Lloyd's from calling down on those guarantees. The
ultimate aim was not to secure damages but to force Lloyd's to
declare the members' contracts with them void, the grounds being
that the members agents had been selling securities in breach of
the Ontario securities laws.

The seventy members on the McCarthy Tetrault writ had
letters of credit with their various banks ranging from £5,000 to
over £250,000. If the action was successful it would shave over
£10 million off Lloyd's asset base as well as setting a powerful
precedent.

In August 1991 Mrs Levin and the lawyers Glenn Smith and
Alan Lenczner travelled to London. Their aim was to gather

further information and they talked to a number of informed parties including John Peel, who had advised them in Toronto, Oliver Carruthers, the editor of the *Digest of Lloyd's News*, Colin Hook, the Chairman of the Feltrim Members Association, and Roger Bradley, a retired working underwriter of thirty years' standing and an external member on Feltrim.

Bradley was a particularly expert witness. He did not speak publicly to the press but his contacts were legendary and he was a unique and priceless source to anyone trying to penetrate the mysteries of Lloyd's. The three Canadians visited him at his home in Surrey. They came away so impressed that a few days later they telephoned him from Ontario and invited him to Canada.

Bradley was due to arrive in Canada on 29 August 1991. On 28 August he telephoned Jacki Levin and McCarthy Tetrault. He told them he was unable to travel after all.

Later, it would be thought by the Canadians that Bradley was 'scared' in that as a Feltrim member with large losses he would lose his deposit and be faced with a serious cash crisis if he agreed to travel to Canada. In a subsequent affidavit to the Ontario Court of Justice the Corporation of Lloyd's claimed that Bradley had already released his deposit and had not been pressured in any way by Lloyd's.

The truth was at variance with both versions. Bradley had been pressured, but indirectly and through the unexpected channel of the Feltrim Members Association. Lloyd's were well aware that he 'knew too much' but there was no financial pressure they could have brought to bear. Bradley was a cash depositor at Lloyd's whose house and assets were in his wife's name and in any case he had voluntarily suspended himself from underwriting. Lloyd's could not put that kind of pressure on him.

The pressure had been applied in a different way. Colin Hook was Chairman of the Feltrim Association and he enjoyed a close relationship with David Coleridge. Hook told Bradley, 'If you go to Canada, we'll lose Sir Patrick Neill' — a reference to the fact that Neill was conducting the long-awaited Feltrim inquiry. As a Feltrim member with an interest in the Neill findings, Bradley felt he had no choice but to agree.

Jacki Levin and her friends in Ontario were initially disappointed by Bradley's last-minute decision not to board the aeroplane to Canada. Later Bradley learned that Colin Hook had been warned by David Coleridge to 'keep control of his members' – a warning Hook was also given about Christopher Thomas-Everard.

This struck some Feltrim members as odd when they were supposed to be part of an action group protesting at a major syndicate disaster and possible failures of self-regulation. Hook was not supposed to be beholden to Coleridge and Coleridge was Chairman of Lloyd's and not Chairman of the Feltrim Association. What was going on?

But Bradley was quietly confident and continued to advise the Canadians with a stream of faxes and telephone calls. Although he shared the reservations of his own Association he reassured the Canadians. With or without his presence, he told them, they would win.

In New York City the attorney Dale Schreiber and his law firm Proskauer Rose Goetz and Mendelsohn got ready to issue a writ against Lloyd's of London.

In San Francisco, the Northern California branch of the Association of Lloyd's Members prepared to hold a meeting to decide who was right: Leboeuf Lamb Leiby McCrae or Proskauer Rose Goetz and Mendelsohn; and whether or not Dale Jenkins, John Roby, Andrew Grossman and the sixty others on the Proskauer writ were misguided or just plain crazy.

Ralph Bunje was the ALM regional co-ordinator in Northern California. Bunje was a Gooda Walker member but admitted his losses were only a third or even a quarter of many of those on the Proskauer ticket. He was not unsympathetic to the Proskauer case but in his memo approved by Leboeuf Lamb and circulated in advance to his members, he hinted heavily that the case would fail.

Most of the people I have spoken with have firmly indicated to me that they do not intend to join Mr Jenkins' legal action . . .

I tend to be a bit defensive about the idea of our paying out, or risking even more money, on top of our already existing losses at Lloyd's . . .

. . . it would be highly unlikely that a U.S. Court would find that Lloyd's membership amounted to an 'investment' and thus a 'security' . . .

While I believe there may be numerous cases of incompetence, negligence and perhaps downright fraud in certain individual cases, and that the Society of Lloyd's is in serious need of reform, I am not convinced as of this date that the proposed Jenkins litigation will be productive. In fact, I can conceive of it being more counterproductive . . .

What if I have a smaller loss, a profit, or intend to continue underwriting in the future? How will this action protect me? If it succeeds in hamstringing Lloyd's Names or activities in the United States, what potential negative effects would that have on me as a continuing Name?

Andrew Grossman had unearthed the SEC Form 'D' question that underpinned part of the Proskauer case. Grossman fired back from Geneva:

It appears unlikely English law will offer any remedy for this gross rape of the middle class investors so recently induced into Lloyd's membership. This is no time for self condemnation, for saying that you 'knew you could lose everything'; you 'took the chance'; that is Lloyd's-speak. Lloyd's knew you could lose everything too, and they took advantage. But U.S. investor protection laws exist to protect you. It is your right as an American to invoke them just as much against Lloyd's as against any more conventional promoter who seeks to skirt the law. I cannot help but infer that Bunje's memo is aimed at supporting Lloyd's efforts at delaying action by U.S. investors until after the statute of limitations has expired. It is, of course, only then that investors will learn how truly horrendous their 1989 losses will be. Only (if preliminary results are to be believed) to be followed by further big losses in 1990 and 1991.

'Finally,' Grossman wrote in some desperation, 'remember this: it was only because of a 20-year cyclical run of good luck that even the most incompetent, the most reckless of agents made profits. And during those years when Lloyd's was supposed to be "regulating" itself the incompetent, reckless and unscrupulous insiders ratcheted up their salaries and fees and took on for their clients greater and greater risks at lower and lower premiums. So that when the cycle inevitably turned and the day of reckoning came the house of cards fell, the clients were ruined . . .

'Foreigners,' Grossman concluded, 'should not expect to be treated equally in their courts. In 1933 Congress wrote laws to deal with such abuses and Lloyd's knew about those laws when it came to America. You should not hesitate to claim your legal rights, whatever Lloyd's and its acolytes may say.'

The San Francisco meeting found in favour of Bunje rather than Grossman.

One Southern California member was threatened with repercussions against his own insurance business if he joined the Proskauer suit. The member retorted that he could live with this but many of the North California members who did not even work in the insurance business were not so sure. The Proskauer suit would go ahead without them.

Ironically, a few months later Bunje himself would write to Grossman and tell him he was doing a wonderful job.

The 31 August deadline for members to meet solvency for the

coming year had passed with many members, having not paid their cash calls, still technically insolvent.

Many British members were taking drastic measures in the hope of staying in Lloyd's and trading their way out of their losses. Houses and woodlands were up for sale and children withdrawn from private schools. Some parents frantically channelled money into school fee funds in the hope that it could not be touched by Lloyd's.

Many children who remained at their expensive schools became targets for the derision of their peers, derived no doubt from their peers' parents. The whisper went out: 'He's the one whose Daddy can't pay his bills at Lloyd's . . .'

Paintings and other works of art that had been in the same hands for many years began appearing in auction houses. One of the more bizarre manifestations was a rise in marital breakdowns but a fall in divorce settlements; with an unknowable number of open years, you could not seal a deal.

Into all these members' lives like a bombshell came the latest news: the 1989 year losses would be as high as £1.5 billion.

Chatset, the independent consultants founded by Charles Sturge and John Rew, forecast a 'pure' loss of £1 billion on the 1989 underwriting year, to which had to be added losses from earlier open years. This was three times worse than the cash calls in 1991 and the losses were not expected to stop there. There would be more cash calls in 1993.

About £340 million of the 1989 losses had been paid out in the form of cash calls. There had also been advance cash calls of £114 million for the losses on the 1990 underwriting year. Chatset calculated that these figures, if added to the 1988 losses and to the £80 million paid by American Names in Federal Income Tax, meant a total cash outflow from Lloyd's in 1991 of over £1 billion; this was nearly one third of the total profits paid out to members over the previous twenty-four years.

Chatset had carried out a survey of members. They found that 38.5% of them had paid out over £50,000 in 1991 (the

Lloyd's estimate had been 2.1%). Lloyd's had estimated that 70% of members would be net losers; the true figure was 85%.

It was also thought that, in spite of the confusion over who was solvent and who was not, over 5,000 members would resign. There would also be fifty fewer syndicates, bringing the total down to below 300 from 437 in 1980.

Lloyd's declared that Chatset were 'in it to sell as many copies of their book as they can, so the more sensational the stories, the better.' But Lloyd's did not dispute the Chatset figures.

David Coleridge, whose own income from salary and dividends was £1.2 million a year, made a general criticism of highly-paid members agents and underwriters. The latter included 'Time Bomb' Terry Green of Gresham 321 who was paid £353,220 in 1990 and was reputedly calling in £26 million from his members for 1989 and 1990, and Derek Walker, the underwriter for Gooda Walker 290. Walker was revealed to have received £300,000 in pay and commission the previous year, while the syndicate had made losses in 1988 and 1989 of nearly £300 million. Gooda Walker was by this time in liquidation.

The Rowland Task Force, commissioned by Murray Lawrence and inherited by David Coleridge, proceeded calmly with its investigations into how Lloyd's could be made leaner, fitter and hungrier for the challenging 1990s. The members met regularly, their findings were stored on a separate computer system and the disks were put away every night under lock and key at 1, Lime Street.

Roger Bradley, the former working Name and external member of Feltrim who was advising the Names in Ontario, had written his own report some years earlier. It was called *Towards 2000*. In his report, Bradley had called for a shake-up of the market from top to bottom.

Bradley's report was resurrected by the Rowland team only to be put back on the shelf. 'You're way over the top, old boy,' one of them cheerfully told him.

More syndicates, once bright stars, joined the black holes in

Lloyd's darkest firmament. As well as Feltrim 540/2 and 847 and Gooda Walker 290, 298 and 387, there now came Rose Thomson Young 255; Devonshire 216 and 833/4; Poland 104; Octavian 384; Secretan 367, and Wellington 406 and 448, whose members included the hero of the British forces in Operation 'Desert Storm', Sir Peter de la Billière.

While Sir Peter had been defending Western interests in the Gulf the Wellington syndicates had been calling for cash from him in a controversial reserving policy supposedly for claims 'Incurred But Not Reported'; known at Lloyd's as 'Imagined But Not Real.'

These reserves seemed to some members to be more for the benefit of the syndicate managers than the members; some of whom were already in combative mood after their losses on the spiral.

Out went the cash calls – but this time they were met by the writs from the overseas members. Among the British members there was just too much politicking and jostling for position for effective action to be taken as early as it might have been.

The Society of Names led by Tom Benyon was rubbished by the Association of Lloyd's Members as a renegade splinter group unrepresentative of the interests of Names. The Association of Lloyd's Members was derided by members of the Society of Names as a front for the Committee and Council of Lloyd's. The Gooda Walker action group did not see eye to eye with the Feltrim action group and within the Feltrim action group there were murmurings of mutiny. The Pulbrook 334/85 action group did not see eye to eye with the Feltrim action group but then they did not see eye to eye with the Gooda Walker group either.

What was the matter with these people, the Canadians and the Americans wanted to know? Why didn't they just get together and fight instead of fight together and get nowhere?

These divisions suited Lloyd's and Lloyd's did little to heal them. But even Lloyd's could go too far.

When David Coleridge described Tom Benyon as a 'busted flush' in a *Post* magazine interview Benyon sued him for libel. Benyon had only wanted £2,000 or so, but Lloyd's unwisely let it be known that Coleridge's costs were being met by the Corporation of Lloyd's: a questionable act of generosity towards a man alleged to have committed libel and who himself enjoyed an income of £1.2 million a year.

The result was that Benyon sued and obtained £25,000 and won. He was able to point out that this was at a cost of roughly £1 for each Lloyd's member.

Why did the British members bicker and politick and fight each other as much as they fought Lloyd's? The likely reason explains both their behaviour and the different behaviour of their Canadian and American counterparts.

Lloyd's had appealed above all to the snobbery of the British as an exclusive club to which they were privileged to belong. Lloyd's was the ultimate badge of belonging in a society which was hypocritical about greed and wealth and which preferred to describe as a vulgar slur the unpalatable fact that its citizens were defined not by their health or their spirituality but by their wealth and possessions. The British members were every bit as grasping and materialistic as the Canadians and the Americans whom they liked to describe and dismiss in those same terms; they simply had more sophisticated and entrenched motives for concealing the fact.

How could you possibly want to bring down or destroy such an exclusive club of which you were so privileged to be a member? To the British the thought was simply too terrible for words . . . no longer to be all for one and one for all . . . no longer to be a member . . . no longer to belong.

The Americans and Canadians by contrast simply did not feel this way, about greed, about wealth and above all about the club of which they were supposed to be so privileged to be members. They thought they had been sold a good investment as they might be sold a good mutual fund and you did not 'belong' to a good mutual fund in the same way that you belonged to Delta Gamma or Beta Theta Pi. When it came to the crunch, membership of a club which did not consult its members before introducing a 20,000% hike in membership fees was about as prestigious as membership of a failed Savings and Loan.

It did not suit Lloyd's at all, therefore, when, as well as the Canadians, the American members showed that, when it came to the business of legal action, at least they meant business.

New York City, 21 October 1991

FOR IMMEDIATE RELEASE

DATE: October 21, 1991

FROM: PROSKAUER ROSE GOETZ &
              MENDELSOHN
              1585 Broadway
              New York, New York 10036
              (212) 969-3000

RE: AMERICAN INVESTORS' LAWSUIT
              AGAINST LLOYD'S OF LONDON

CONTACT: Dale A. Schreiber
              Minna Schrag

NEW YORK, NY – Charging violations of the registration and anti-fraud provisions of the federal securities laws and the federal RICO legislation, 64 American investors (known as Names) in insurance syndicates sponsored by Lloyd's of London have brought suit in the U.S. District Court in Manhattan against Lloyd's, its Council and Committee, 266 syndicates, 16 members agents, 42 managing agents, and 59 of their principals.

Generally, Lloyd's Names are investors in Lloyd's-sponsored syndicates that write insurance and reinsurance for aviation, maritime, transportation and other risks. The syndicates operate for a calendar year. The Names are recruited annually by members agents who are approved and regulated by Lloyd's. The syndicates are managed by managing agents who are also approved and regulated by Lloyd's.

Lloyd's Names generally have unlimited liability for their shares of syndicate losses. The plaintiffs, like all Lloyd's Names, have pledged cash, letters of credit, bank guarantees, and other forms of collateral with Lloyd's to secure their losses.

The plaintiffs have been notified that their personal losses for 1988, 1989 and 1990 syndicates already exceed (US) $9 million. Their personal losses for those years, earlier open years, and 1991 could be far greater . . .

The suit charges that investments for each year in Lloyd's syndicates are 'securities' under the Securities Act of 1933 that require registration with the SEC . . .

In addition, in charging anti-fraud violations under Section 12 (2) of the 1933 Act and SEC Rule 10b-5, the suit alleges that Lloyd's, the members agents who have actively recruited American investors in the United States, and other defendants have actively downplayed the practical import of the Names' unlimited liability, while misrepresenting or failing to disclose serious risks in plaintiffs' syndicate investments.

These include denying plaintiffs participation in profitable syndicates, inadequate reinsurance coverage, secret and excessive compensation paid to insiders, the so-called 'LMX spiral' by which catastrophic risks reinsured by a particular syndicate were transferred back to that syndicate without the knowledge of the member Names (while the syndicate was paying exorbitant commissions for the placement of this ineffective and detrimental reinsurance), the secret withdrawal of 80% of one syndicate's capital by Lloyd's resulting in massive losses to its member Names, and secret assumptions by syndicates of losses earlier incurred by other syndicates.

Under their RICO claims, the plaintiffs seek treble damages
and attorneys' fees.

RICO stood for 'Racketeer Influenced Corrupt Organisation'
and was a provision of the Organised Crime Control Act of
1970. Was this really the same Lloyd's of London of which
Murray Lawrence had spoken in Chicago?

In London Alan Lord publicly professed astonishment at the
Proskauer writ and the SEC Form 'D' exemption inquiry. Lord
also professed to be surprised at the news that an inquiry was
being conducted by the Senate Permanent Subcommittee on Investigations into the way Lloyd's solicited members in America. The
chairman of the Senate Subcommittee was Senator Sam Nunn,
one of the most prominent politicians in America.

Although it was not publicly known at the time, Senator
Nunn, the Permanent Subcommittee on Investigations and its
Deputy Chief Counsel John Sopko (a former organised crime
prosecutor) were deeply concerned about the effects of problems
in the insurance business and particularly at Lloyd's on the interests of American policyholders. Sopko and his associates began
a deep and wide-ranging investigation into Lloyd's which would
bring them to London early in 1992.

Alan Lord publicly professed astonishment and surprise, but
privately, in the words of Robert Hiscox, it was war. Lloyd's
took the Canadian and American legal actions seriously enough
to make aggressive counter-moves aimed at preventing them from
resisting the drawdown on their letters of credit and forcing them
to pursue their actions through the British courts.

Dale Schreiber, the attorney acting for the American members
on the Proskauer case, was a rough, tough lawyer with a record
of success in Wall Street legal battles and in cases against large
American companies. Schreiber had a war chest of $1.5 million
and maintained that the American members were not motivated
by greed.

'If they get three times damages they could make money,' he said, 'but I don't think that's their objective – they just want to recover from the devastation and get on with their lives.'

If the Federal District Court in New York City ruled in Schreiber's favour, Lloyd's would not only have to cover the American members' $9 million losses and pay treble damages. They would also have to go on meeting the claims that had caused those losses for years to come.

As one London lawyer specialising in insurance litigation put it: 'American Names are still picking up the tab on some of the open years. If they get off the hook, the money will have to come from the Central Fund – which is not a bottomless pit.'

This prospect and the legal precedent it would set for other distressed and aggrieved members was what Lloyd's most dreaded. If the British members successfully adopted the litigious mentality of the foreigners, there was the likelihood of a real threat to the solvency of Lloyd's.

Lloyd's lawyers in New York City, Leboeuf Lamb Leiby and McCrae, were dismissive of the Proskauer writ.

'A group of people have lost money,' said Sheila Marshall. 'They're floundering around trying to find some strategy that will make them money.'

But the signs for Leboeuf Lamb and for Lloyd's were worrying. As the SEC letter to Congressman Pease, of whom the Proskauer litigant John Roby was a constituent, had revealed, the feeling at the SEC was that the litigants might have a case to pursue in America. The FBI were working in tandem with the Senate Subcommittee and were also antagonised by Lloyd's attempts to prevent Roby, a former FBI agent, from pursuing his case as an American citizen in America.

Either the Chief Executive and his colleagues on the Committee and Council of Lloyd's were badly out of touch with the strength of feeling among the Canadian and American members, or they had decided it was time for the gloves to come off and that Lloyd's was going to teach these impudent foreigners a lesson. The latter was the more likely explanation.

At 1, Lime Street a defensive atmosphere began to percolate through the building. A notice appeared on the bulletin board to the effect that no one was to talk about the affairs of Lloyd's 'to anyone outside the Lloyd's community.'

Alan Lord was in his sixth year as Chief Executive and was due to retire in the following year, 1992. Lord had no plans to preside over any major changes in the structure of an institution to which he felt so proud to belong, even though he had many times declared that he would never have become a member because 'it was a twenty year commitment.'

Unlike his predecessor Ian Hay Davison, Lord did not appear to attach particular importance to the media. His Media Relations Manager, Nick Doak, who had been so irritated by the invitation to Melvyn Bragg to advise David Coleridge on 'how to manipulate the media', admired Lord's 'bluff Inghamesque way with the press': a reference to Bernard Ingham, the controversial press secretary to Prime Minister Margaret Thatcher.

Doak was ready with an Inghamesque dismissal of the complaints of the American members.

'If they say none of the American Names have been members of Lloyd's,' he declared, referring to the SEC Form 'D' controversy, 'and losses should be repaid, then profits should be repaid as well.'

Doak did not seem to understand that if profits had been paid there would have been less likelihood of legal action. It was no secret that money was what motivated people to litigation; and there was no more motivated a litigant than the member who had not received any profits in the first place.

* * *

Lloyd's was like a sweater with a loose thread, Christopher Moran had said. When you pulled the thread the whole thing started to unravel. It seemed a lot of people were pulling on a lot of loose threads and the whole sweater was in danger of coming apart at the seams.

In Ontario the members were pulling hard to prevent their banks calling in their letters of credit. In New York City they were calling for their contracts to be voided and for treble damages. In California, too, members were consulting lawyers and making their own investigations in spite of the early misgivings of the ALM.

In Britain the members of action groups had the potential to unite and pose by far the biggest threat to Lloyd's credibility and its solvency; their willingness to do so was still uncertain and the decision lay in their hands.

In London at the High Court, Anthony Boswood QC for the Outhwaite 1982 members was giving Dick Outhwaite an increasingly uncomfortable time in the witness box.

'It is probably the case,' he told the judge, 'that never in the commercial history of the City of London has so much of other people's money been lost by the single-handed negligence of one man.'

The long tail furies that had devastated Outhwaite in 1982 had also brought down Pulbrook 334 and inflicted damage on Merrett 418. The Merrett members had an additional grievance. Many of them had been brought onto the syndicate after Merrett had written the eleven asbestosis 'run-off' policies and these members had inherited the claims and the large losses they incurred; when, they claimed, like Outhwaite, Merrett should have admitted defeat and left the year open, instead of 'dumping' the losses on the new members.

Ken Lavery was the Ottawa accountant who had said to himself at the time he was elected: 'I started out with zippo and I figure I am a pretty clever fellow.'

Ten years later Lavery did not feel so clever as a member of Pulbrook 334 and Merrett 418.

Lavery wrote to Lloyd's: 'When you review the list of the 1,959

Names (1982) helped by the . . . 2,089 Names (1983 to 1985) you find many familiar names . . . five members of the 1990 Council of Lloyd's appear in this group, including the current Chairman. I am only pointing this out to show how very difficult it is to find disinterested people to deal objectively and fairly with these issues.'

Lavery also claimed that, although the membership of Merrett 418 had increased in size by 83% between 1982 and 1985, the business it did increased by only 1%.

Lavery was by this time retired and living in Oakville, Ontario. As Jacki Levin had found, Ontario was a long way from London when it came to gathering information. But Lavery had been confident that his questions would be answered by the self-regulatory system that existed at Lloyd's as a result of the 1982 Lloyd's Act and the 1987 Neill Report.

He was rudely surprised to find that, although he paid his losses and compiled a file of material six inches thick, his questions were ignored by the gentlemen in London.

Lavery had persuaded the Association of Lloyd's Members to organise a meeting of the Merrett 418 1985 Association at the old Town Hall in Chelsea.

The association decided to elect a committee and take legal advice.

'I thought "bugger this",' Lavery told this author, 'my view was that Lloyd's were unable to regulate themselves. I find it incredible, coming from a country with our securities laws. My criticism is of the system and the culture and the UK Government.

'It's a bad advertisement for Britain. There is this huge problem and the British seem unable to deal with it. You have got to get rid of Chamberlain,' Lavery concluded, meaning David Coleridge, 'and bring in Churchill' – meaning Ian Hay Davison.

Once again it had taken an overseas member who was not mesmerised by the thought of no longer belonging to 'the club' to liberate the repressed feelings of the British members.

But, for one foreign-born British member whose lifelong aim

had been to manipulate the club and whose lifelong claim had been that the club had never accepted him, there was no such liberation.

Gran Canaria, 4 November, 1991

The *Lady Ghislaine* cruised on sleekly into the night, her captain and crew unaware of the splash of a man going over the side and the mounting tensions that he could no longer ignore. Later, controversy would rage over whether or not he had taken his own life, and, if so, which of his many troubles had driven him to commit suicide. For Robert Maxwell, a member of Lloyd's through Willis Faber, and an Outhwaite litigant, was a £20,000 line on Feltrim 847 the final straw?

* * *

Loose threads in the sweater . . . the attempt to force the American members to abandon their claim to an American court hearing would quietly founder. The forbidden voices leaking information about Lloyd's affairs 'outside the Lloyd's community' grew louder and more numerous. Dick Outhwaite was under heavier fire still in the witness box; from Ulrich von Eichen, an expert witness from Munich Re.

The Gooda Walker and other spiral syndicate members obtained expert opinion from the eminent barrister Gavin Leightman QC regarding the 'retrocession' or reinsurance practices of the spiral:

'A retrocession or a series of retrocessions would be held to be voidable if it could be established that:

1. A retrocession or a series of retrocessions were entered into otherwise than for the benefit of the Name. (This would be a breach of the managing agent's fiduciary duty to the Name.)'

Lloyd's announced loss reviews into the Devonshire syndicates 216 and 833/4 in the hope of staving off legal action.

The Devonshire members, victims of the entry of Hurricane Hugo into the spiral, were not so sure; and, in any case, Lloyd's still wanted them to pay their cash calls. The members set up an action group.

Among the Devonshire members was Lady Patricia Ashmore, whose husband was former Master of Her Majesty's Household and Extra Equerry to the Queen. Lady Ashmore was also a Feltrim member. The Queen was known to be concerned at the losses suffered at Lloyd's by close associates and members of the Royal Family.

Four thousand members were leaving and only 171 were coming in. More syndicates were closing or merging, further reducing the capacity of the market to underwrite insurance business. Privately, on the twelfth floor of Lloyd's, the estimates of the likely loss of members had by this time reached the 10, 000 mark: nearly half the membership.

Downstairs on the floor of The Room it appeared to be a case of business as usual.

1, Lime Street, late November 1991

Ken Lavery showed his membership card and strode onto the marble floor of The Room. Far above him the glass roof muffled the light from a grey winter sky.

Lavery walked over to the Merrett box. It was 4 pm and Stephen Merrett was sitting there. Lavery was impressed.

Lavery was 6 feet 4 inches tall. Merrett looked up at him and stood up. Lavery put out his hand, took Merrett's, and gave it a vigorous shake.

'My name's Ken Lavery,' he said, 'and I'd like to buy you a cup of coffee.'

There was silence for what seemed like a long time.

'Why?' said Merrett.

'Because we have things to talk about.'

'Do we?'

'I think we do,' said Lavery.

There followed to Lavery's surprise a tirade from Merrett about what Lavery had been saying about him in the press. At the same time Merrett was still trying to wrest himself free from the Canadian's handshake.

Eventually Merrett succeeded in doing so.

'OK,' said Lavery, 'I didn't come here to engage in a pissing contest on the floor of Lloyd's,' and he walked away from Merrett, from Lime Street and from his Lloyd's membership.

* * *

Loose threads in the sweater . . . a dismal wet winter night in central London. In Commonwealth House on Northumberland Avenue, just round the corner from Whitehall, a group of people were gathered in a basement. On a dais were Tom Benyon, Alfred Doll-Steinberg, leader of the Gooda Walker group, and others.

In the audience, ruined and near-ruined men and women recounted their experiences, unique they had thought to themselves, and virtually identical as they now discovered to each other's. For the first time they were able to discuss the nightmare into which they had entered and from which there was seemingly no escape. For the first time they began to show emotions other than fear, self-pity and guilt. For the first time it was becoming clear to these hitherto decent, honourable and law-abiding British members that some of them were not going to pay.

Afterwards some of them ran through the rain to the nearest pub.

The main topic of conversation was the Hardship Committee.

'A friend of mine's father offered to buy her house to help her out,' said one, slowly sipping a beer. 'He lives in the Isle of Man. When the Hardship Committee got to hear of it they tried their hardest to persuade her that they should go to the Isle of Man and "dissuade" him from doing so.'

'I know another case,' said another. 'This time it was a member's children who offered to buy his house from him. The Hardship Committee told him they took a dim view of this. Some creepy little accountant must have told them that property they acquire now is a good asset in the long term.'

'I hate them,' said another. 'The Hardship Committee create hardship, they don't relieve it. They want you buried so deep and so dark you will never be heard, never get out. Apparently four out of five people who go to them back off in horror. Is their condition of silence sustainable in law? What an appalling insult, to "allow" people to go on living in their own homes, as if it is they and not Lloyd's who have offended.

'I am looking to escape offshore,' he went on, 'possibly to the Channel Islands. Or America. When does the statute of limitations expire in the USA?'

There were many such voices, but one remained silent throughout the conversation. Christopher Thomas-Everard had been recognisable at the meeting because of the brown tweed suit he was wearing and the calm lucidity of his observations; he seemed to know more about Lloyd's than all the rest of the people in the meeting put together. He also had the facts and figures to prove it.

In the pub he pulled them out of his briefcase like a conjuror pulled rabbits out of a hat.

'Have you read the Chester Report into Oakeley Vaughan? As you know, it was never published. Would you like a copy?'

This was a man to be reckoned with. Later, in the farmhouse on the hill in Somerset, he made it clear he could be of help and needed help in turn. But for the time being he did not want to be identified in the press. He agreed to be known as 'the sheep farmer.'

Loose threads in the sweater . . . as the sheep farmer was discovering, Lloyd's was a steep learning curve; and although the view became clearer, the climb became even steeper on the way to the summit.

A Conversation in a City Chop House

Angus Runciman was not a member of Lloyd's. After a career in 2nd Battalion the Parachute Regiment, where he had missed the Falklands War by a whisker, he had become an insurance analyst with Banque Nationale de Paris. He held forth over a mixed grill.

'What you have to understand,' said Angus, 'is that, when you compare Lloyd's with other European insurance institutions, certain interesting things emerge.

'On the one hand, Lloyd's premium income is £5 billion or whatever and that is not a lot different from Munich Re. On the other, in spite of its Germanic secretiveness Munich Re does publish some sort of detailed annual accounts. Lloyd's doesn't. And it is possible to analyse these accounts and draw certain conclusions about Munich Re and Lloyd's of London.

'Take the question of reserves. In the case of Munich Re an informed guestimate would put them at £15 billion. Now £15 billion is not necessarily a lot of money but it is a lot of money compared with the £500 million or whatever in the Lloyd's Central Fund.

'So where are Lloyd's comparable reserves? (Munich Re by the way are prudent as well as secretive and they still worry that their own reserves are too low.) Lloyd's would point to its premium investment funds, and to the assets of its members. Unlimited liability, it proudly reminds you. The time-honoured boast. OK. But what exactly are those members' assets?

'Say there are 26,000 members (it may go down to 22,000 by the end of the year or even lower than that . . . if it does, it's serious). Say on average they are worth £600,000 – that's property, equities, pensions, bank guarantees, ready cash and cufflinks. That's 26,000 times £600,000 equals £15,600,000,000 – around £15 billion – around the same as Munich Re.

'But does Lloyd's really have access to that sum? All Munich Re has to do is write a cheque to the policyholders and say to its shareholders, "bad news, kamerads . . . no dividend this year." It doesn't have to send in the bailiffs. And who is to say that, faced with such claims, Lloyd's Names will actually pay?

'After all, the idea was that they would never actually have to do so. How else were they persuaded to become Names otherwise? And many of them do not have that £600,000 or whatever in liquid form. They would have to sell everything. And people won't do that.

'So there is a major doubt there, and it is a doubt also in the mind of the potential client who is looking for insurance cover. After all, if my car plant burns down in Turin will Lloyd's actually be able to pay for it? If I am a direct insurer and I cover the risk that an avalanche will smother Zurich, should I go to Lloyd's for reinsurance cover or somewhere nearer home? After all, I am a big European direct insurer with some big subsidiaries, and I am therefore more likely to be able to survive the claim. So I won't go to Lloyd's and pay Lloyd's rates, I'll go somewhere else which is part of a big risk-spreading institution which does not rely for its funding on the equity tied up in hundreds of Home Counties rectories.

'I don't think in the light of these factors that unlimited liability is a viable boast any more. I think too that Lloyd's will increasingly become the last port of call for reinsurance. The big European insurers will get more and more of the bread and butter business and Lloyd's will get the higher risk business which will make it more volatile and less attractive to Names. The 1988 catastrophe losses have reduced their wealth and their underwriting capacity and are deterring new investors from becoming members.

'I think Lloyd's are very worried. There is definitely a big PR offensive going on. They want overseas Names because they are more likely to benefit from tax concessions in a way that the British Names have not done since Maggie lowered taxes. But Lloyd's are still not thinking in a European way. They never liked foreigners and have always regarded them as a

necessary evil. They were even worse than women. 1992 will be
a grimly appropriate year for such a xenophobic and introverted
establishment to announce record losses of over £1 billion.

'*Anything else?*'

'Well, there's the new London Underwriting Centre in Minster
Court. That's going to do what Lloyd's does just as well, but at
more reasonable rates.'

Angus contemplated his beer:

'I think we are seeing the end of a Great British Club. External
regulation must come if Lloyd's is to survive at all. But I think
there is a lack of will and a complacency among people who have
made a lot of money and will not look out of the window.

'I don't think Lloyd's has a future in its present form.'

'*Anything else?*'

'Cheers.'

* * *

Christopher Hitchings was not a member of Lloyd's either but
he too was an insurance analyst and a director of Hoare Govett
Investment Research and he did not agree with Angus Runciman.
At a seminar for professional advisers held at Lime Street he put
his point of view:

'If the pattern of the 1960s is followed,' said Hitchings, 'that
paves the way for a substantial upturn in profitability in the
1990s.

'Lloyd's will gain even more than the insurance companies
from this,' Hitchings went on. 'Lloyd's is, in market terminology,
a wholesale market. What this means is that it is the market of last
resort: the market used when the mainstream insurance market
does not want or cannot write the business.

'A period of structural overcapacity has a double effect on
Lloyd's. The rates fall and the volume of business falls. This
puts pressure on expense ratios and underwriters, unable to write
external business, resort to reinsuring each other. A major loss,

like Hugo or Betsy, reverberates around the market magnifying its effect . . . Lloyd's results do not compare as favourably to those of the insurance industry generally as normally, and can be horrendously bad.

'I am a supporter of Lloyd's,' Hitchings told a sympathetic audience, 'and I think great care needs to be taken in changing it. Over the past 40 years, the average Lloyd's syndicate has achieved profits of 9 per cent of net written premiums: the average insurance company has achieved just 3.7 per cent. Whatever has generated that needs to be preserved since, if the gap were closed, Names might just as well forsake unlimited liability and buy insurance company shares . . .

'I am sure you appreciate that 1989 and 1990 will be very difficult years. 1991 may be better; it may not. Cycles turn,' Hitchings concluded, 'when underwriters and their capital cease to believe that they will.'

*   *   *

Loose threads in the sweater . . . storm clouds were gathering over Lloyd's that winter. In the High Court Dick Outhwaite was being shot to pieces by the man from Munich Re; and there were those on the Council of Lloyd's who said that if Outhwaite lost this one then Lloyd's was doomed, because he had done nothing out of kilter with the rest of Lloyd's during the underwriting year in question. Others said he deserved to win (or lose) for precisely this reason.

Lloyd's announced more loss reviews. The long tail casualty Merrett 421 had posted a loss of 574% or minus £57,400 for every £10,000 line. Mackinnon Hayter 134 and 184, the market's first stop loss syndicates, had racked up losses on the 1983 year of over 1,000%; minus £100,000 for every £10,000 line. Again, the message was: 'pay now, sue later.'

The Hardship Committee was revealed to be allowing single distressed members who accepted its terms an income of £9,000 a year. For a couple the figure rose to £14,000. The tactic of many distressed members was to go through the motions of filling in and posting off the questionnaire in the hope of buying time, while their members groups took legal advice as to whether or not they could avoid paying up.

One such member learned from a source at Hardship headquarters in Chatham that, of the seven hundred members who had approached the Hardship Committee, fewer than two hundred had gone through the process and entered the ultimate oubliette. But two hundred members going through the Hardship process also meant two hundred more members' losses to be met from the Central Fund: losses which in many cases exceeded the assets of the members in question.

Bill Brown of Walsham Brothers had broked many of the reinsurance risks to Feltrim and other spiral syndicates whose members were the Hardship Committee's principal customers. Brown was revealed in his 1990 accounts to have taken a £792,000 pay cut; reducing his annual salary by 10% to £7.3 million, or £1 a second. But Brown was merely the best-paid and not the only example of his kind.

Lloyd's succeeded in preventing the Ontario members from obtaining an injunction against Lloyd's claiming against their banks. But the Ontario members succeeded in preventing those same banks from calling on their letters of credit. The legal argument was now somewhere in the middle of the Atlantic.

Lord Alexander had wrestled with the Hardship Committee and was looking right into the financial abyss when Lloyd's tried its latest ploy to deny legal redress to the members of Oakeley Vaughan. This was to question a High Court verdict that the Law Lords had already given in the plaintiffs' favour.

In a letter to Lloyd's QC David Johnson, Lord Justice Nourse made his feelings uncommonly plain:

'... your invitation to the court to reconsider its decision to allow the appeal is inappropriate and, in our experience, unprecedented. It would have been inappropriate even if the ground advanced had been a sufficient basis for invalidating the decision, which it most clearly is not . . .'

Johnson promptly announced that the Oakeley Vaughan case had gone on longer than he had expected, and that other commitments meant he would not be available during the early months of 1992.

Lloyd's meanwhile were petitioning the House of Lords directly to have the issue heard separately of whether or not it owed 'a duty of care' to the Oakeley Vaughan members. Lloyd's would succeed in its petition and the case would be further delayed; apart from the apparent injustice of this, a further absurdity was that more costs would be incurred and these would fall on Lloyd's own members, since the judge had decreed that the costs of both sides in the action should be borne by Lloyd's.

In another place, too, the members were becoming increasingly restive.

The House of Commons, December 1991

The Central Lobby of the House of Commons was a magnificent place for what began as a depressing conversation.

'I began underwriting in 1986, so the timing couldn't have been worse. I am a farmer and landowner – I wanted a return from assets that were not yielding money. So it seemed sensible to pledge them as security for Lloyd's.

'I say this against myself, but I used a bank guarantee for my Lloyd's deposit. It's an easy thing to do and I am not absolutely certain that it is sound. I think a lot of banks have not been looking too carefully at the asset value of their clients – in return for their one per cent guarantee fee. I think that facility is perhaps dangerous – a rosy path to oblivion.

'But I need the money to live on. My farm doesn't pay much and I have a portfolio of shares which has taken a pounding. Being an MP is a net drain and it is a very demanding job.

'As a Member of Parliament and a member of Lloyd's I

suppose I could say that members of Lloyd's would like the same tax concessions as small businessmen. That was floated in the idea of writing back losses before the last Budget but it got nowhere. It would have looked like special pleading and it was a non-starter.

'But there are about sixty of us here in the Commons and next year's results don't look too good either. So this is obviously a subject mentioned by a lot of people in the submissions to the Chancellor and Treasury Ministers which will take place between now and the end of January. We all trot off in little groups and give our views. Those of us who are also members of Lloyd's are co-ordinated in the House in a little group.

'Do you know, I think there is a world of difference between being a working member inside the market and an external member. Do you think so? Do you know anyone else who thinks so? You do?'

* * *

Unlike sixty of his MPs and several members of his Cabinet, the new Prime Minister, John Major, was not a member of Lloyd's. If anything he was an advertisement for the refutation of the idea that 'first generation don't even speak.'

The Prime Minister seemed unwilling however to depart publicly from what sounded like a brief dictated and passed to him from the Committee Room on the twelfth floor at 1, Lime Street.

Just before Christmas he made a speech at the opening of the new offices of the broker C. E. Heath at 133, Houndsditch, just down the road from the deserted offices of Robin Kingsley's Lime Street Agencies.

'As competition intensifies in Europe and worldwide,' the Prime Minister declared, 'we do have in this country one priceless advantage over actual and potential European competitors. And that priceless advantage which we should never spurn or lose is the international fame and standing of Lloyd's of London.

'It is at the heart of the London insurance market. It holds a worldwide reputation for innovation and for the security that unlimited liability brings. A great deal, I know, is made – particularly by those at the heart of the problem – of Lloyd's recent underwriting losses. I know for some they have been serious, but they do need to be seen in some perspective.

'The 1988 losses,' the Prime Minister went on, 'the first for 20 years since 1967 – were fully covered by increased reserves for liabilities. Those reserves will place the market in a much stronger position. And the important point is that Lloyd's knows the future lies in expanding abroad.

'It is actively seeking to extend its overseas representation both in Europe and elsewhere. And I do not have a single shred of doubt that UK insurance can face up to the more challenging world of the 1990s and take markets abroad that currently are in the hands of other people.'

It would have been naive in the extreme to expect the Prime Minister to criticise Lloyd's, given the enormous press coverage that would have been given to any such criticism. Yet so much of what he said was patently unsustainable. While it was proudly reported in *Lloyd's Newsletter*, elsewhere it aroused roars of laughter.

'Has the Prime Minister been elected to the Lutine Lodge?' asked one former broker.

Such adherence to what read and sounded like a Lime Street PR hand-out did little credit to the former Chancellor of the Exchequer and the present Prime Minister of Great Britain.

It was time to solicit the opinions of another staunch Conservative Party supporter. This one knew too much, however, simply to mouth the party line.

Grosvenor Place, London, December 1991

A week after the Prime Minister's remarks, Ian Hay Davison sat in his office near Hyde Park Corner winding a small and attractive carriage clock; not the large and ugly item that had been presented to him by Sir Peter Miller.

Davison had not been idle in the six years since he had ceased to be Lloyd's first and last externally-appointed Chief Executive. He had been appointed to develop a blueprint for the Hong Kong securities market. He had been active in business and was a director of the *Independent* newspaper. He was Chairman of the Conran conglomerate Storehouse plc. He was comfortably off and could retire any time he liked.

But, somehow, the man to whom the Governor of the Bank of England had said, 'After that, all sorts of things will be possible for you,' was no longer regarded as being in the forefront of the City. Davison was not a yesterday's man; but his career seemed frozen in time, like the speedometer of a car at the moment of impact.

In 1987 he had published *A View of the Room*, an authoritative but circumspect account of his extraordinary years at Lloyd's. Now he was able to speak openly about the dramatic circumstances of his arrival, presence and ultimate departure. Strangely however, in spite of the mounting publicity about Lloyd's, no one had yet bothered to seek him out. He was surprised but not vain or insecure enough to mind.

Over the next hour Davison talked memorably and candidly about his years as Chief Executive and the personalities who had supported him and dogged his every move.

'I always got on with the people in The Room,' he said, a remark confirmed by many who worked there. 'But my relations with the Corporation staff (the permanent administrative employees) were pretty difficult. I was being paid three times as much as they were for a start. Not many even in the top rank survived . . . there were some real puddings sitting there. But I did not succeed in bringing in a cadre of competent executives who stayed – that just didn't work.

'I had a mixed press with the Council,' Davison went on. 'They were a pretty rum bunch. The fundamental difficulty I had is that I conceded that the Council actually had a role to play in rule-making – poachers make good gamekeepers – but for me to expect the players to act as the referees and apply those rules fairly was naive. They were quite shameless in some cases about why they were on the Council – one of them' (he named a leading underwriter and Council member) 'said to me, why do you think I am on the Council? Because I want to find out what is going on before other people do!

'It is an insider's market. But I don't know how else such a market would work. It goes without saying that a rehash of the Financial Services Act would bring Lloyd's under external regulation.'

The carriage clock ticked on his desk. Davison was coming to the end of the time he had to spare.

'Matters have now reached a stage,' he said quietly, 'that unless Lloyd's and the authorities take some fairly serious steps to restore confidence by the investors in Lloyd's, its future must be in doubt. One option might be to contemplate liquidation and the foundation of a new body.'

'*Are you serious?*'

'Would you laugh? The most famous thing I have ever done is to be Chief Executive of Lloyd's. I resigned and all my predictions have come true.'

* * *

Loose threads in the sweater in the first days of 1992 . . . Lloyd's had apparently abandoned the writs it had taken out in the Commercial Court in London seeking injunctions to restrain Dale Jenkins and John Roby from bringing an American legal action and soliciting others to do so. Lloyd's had brought suit against four overseas Names in Australia, the Bahamas, South Africa and New York.

Lloyd's were told by the judge to 'get on with it' in the case of Oakeley Vaughan; nearly ten years had passed since the Chester

Report had been commissioned, delivered and put on the shelf, its explosive contents withheld from the syndicate members.

A figure in a brown tweed suit was to be seen entering the old MI5 headquarters in Curzon Street; the sheep farmer was visiting the Kroll private detective agency. A suggestion had been made that it might be a good idea to unleash some ex-SAS bloodhounds on the gentlemen of Lloyd's of London.

Many of the largest and oldest syndicates such as the Janson Green marine and non-marine syndicates were leaving open the 1991 underwriting year; no accountant or actuary could be found to certify 'true and fair' that the last had been seen of the long tail furies, the asbestosis and pollution claims underwritten in the 1940s, 1950s and 1960s.

Over 5,000 members – nearly 25% of the membership and £3 billion of Lloyd's £18 billion asset base – had joined fourteen action groups in the belief or delusion that their losses were not the product of a well-regulated market. Devonshire 216, Feltrim, Gooda Walker, Merrett 418, Merrett 421, Oakeley Vaughan, Outhwaite 1982, Poland, Pulbrook 90, Pulbrook 334, Rose Thomson Young 255, Warrilow 1984, Mackinnon Hayter 134 and 184 and Lambert 604 were all trying not to bicker and politick with each other. There were signs of a consensus about legal action.

The Rowland Task Force Report, *Lloyd's: a route forward*, was published amidst great expectations, many of them false. Few members knew or remembered that the telephone call by Murray Lawrence to David Rowland in Hong Kong had been the beginning of an initiative to strengthen the market's capital base and reduce its costs, rather than write a charter for its members.

Yet the crisis of the membership had become so deep and so sharp in the year since Rowland had been commissioned that the misconception was correspondingly magnified. The result was that Lloyd's liked the Rowland Report for the very reasons the distressed members disliked it; because it proposed a way ahead for the market.

David Coleridge and the Council of Lloyd's promptly accepted nearly every one of the Rowland proposals: that divestment of brokers and managing agencies should be reversed, that limited corporate capital be solicited, that a fund be established which in effect would mutualise extreme losses, and that this fund would help distressed members in future. But they rejected the proposal that the Council should be scrapped in its present form and that Lloyd's should be run by a professional board of externally-imposed managers.

Prominent among the opposition to this proposal were David Coleridge and the Chief Executive, Alan Lord. Lord argued that regulation would suffer. Besides, the change would require new legislation, a new Lloyd's Act; and unlike his predecessor the Chief Executive did not seem convinced that a new Lloyd's Act was a good idea.

Others on the floor of The Room were not so sure about Lord's response: 'We don't want someone who can prepare beautiful papers for a meeting,' said one, 'we want someone to run the bloody thing.'

There was anger too at Lord's attitude among external members which overflowed at one action group meeting. One distressed member, himself a former senior civil servant, called for Lord's immediate resignation, to loud applause.

Lloyd's liked the Rowland Report and the external members disliked it.

'The Report . . . points the way in a lucid and constructive manner to a profitable long-term trading future for Lloyd's,' David Coleridge wrote to all members. 'The Council will approach in the same spirit its urgent task of evaluating the Report, and will not shrink from necessary but difficult decisions.'

At 1, Lime Street, the mood was exultant.

'Is there some more wine on the go?' yelled one press officer at the conference called to announce the Task Force's findings.

Lloyd's announced a multi-country travelling roadshow to spread the good news of the Rowland Report to members as far apart as London, New York, Chicago, San Francisco, Perth, Sydney, Christchurch, Wellington and Johannesburg.

The press were forbidden from attending; but there was nothing to stop an interested party being placed on the list in London as an elderly member's 'independent financial adviser': 'Lloyd's,' announced one speaker at the roadshow in the City, only a mile or so from the Lloyd's building, 'is the pivot of the London market – and London is the most important insurance market in the world.'

'We have the best underwriters,' said another speaker, 'the best expertise.'

'We're looking again at the governance proposal,' said yet another, referring to the proposal rejected by Alan Lord and the Council, 'we're setting up a high-powered working party – under Sir Jeremy Morse. We're not asking for anything retroactive,' he added quickly.

All spoke, they stressed, 'first and foremost as Names'; yet one was a stop loss underwriter, and another was a former Deputy Chairman of Lloyd's and a members and managing agent. The audience, mainly external members, remained sceptical.

Others were sceptical too.

'Given the catastrophes and liabilities that have beset the industry,' said Charles Sturge of Chatset, 'I think Rowland had very little room for manoeuvre.'

'This Report is an inside job,' said Ken Lavery.

'This may be the first time Lloyd's has put the outsiders first and not the insiders,' said Tom Benyon, 'but it does nothing to help the many distressed members.'

'The distressed members are being put in a bag and dropped in the river,' said Clive Francis.

'We're being packed into railway carriages and sent over the cliff,' said the sheep farmer.

Lloyd's liked the Rowland Report and the distressed members disliked it. But the irony was that the latter view now eclipsed the former and the distressed members were seen as holding the initiative. No matter that the Task Force had in fact succeeded in addressing its original remit to the satisfaction of the people who had commissioned it in the first place: the Chairman and Council of Lloyd's.

David Rowland himself had said: 'It's almost as if a conspiracy existed within Lloyd's against the outside world.' Rowland was Chairman of Sedgwick, one of Lloyd's largest brokers, which only channelled 12% of its premiums into Lloyds; which the speakers at the multi-country roadshow were calling 'the pivot of the London market', which in turn was 'the most important insurance market in the world.'

In the end none of these things mattered because what did matter was that there had been a massive change of perception. The crisis of solvency and confidence among members around the world was now so deep that the Rowland Report was severely criticised in the serious press for failing to achieve what it had never set out to do.

After the Task Force Report was released the row broke on a big scale in the press and would not go away.

'All this is merely rearranging deckchairs on the *Titanic*,' said the *Independent*. 'Unless Lloyd's comes up with more radical solutions to attract new capital, another report will be needed after a further five years – if, by then, it is not already too late.'

'Lloyd's needs bolder reform,' said the *Sunday Times*. 'The Rowland taskforce will go some way, but not far enough.'

The twenty-year experiment with external members, brought about by the Cromer Report, had ended with Rowland. But the time bomb identified by Cromer, ignored by the Committee of Lloyd's who placed his report on the shelf, and subsequently missed by Fisher and the Council, had finally exploded and decimated parts of the membership.

For many the peaceful death of 'the Grobfather' Kenneth Grob at home in palatial surroundings in the South of France was an ironic and timely reminder of the way the market insiders had driven a coach and horses through the act of 1982. Grob and three other so-called 'expert witnesses' who had testified before a credulous cross-party committee of MPs in 1982 had subsequently been damningly criticised by the DTI investigation. But ten years on, in 1992, MPs and Parliament and the DTI would not be so gullible.

Two weeks after the Prime Minister's remarks I sat with the sheep farmer, Christopher Thomas-Everard, in the office of John Redwood, then Minister for Corporate Affairs at the Department of Trade and Industry. Redwood, a formidably intelligent and articulate man, was initially sceptical about the idea that insiders had stitched up much of the low-risk high profit business for themselves at the outsiders' expense. He articulated the view that since 1982 Lloyd's had no longer had this kind of problem.

Thomas-Everard listened and then explained patiently how it was done, pushing documents across the Minister's desk. The Minister for Corporate Affairs and his staff were visibly shaken. At the end of our conversation he thanked Thomas-Everard profusely and asked for immediate copies of his researches.

It was a misty afternoon in London; but the next morning in Somerset Thomas-Everard woke up to a clear day.

Loose threads in the sweater . . . four thousand Gooda Walker members received cash calls for £20,000 each for the 1989 and 1990 underwriting years and many announced that they were not going to pay. Fewer than ten per cent would pay and repayment of a further £90 million in claims would threaten to fall on the Central Fund. Ken Randall, the former head of regulation at Lloyd's who had investigated PCW and Oakeley Vaughan and been an ally to Ian Hay Davison, was appointed to investigate the increasingly murky affairs of Gooda Walker syndicate 290. Alfred Doll-Steinberg, the Chairman of the Gooda Walker Action Group, produced evidence refuting the claim by Lloyd's that LMX syndicates had earned 15 to 25 per cent per annum; in the five years before 1988 Gooda Walker 164, 290, 298 and 299 had made an average profit of just six per cent per year. Since 1988 their known losses averaged 148 per cent.

Then came the latest bombshell; Chatset announced that the estimated overall Lloyd's losses for the 1989 underwriting year would exceed a staggering £1.3 billion. These would fall during the next few months on the shoulders of already hard-pressed and distressed members.

Many could not take in the implications of the Chatset figures. But according to Chatset there was worse to come; a further loss of £1.1 billion on the 1990 year, due to be paid in 1993, and a loss of £800 million on 1991 to be paid in 1994. The total was £3.2 billion; and the letters were already going out for cash calls which if Chatset was right averaged £100,000 across the market.

Members faced losing half their existing deposits after the 1989 losses and all their deposits by the time it came to pay the 1991 account. Somehow they would have to find an extra £6 billion to replace these reserves; yet 4,000 members had resigned in the past year and 6,000 were in litigation. This would also cause problems for many branches of the major banks who had so readily granted members guarantees and letters of credit.

Privately even David Coleridge was rumoured to be conceding that 1992 would see 10,000 members unable to go on underwriting in the market. No wonder he kept this private; not only would this leave the fifty per cent who remained underwriting with one hundred per cent of the burden, but such an exodus would somehow have to be managed if the members and Lloyd's itself were not to be trampled to death in the rush.

Lloyd's denounced the Chatset figures as 'unnecessarily pessimistic and alarmist'; but could offer no better news on underwriting year 1989 and only marginal consolation in the case of the underwriting years 1990 (another loss) and 1991 (a possible profit).

If these figures were true, they could only mean one thing. Lloyd's was running out of money.

What did this mean?

The terrifying fact was that nobody seemed to know.

The bickering and politicking among the action groups diminished and this may well have been connected with the announcement of the Chatset figures. Minds were focussed firmly on legal action. The most prominent figure in this respect was Michael Freeman.

Freeman was a squat, aggressive lawyer who was prepared to attempt the ploy considered and rejected three years earlier by the Outhwaite barrister Anthony Boswood QC. This was an injunction to prevent Lloyd's members agencies from drawing down on members' security at Lloyd's to meet cash calls. The grounds were that the draw down procedures were allegedly defective.

Freeman aroused intense controversy in legal circles. Some lawyers claimed he was making misleading claims and others claimed he was touting for business. But, to many of the distressed members of syndicates such as Feltrim, Gooda Walker, Devonshire, and Rose Thomson Young, Michael Freeman was their last hope.

'I thought St Michael lived in a High Street store until I met you,' cried one woman at his seminar at the Cumberland Hotel in late January 1992.

Lloyd's took Freeman sufficiently seriously for their internal solicitor, John Mallinson, to remind members agencies that 'they held the purse strings'; dire consequences would befall any members agency who did not collect the money.

Lloyd's declared that, instead of eight specimen plaintiffs on one writ, as Freeman had originally planned, each aggrieved individual would have to file his or her own writ.

Freeman and his staff promptly printed six hundred of the appropriate forms and were swamped with enquiries from members of spiral syndicates facing massive cash calls.

As Freeman pointed out, the members agencies would be delighted if he succeeded in bringing the injunction. They would not have to draw down on their members' reserves and suffer a massive drop in their members' underwriting capacity.

But there were members agents whose actions had already brought themselves and their members to the point of no return.

Ham Common, Surrey, late January 1992

'I am very distressed,' said Robin Kingsley.

Kingsley had talked for a long time about his early career and the origins of Kingsley Underwriting and Lime Street Agencies. The good years were over and the nightmare had started and a lot of people wanted his blood.

'Buf if you are going to do business with people in Lloyd's,' he went on, 'you have to trust them. If you don't, you shouldn't be there.'

Kingsley was talking about the syndicates on which he had placed so many of his members. He could have been talking about the trust his members had placed in him.

'The Excess of Loss syndicates like Feltrim and Gooda Walker were successful in their day. We did not know the extent of the reinsurance within the market.'

'Not everyone is picking on us,' Kingsley said, 'but look at all the other agencies who supported those syndicates!'

'*But in many cases you placed more of your members on those syndicates than any other members agency.*'

'We felt if you backed a syndicate, you backed it, not with only a small proportion of your Names.'

'*Why did you not tell your members sooner about the change in policy concerning Errors and Omissions insurance? You told many of them too late for them to be able to put in a claim.*'

'I know some members are claiming they should have been told earlier,' Kingsley said, 'but the cost of taking out Errors and Omissions policies was astronomical. And you could never divulge the actual indemnity purchased because the Errors and Omissions underwriters could possibly claim you were exposing them to suit . . . under the terms of the insurance contract it could have been voided by the underwriters.

'The trouble with Lloyd's,' Kingsley went on, 'is that when things are going well, by and large most people are happy. When things are going badly, acrimony creeps in.'

The silences were growing longer in the drawing room of Sudbrook Lodge, the Carolean house he had bought with part of his wealth.

'Why are these members in America and Canada now saying they were "recruited"?' asked Kingsley. 'Probably because they have lost money; the fact is that things went very badly wrong for them from the word go. Now they cannot believe their members agent is telling them the truth.'

'*What is the truth?*'

'The truth is that there was no question of recruiting. It is a deliberately derogatory word. I can't comment on the Proskauer case except to say that Lloyd's had an understanding with the IRS.

'It was totally unique. We couldn't sell to them. Under IRS rules Lloyd's was an exempt private placing. Every year I would go and see Sheila Marshall at Leboeuf Lamb in New York. We were not allowed to make presentations. We could only see people together if they were already members, and that was to talk generally about the current position. We had to see a candidate on his or her own or with an adviser, and that is what we always did.'

'We weren't having trouble finding members in Britain,' Kingsley continued, 'absolutely not. But we were worried about the UK tax climate and it seemed common sense to attract members from countries without those problems . . . like America, Canada, Australia and New Zealand. We even foresaw a time when half the membership would come from overseas . . . particularly the United States of America.'

Kingsley appeared to have plenty of time on his hands.

'What happens to a members agent when syndicates on which you have placed a large number of people hit hideous trouble?' he said. 'It is devastating.

'People who have become very good friends over the years are desperately affected. And one's own family. Relationships are strained. Staff are worked harder and harder. Many clients leave and new ones do not apply. You lose your clients. You lose your business.

'Will I be able to stay in this house? I don't know.

'It is a nightmare for all Names who make huge losses and always has been.'

Kingsley appeared to have plenty of time. He drove to the station.

As we parted he said quietly: 'These are very harrowing times.'

* * *

Suddenly all the loose threads were pulling at once . . . and the sweater began to come apart.

Lloyd's caved in over the Outhwaite case and made a £116 million offer to the members of the 1982 Association. Ironically the burden of this would fall on the Errors and Omissions syndicates which many members alleged had traditionally creamed off 'insider' business.

The Outhwaite settlement would cover 80% of the 1982 losses to date; but it was impossible to estimate or cap the members' future losses. Outhwaite himself did not and never would concede negligence.

The 250 Warrilow members won a £4 million settlement of the 1985 losses. This was only 25% of their losses and like Outhwaite it was impossible to quantify what their future losses might be. Like Outhwaite, they would have to use some of the settlement to purchase stop loss insurance for the indefinite future. The Outhwaite claims could continue coming in until the 21st century.

Both settlements were restricted to the members of the action groups who had subscribed to the litigation. This led to unseemly pushing and shoving by members who for one reason or another – in some cases because of the Murray Lawrence letter – had chosen not to support the actions. Others had simply been too mean to do so and now tried to beg or bribe their way onto the legal ticket.

The solicitors handling the Outhwaite case even received 'copies' of letters the originals of which members intimated had been 'lost in the post.' Other non-litigating members offered a percentage of any money recovered to the solicitors if they would falsify the paperwork and include them in the settlement.

Peter Nutting professed himself cautiously pleased. 'It's the best deal we could do and that's why I think we should accept it,' he told his members at a meeting at the Central Hall, Westminster. They agreed with him; but unknown to Nutting and his members the Outhwaite settlement was not settled yet.

Tom Benyon knew that this was the best he could have managed; but he was disappointed with the lack of acknowledgement from some of his members. 'They seem to think the Warrilow 1985 Association is some kind of branch of the National Health Service,' he said. 'They have all the qualities of a dog without the loyalty.'

There were rumours too of an impending settlement in the case of Oakeley Vaughan.

Why were these long-running claims apparently about to be settled? One likely explanation is that word had gone out from the twelfth floor at 1, Lime Street that these were small beer by comparison with the £1.3 billion to be paid in 1989 and the £3.2 billion losses over 1989, 1990 and 1992. Settling these claims would secure some much-needed goodwill.

The message read and understood by the other action groups was simple: legal action always led to victory. But there were no winners in the sense that the burden of settling these claims fell on the Errors and Omissions syndicates – and therefore on the

Errors and Omissions syndicate members – within the Lloyd's market.

The loose threads were all pulling at once . . . six weeks after the Prime Minister's remarks the row over Lloyd's exploded in Parliament.

Tom Benyon, Alfred Doll-Steinberg and Christopher Thomas-Everard were the men responsible for the outburst of indignation on the part of the sixty Conservative MPs who were also Lloyd's members.

Benyon was the former MP and experienced lobbyist; Doll-Steinberg's was the amiably sharp analytical mind; and Thomas-Everard had supplied them with copies of the researches he had supplied to the Minister for Trade and Industry.

After a long struggle, the sheep farmer had culled reams of facts and figures from computer databases and other sources. These facts and figures underpinned a set of questions Benyon and Doll-Steinberg presented to MPs at Westminster.

The MPs were advised to ask the same questions of the Chairman of Lloyd's:

Can you please explain about preferential access for working members?

Why are the disastrously bad syndicates composed almost entirely of external or retired members?

Why do you not allow the terms of reference for Sir Patrick Neill's Loss Review Panel to investigate the 1990 year of syndicate 540?

Is it not correct that every time external members of syndicates have banded together, they have won their case or a settlement of their claim for negligence? What is the latest position?

Why does Lloyd's refuse to give the addresses of syndicate members to Action Groups?

Chatset correctly predicted that 1988 would be a loss

while Lloyd's were still forecasting a profit of £240 million. Might they not also be right for 1990 and 1991?

Why did Lloyd's allow the excessive recruitment of many small investors with assets of only a bank guarantee of £100,000 on their house?

Do Lloyd's underwriters agree with the Chairman of the ILU [Institute of London Underwriters] statement last week that most premium levels are still completely inadequate and will continue to be of little profit for another three years?

How much of the central fund is already earmarked for PCW losses and insolvent Lloyd's members?

If Lloyd's agents have been taking underwriting salaries of over £200,000, agency directors salaries of £100,000, substantial dividends on their agency shares, and large returns from restricted access insiders' syndicates, while making losses for their members, do you not consider that the Lloyd's market practitioners should arrange a mutualisation or pooling of the LMX losses dumped on external members?

Is there not a structural rottenness over the conflicts of interest or the regulators within Lloyd's, which can only be met by outside regulation under the Financial Services Act?

David Coleridge was handed these questions at a meeting of the Tory backbench finance committee on the night of 11 February 1992. Those present confirmed that as he read them he began to shake.

The MPs then proceeded to interrogate him in a way that made the 'roasting' of their last meeting feel like a modest sunlamp. They were not satisfied with his answers.

'There are a lot of people who can't tell a loss from a scandal,' Coleridge told them.

Asked whether or not he would grant access to the Lloyd's computer database in order to substantiate or disprove these allegations, he did not answer.

The MPs were not amused. They were so angry that they

leaked the questions to their opposite numbers in the Labour Party, two of whose members tabled five Commons motions based on the questions.

'TORIES DECLARE WAR ON LLOYD'S,' read the headline in the *Independent*. 'MPs LEAK CLAIMS THAT INSIDERS ARE CREAMING OFF BEST BUSINESS.'

'LLOYD'S IS "GRINDING TO A HALT" IN CASH CRISIS,' read the headline in the *Independent on Sunday*.

'IS IT TIME TO PUT LLOYD'S INTO LIQUIDATION?' read the headline in the *Evening Standard*.

The last headline was above an article which contained the following lines:

> 'Lloyd's tried to pretend it was still a gentleman's club long after its morals had fallen below those of a Lebanese casino. How and why did it all go so wrong? In the course of a year spent writing a book about Lloyd's I have thought of a number of answers . . '

The article was written by this author and apparently enraged the Chairman of Lloyd's to the extent that on the following day Lloyd's issued a press statement.

> The chairman of Lloyd's, David Coleridge, made the following statement, Saturday 15th February:
> 'The *Evening Standard* article published yesterday about Lloyd's was read by me and no doubt by members of Lloyd's, with fury and dismay. It is impossible to list in this short statement the falsehoods it contained. Suffice it to say that whilst Lloyd's has always welcomed constructive criticism, the *Evening Standard* article was a disgraceful and wholly baseless attack upon the integrity and solvency of a leading City institution. Accordingly, Lloyd's will take all appropriate steps to seek redress, including, if necessary, the bringing of legal proceedings.'

The press statement, like the article, was widely reported. No legal action was forthcoming although the Chairman of Lloyd's did receive a number of letters from affronted Lebanese members. Coleridge himself felt moved to write a long article of his own in the *Sunday Telegraph*:

No LEBANESE CASINO AT LLOYD's
The media, once more, is full of allegations of scandal at Lloyd's of London. As is usual, the allegations are made by those who have little knowledge or real interest in Lloyd's, its regulation or its working practices. Instead, we are used as a stalking horse and a whipping boy . . .
'Excess of Loss is a highly-geared business,' Coleridge went on. 'When incidence of catastrophes is normal, it yields high profits; high incidence produces high losses. But, contrary to recent vulgar assertions, it is not a kind of Lebanese casino; it is an essential means of providing cover and liquidity for the insurance market . . .
'We enter 1992 leaner, fitter, more efficient and eager for business now the insurance cycle has turned and rates have hardened . . .'

Unwilling to become involved in the story, but also unwilling to be patronised in this way, I decided to release information that could not have been gathered by someone with 'little knowledge or real interest in Lloyd's.'
I passed the Gilkes letter about the spiral to a national newspaper which reported it on 23 February with the headline: **'Lloyd's failed to act on warning four years ago.'** I liaised with action groups seeking to communicate with individual members around the world, and with individual members around the world seeking to communicate with action groups. I testified in London to Senator Nunn's Senate Permanent Subcommittee on Investigations. I subscribed to Ian Hay Davison's maxim: 'Sunshine drives away the mist.'

I regretted having to do this. But I also regretted not having acted sooner to show that had any moral high ground ever existed in this affair, it most certainly was no longer occupied by Lloyd's.

Suddenly all the loose threads were pulling . . . Paul Marland MP had lost a lot of money through Peter Cameron-Webb. Marland had switched to the Gooda Walker agency in the mid-1980s hoping to claw back his losses, only to lose another fortune from the syndicates on the spiral. A few days after the row blew up in Parliament Marland and other members of the Houses of Commons and Lords faced Coleridge at 1, Lime Street.

They had seen the slide show and had the easy question and answer session. Now they began the serious questioning.

'In which of your three capacities are you appearing here?' asked Marland smoothly. 'As the Chairman of Lloyd's, as the man responsible for regulation of the market, or as the Chairman of Sturge Holdings, from which you earn over £800,000 a year?'

Coleridge looked around at his colleagues but they were unable to help.

'My Sturge salary,' he said, 'is £75,000 a year. I am paid nothing for being Chairman of Lloyd's.'

Marland was enjoying himself.

'What about your other income?' he said.

Coleridge shrugged.

'I do have a considerable private income,' he replied.

Lord Alexander spoke for the House of Lords and the Oakeley Vaughan members.

'Has Lloyd's any sense of duty to its members?' he asked simply.

Coleridge could not reply.

Shortly afterwards, the *Sunday Times* made a suggestion unprecedented in a British newspaper. It called for the resignation of the Chairman of Lloyd's.

There was no longer any way it seemed in which Lloyd's could stop itself coming apart at the seams.

Lloyd's furiously denied seeking aid from the Bank of England and cited its '£18 billion from premium income and assets that belong to Names.' Alan Lord also irritably cited this figure in response to the suggestion from Ian Hay Davison that the crisis of confidence was such that Lloyd's would not survive the end of the century.

'The Lloyd's policy is still backed by £18,000 million,' Lord declared, 'and premium rates are rising.'

But one experienced market source claimed that the figure of £18 billion dated from 31 December 1990 and had to be balanced against £12 billion in liabilities including claims 'Incurred But Not Reported'; leaving available assets of only £6 billion, much of which consisted of bank guarantees secured on such volatile and depreciating items as shares and property.

Furthermore, there was no evidence of hardening premium rates.

'I was on the Janson Green underwriting box in 1968,' the retired underwriter Roger Bradley told this author, 'when the claims came in for Hurricane Betsy. Peter Green gathered us all round the box and told us what we were going to do: "We're not going to raise rates by 10% or 20%," he told us, "I want them raised by 100%–1000% if necessary." And we did it,' Bradley went on, 'we turned round the market. But that is not happening in 1992.'

Lloyd's also vigorously denied the charge that insiders had profited at the expense of outsiders. But it was forced to appoint Sir David Walker, outgoing Chairman of the City's main regulatory body, the Securities and Investments Board, to head an enquiry into the allegations in question.

Sir David Walker had to weather considerable scepticism about his appointment because, although he was not a Name, he was an *ex officio* member of the Council of Lloyd's. In a climate where reasonable doubt was often indistinguishable from paranoia such scepticism was understandable. Eventually Sir David was able to go ahead with his investigation into such matters as preferential syndicates for insiders and 'dustbin' syndicates for outsiders, and the spiral.

A main plank of the Thomas-Everard allegations was that many of the 'working' members claimed by Lloyd's to be on the spiral syndicates were no longer in fact working in the market; this particularly applied to Feltrim 540/2. A further Thomas-Everard allegation was that, while working members commonly had lines of £10,000 on such syndicates, many external members had much higher lines.

The most tragic case of this was the Cumbrian farmer who had been encouraged to raise his line on Feltrim to a staggering £75,000 at a time when it was known within the market that Feltrim was to be placed under investigation. With cash calls of over £700,000 the farmer's lands were sold and he was ruined.

Lloyd's also cited numerous statistics to prove that working members could be on disastrous syndicates and external members could be on syndicates that did very well even in such troubled times as these.

On 25 February 1992, Miss Barbara Merry, the Manager of the Solvency and Reporting Department, sent the following internal memo to David Coleridge. She copied it to Alan Lord and the Head of Regulatory Services, Bob Hewes:

SUBJECT: Information re: CT-E (Christopher Thomas-Everard) points

CT-E has identified a selection of syndicates which demonstrate his theory of insider preference.

An alternative selection may be made which demonstrates the opposite (either that heavy loss making syndicates have an imbalance of working members compared to the average or that high profit making syndicates have an imbalance of external members compared to the average) as follows:

Loss makers	% Workers (average 12%)
764	42
455	35
1035	24
411	25
727	30

Profit Makers	% Externals (average 88%)
204	94
838	95
554	95
184	95
253	95

Yet crucially these statistics, given for the disastrous 1988 under-writing year, did not state how many of the working members were actually working, did not state what size lines they were writing, and did not above all state the size of the syndicates: a key factor in that, the smaller the syndicate, the higher generally the number was of working members.

If they had stated these things, they would have had to state that, of the 'Loss Makers', syndicate 764 had only 624 members in 1988; syndicate 455 had only 150; and syndicate 411 had only 551.

Likewise, of the 'Profit Makers', syndicate 554 had only 197 members in 1988; syndicate 184 had only 77; and 253 had only 231. These were small syndicates with small capacities.

Alan Lord gleefully seized on these figures (without the above analysis) to declare in the letters page of the *Independent* of 12 March 1992:

'Selectively proved data can prove anything ... We took the decision to release the information that had been collated so far to make it clear that this market has nothing to hide.'

Miss Merry had a further statistic which she felt she should share.

'In addition,' she noted to the Chairman, 'you might wish to note that in excess of 350 man hours has been spent on CT-E related work at an approximate cost of between £35,000 and £40,000 . . .'

As far as the cost in man hours to Thomas-Everard was concerned nobody seemed to mind.

Sir David Walker however took the Thomas-Everard data seriously enough to write to him two weeks later on 9 March 1992:

'I am aware of the considerable interest you have shown in this area. If there are, and I anticipate that there may be, matters which you would particularly like to draw to my attention . . . it would be a great help if you were able to put them in writing . . .

'Mr Foster [the Walker inquiry's secretary] tells me you spoke to him last Friday and have offered to make available a substantial computer database. I have asked him to look into arrangements for handling the computer data you have offered . . .'

David Coleridge had written to Sir David Walker a week earlier:

'I was asked to consider whether Lloyd's would make available to members of the action groups information about the number of working and external Names on particular syndicates. I did not give a final answer at that time, but I have now had the opportunity to review the matter at greater length.

'Our conclusion is that such information should not be available on a selective basis, either in terms of who may be entitled to receive it or which syndicates should be covered. Instead we have decided that we should make available to all members of Lloyd's information about the number of working and external Names on every syndicate and the aggregate values of those participating for each of the last six years, 1986–1991. Similar information for 1992 will be made available as soon as it is ready and each year's data will similarly be made available in the future . . .

'In view of the clear interest of the Names' action groups in this information I am sending a copy of this letter to each of the action group representatives who attended our meeting together with a full set of the syndicate data. I should stress that I cannot guarantee the complete accuracy of the data. It has been collated from systems that were not designed originally with this kind of service in mind and some of the data may be less than completely accurate, especially for the earlier years. I am afraid that without a massive commitment of resources to check every Name's categorisation individually, we cannot wholly eliminate this risk.'

Coleridge's letter was dated 28 February 1992. Less than a month later, analysis of Lloyd's data would confirm that insiders had profited at the expense of external members. Lloyd's would also admit that there was 'some potential conflict' of interest in the activity of brokers to the syndicates on the spiral.

Thomas-Everard meanwhile was discovering new and interesting facts about the working membership.

Clause 2 (1) of the 1982 Lloyd's Act stated that a working member was one who 'occupies himself principally with the conduct of business at Lloyd's.' But according to Lloyd's 'Brown Book' which listed the working members and their details, 2,000 of the 6,000 working members of Lloyd's were not even working.

One working member was a director of a members agency who had joined Lloyd's in 1928. Another had joined Lloyd's in 1938. Both were on Feltrim.

Many working members only wrote small premium incomes

and therefore escaped the spiral simply because they were on a smaller spread of syndicates than outsiders.

This and the fact that many others listed as 'working members' were in fact retired suggested that there was even less evidence to support Lloyd's claim that working members had suffered significantly from being on the syndicates on the spiral.

Coming apart at the seams ... having distanced itself from the Bank of England stories, Lloyd's passed a by-law enabling it to borrow from its own central premium trust fund, set up to provide deposits in countries that required underwriting by foreign insurers to be backed up locally.

Standard and Poor, with Moody's, were the world's leading credit rating agency for businesses and financial institutions. They expressed doubts about Lloyd's solvency and its ability to collect funds from its members. They said this was 'of considerable concern from the policyholder's perspective.'

The reaction of Lloyd's was swift.

'I deplore,' said David Coleridge, 'the action of a respected and responsible organisation such as Standard and Poor in issuing a misleading and potentially damaging statement.

'I am much encouraged,' Coleridge went on, 'by the continued support being shown by the producers of Lloyd's business and by policyholders throughout the world.'

This was insane; no business or financial institution publicly criticised a Standard and Poor statement any more than a test cricketer assaulted an umpire. The worst thing Lloyd's could have done was try to bluster its way out of a corner by treating the world's leading credit agency like an impudent schoolboy.

The result was that even greater attention was focussed on its solvency and the insolvency fears deepened. Lloyd's too increased the pressure to counter-act this possibility. On 9 March 1992 this letter was sent out from Lloyd's Membership Department in Chatham, Kent:

'You will be aware that a number of recent cash calls
have met with a poor response. Accordingly it is necessary
to take special measures in order to accelerate the normal
process for the release of Names' deposits to syndicate funds.
    'By formal resolution the Council of Lloyd's decided
on March 4 to pursue this action on a blanket basis.'

An accompanying letter warned: 'The Council may, without
giving further notice to you, take steps to draw down on your
deposit for the necessary amount.'

The seven hundred members on the Michael Freeman writ
could not be touched by this since a court undertaking had
frozen their deposits until the case was heard. A Lloyd's official
acknowledged that the 'blanket basis' could drive thousands of
other members to take the same kind of legal action.

Members seeking help from the Hardship Committee were
not exempt and received the letters 'pending the outcome of
your application.'

The bulk of the cash calls involved were for loss incurred
by claims within the spiral; the original claims had been paid
off long before.

Lloyd's decreed that these letters should be sent out to
members via their members agencies. The result was that some
agencies sent the letters to all their members, some sent them to
some members and not others and some agencies sent out no
letters at all.

Loose threads in the sweater . . . when you pulled them, the
whole thing started to unravel. A big broker was alleged to have
been skimming off insurance premiums since 1983, a year after
the Lloyd's Act had enshrined self-regulation as the guiding force
of the market. Expert witnesses were told to prepare themselves
for a hearing in early 1993. The Chairman and Council continued
to maintain that business had not been creamed off by insiders at
outsiders' expense.

Lloyd's held up the Outhwaite settlement on the grounds that before being released, the funds should also be used to settle losses incurred by Outhwaite members elsewhere in the market. This was regardless of the fact that these losses were on syndicates which had nothing to do with Outhwaite, and the move only served to enrage and distress many members.

Nutting was Chairman of the Lloyd's Names' Associations Working Party, a new group made up of thirteen individual action group leaders. They commissioned a confidential report compiled by John Rew of Chatset and Alan Porter, an accountant.

The report was presented to Lloyd's Council members on 27 April, 1992. It was soberly written, yet it made bloodcurdling reading:

> The Working Party believes that the scene is set fair for five to ten years of litigation which will involve Members Agents, Managing Agents, Directors of Agencies, individual underwriters, auditors, brokers, errors and omissions underwriters and the Corporation of Lloyd's itself . . .
>
> 'Some £1.3 billion of market losses for 1987–90,' the report went on, 'perhaps 50% of total aggregate losses, are concentrated on 6,000 Names on the distressed Gooda Walker, Feltrim, Rose Thomson Young and Devonshire Syndicates, and perhaps £3 billion throughout the whole of the LMX market. A substantial proportion of these losses will be irrecoverable by Lloyd's . . .
>
> 'The total of the losses to be borne 1988–91,' added the report, 'may amount to almost the entire deposits and reserves of all the membership . . .
>
> 'Even if Chatset's projections are only partly accurate (and there is no reason to believe this), the future could well be a bleak one in which increasing numbers of Names are forced into resignation with a cascade effect of unrecovered losses, old year deteriorations and unrecovered administrative costs falling on a diminishing number of survivors. Few Members

Agencies would be left in business; unemployment would be widespread and Lloyd's pass into runoff. Dramatic stuff'
Rew and his colleagues concluded, 'but at least a possibility.'

Council members in London pondered this report and the down to earth solutions it proposed, which read like a company doctor's distillation of Ian Hay Davison and the Rowland Report.
Meanwhile in Washington the Senate Permanent Subcommittee on Investigations digested the reports that Lloyd's had 'borrowed' £350 million from its American Premium Trust Fund, which had existed since 1939 to meet the needs of American policyholders.
Many distressed members faced with huge losses and the choice of bankruptcy or the Hardship Committee began to make clandestine arrangements to salvage what remained of their assets. They liquidated everything they could and hid it in cash behind other people's names, or transported it physically out of the country. Millions of pounds began to find their way to hiding places in Britain, the Channel Islands and on mainland Europe. The burden of these clandestine withdrawals of cash earmarked by Lloyd's to pay losses would fall on the already hard-pressed Central Fund; and failing that on the surviving members, and even, in the event of an emergency bale-out, the Bank of England.

1, Lime Street, May 1992

'I must say the type of book you are writing doesn't particularly thrill me.'
David Coleridge sat behind his large desk on the twelfth floor of the Lloyd's building. The building had recently survived an IRA bomb blast; the Chairman of Lloyd's had the tired but defiant manner of a man under siege:
'Do you think in hindsight, and in the light of what is happening today, that Lloyd's made a mistake in implementing the part of the Cromer Report that recommended finding new outside capital from less wealthy people?'

'I don't know whether the people now suffering substantial losses all became Names because of Lord Cromer's reduced asset test. I imagine some did and some didn't.

'I suppose the truth of the matter is that for twenty years Lloyd's did not really make losses as a market. When you then get a horrific period of large losses it is naturally much better if the members can stand it. You prefer them to have outside income, preferably from working, and if not from working, a substantial income from other sources. If you ask me, the problem is those members who have not got income. It is as simple as that.

'The ones who have done badly,' Coleridge went on, 'are those who joined in the early 1980s and have had losses, have no outside incomes, and whose reserves are either very little or nil. They were relying on not losing and to pay a large loss has caused great problems. If you ask me if that is anything to do with Cromer I don't really think so. But I suppose in retrospect it was unwise to have members with so small an asset base.'

'*Do you agree in any way with what some Americans are saying, that membership of Lloyd's can be described as an investment?*'

'I don't, but it helps Americans to say so because then they think they might be protected by the SEC. We have always made it very clear to the Americans that membership of Lloyd's is not an investment. That's how we have been dealing in America for the last eight to ten years.'

'*What proportion of Sturge members agency Names are Americans?*'

'Probably 20%,' said Coleridge, 'but we have always taken a lot of Americans since the early 1970s.'

'*The Lloyd's average is about 8%, is it not? About 2,000 American members altogether?*'

The Chairman agreed that this was so.

'*Can I ask you about the statement you made at the 1991 Annual General Meeting when you were asked whether or not Lloyd's owed a duty of care to its members. What is this duty?*'

Is it financial? Legal? Moral?'

'The questioner asked: "Would you give a yes or a no, does the Council of Lloyd's have a duty of care?" I had no reason to believe it was being asked for a specific reason, which was part of the Oakeley Vaughan litigation . . .'

'Does it really matter why it was asked?'

'Yes, it does matter. If a legal question is deliberately asked for a particular reason, they should say so first.

'I took the view,' Coleridge said, 'that a member of Lloyd's was asking me as Chairman "Does the Council of Lloyd's care about its members?" My view is that we do care and we have certain duties. We monitor premium income, we have rules and regulations and we have by-laws. We do not interfere or have responsibility when it comes to what business an underwriter decides to put on his books. That is a matter for the managing agent and the underwriter and we as Lloyd's Council and/or Committee do not tell them what to do.

'I'm not even quite sure,' the Chairman went on, 'what "duty of care" means.'

'It's a legal phrase. It's being tested in court as we speak.'

'It's from the law of agency.'

'It seems to me that this phrase "duty of care" is going to be heard more and more frequently.'

'I think,' said Coleridge, 'the members who want to start litigation are doing so against managing agencies on the grounds that the underwriter was incompetent. Their theory is that there must have been incompetence if there was a loss.'

Coleridge did not look as though he shared this theory.

'Do the present big losses affect Lloyd's reputation as far as policyholders are concerned?'

'No,' said Coleridge quickly, 'it helps policyholders when we say we are going to help our members. We have funds here to pay our losses to policyholders. We have the Central Fund of £500 million and assets of £18 billion.'

'These figures are disputed by people like John Rew of Chatset.'

'I've read John Rew,' the Chairman sounded distinctly menac-
ing. 'He is entitled to print what he wants. He is an accountant,'
he added, 'so I imagine he knows what he is doing.

'But we know,' the Chairman went on, 'that the figures we
publish are accurate. I wouldn't know if everyone's got the cash,'
he said, 'but I know the deposits are there – I've got 'em. I know
the reserves held by agents are here. I know we used the known
qualification test of each member to show that he or she had
sufficient assets to become a member of Lloyd's.'

*'Do you have any comment about recent developments in the
Outhwaite settlement, where £116 million in settlement monies
are not being released until members have met other losses in
the market? Does this seem fair?'*

'All Lloyd's have done,' said the Chairman, 'is point out
that funds which arrive from the settlement should form part of
the Name's premium trust fund. That is all. If a member has no
other losses, he can have the money tomorrow.

'We haven't got the money,' Coleridge went on. 'Richards
Butler (the solicitors for the Outhwaite 1982 Association) have
got the money. If Peter Nutting (Chairman of the Association)
is so certain it can be released, why doesn't he release it? I'll
tell you exactly why. Because if he is wrong, we will hold him
responsible for every single pound that wasn't paid.

'Lloyd's wasn't involved in the Outhwaite settlement in any
way, shape or form. We weren't party to the agreement, we
weren't party to the settlement, we weren't party to anything. All
that happened,' the Chairman smiled amiably, 'was that a week
before he was due to pay out the money, he was "reminded" that
it was part of the premium trust fund. Now,' Coleridge positively
beamed, 'if he was so confident, why didn't he just say "F***
you"?'

*'It depends what you mean by "Lloyd's", doesn't it? If Council
members and Chairmen are also major players in the market, then
what is "Lloyd's"? If major figures in the Errors and Omissions
market are Council members, are they "Lloyd's" or Errors and*

*Omissions underwriters? This is where I find it a little difficult
to understand how decisions can be made concerning the management of the market, which at the same time directly concern the
interests of the individuals making those decisions in their
professional capacities as big players in that market.*

'It seems to me an impossible position. Is it really possible
to be Chairman of Lloyd's and Chairman of Sturge Holdings
plc and answer the rather painful and unpleasant questions MPs
throw at you? Don't you find it impossible to give satisfactory
answers because of the contradictions in your position?'

The Chairman of Lloyd's and Sturge Holdings plc thought
about this for a moment:

'I don't think so,' he said.

'I'm not quite sure,' he went on, 'what the conflict is. They
scream at me because they have lost money. They say it's unfair.
They make accusations against the system. We look into it. They
say they have been put on bum syndicates or there is insider
dealing or that the LMX market only exists to enrich brokers
and underwriters. All right. I am not commenting on what Sir
David Walker will find in his inquiry. He may well find some
people have been rather stupid.'

'*Will there be fewer syndicates?*'

'There will be fewer syndicates and there will be fewer members and the number of new members joining will be smaller. The
number of contra-cyclical people joining will be limited because
contra-cyclical people are normally highly intelligent and there
aren't that many highly intelligent people in the world.'

'*Highly intelligent or very rich?*'

'Both. If you're very rich it's nicer.'

'*Have you any advice for your successor?*'

'There is no miracle advice . . . all you can do is the best you
can. I can't tell people what to do. The fact is that our membership
is fragile and has been very badly hurt. We must try to help the
very badly hurt ones. We won't get any thanks but we must show
the world that we care and then we can get on with our business.

'Insurance should be a very dull business,' mused the Chairman. 'We never had any publicity for years. It was a very dull place.'

*   *   *

The bell was tolling for the old ways of Lloyd's that had survived the move to the new building at 1, Lime Street, just as surely as it had tolled for the *Lutine* and the *Berge Astra* and the other ships that had sunk beneath the waves. The bell was tolling for the office of Chairman, and the Council, and the Committee of Lloyd's. The bell was tolling for as many as one hundred and fifty of the three hundred and fifty syndicates that were underwriting insurance business on the floor of The Room. The bell was tolling for ten thousand of the twenty thousand members and for self-regulation and for the 1982 Lloyd's Act. The bell was tolling, and there would be a solvency crisis, and as far as what happened then was concerned nobody seemed to be sure.

At around this time I received a letter which, if held up to a mirror, made perfect sense of the looking glass world of 1, Lime Street:

Lloyd's of London

From the Members' Writing Room

Dear Mr Mantle

I apologise for my very delayed reply to your letter requesting some help towards your book. I can only use as an excuse the fact that as I am sure you will realise the implementation of the Task Force has involved the Members of Lloyd's Council in the most unbelievable pile of work and one's own personal pile of correspondence becomes seriously delayed. I am sorry if I have appeared ill-mannered and apologise for this.

I am afraid I can be of little help to you regarding your book: as a Member of the Council I am in a difficult position as I am sure you can imagine. The Task Force implementations will completely change Lloyd's as we know it. One of the benefits of self-regulation, appreciated only by a few, is that as soon as any dishonourable behaviour comes to light it is pounced on immediately. Were Lloyd's to come under the jurisdiction of the DTI with their past history of speed, it would take far too long for wrong-doers to be brought to justice as we have seen with the Guinness affair, Grob and countless others including Cameron-Webb who slipped through the net because of the DTI's tardiness.

The new Lloyd's is a much fitter, cleaner and regulated place. We do not benefit at all by harping back into the past and I think all Members of Lloyd's are now looking to a brighter future. I have seen far worse examples of dishonourable behaviour in other aspects of City life than I have seen at Lloyd's.

Good luck with your book and I am sorry I cannot be of more help.'

With kindest regards.

Yours sincerely

Rona Delves Broughton

LADY DELVES BROUGHTON

If you held this letter up to a mirror it made perfect sense.

But wait . . . what was that sound?

In the distance a bell was tolling.

* * *

Thelnetham, Norfolk, 1992

Janis Nash had been away a long time. She had not been able to return to full-time work but she had gradually weaned herself off the booze. She had gone on taking sleeping pills and tranquillisers for a long time but now she had weaned herself off those too. She was fifty-eight years old and nobody wanted to give her a job. She did not have a lot of money and she did not desperately mind.

The cottage was at the crossroads in the village of Redgrave, a few minutes from the village of Thelnetham and Lower Lodge, the house where she had lived and hoped always to live with Michael Church. But Michael Church was dead and he had been dead for eight years; he had to die, just as the club now had to die of which he had been a member.

Janis Nash lived in the cottage alone apart from her cat. There was a view across the fields at the front and a garden at the back. She was carrying out extensive renovations and there was dust in the air. The dust fell on the floorboards, and on the windowsills, and on the mantelpiece, and on the photograph of Michael Church: a big, happy man at the wheel of his boat, with the wind blowing his hair.

Janis Nash had moved back here because she had always loved the area and she would always love Michael Church. She did not think of herself as morbid but she felt very close to him. She missed him terribly and after eight years it still hurt every day; but she had come to terms, with his death and with her life. When she had found his body in the barn that day, she had gone running down the lane to the farmer, and he had come back with her and stayed with her until the police came. When she had moved back here, only a few months earlier and seven years later, the farmer had sent her a letter. He said they were glad to have her back.

Janis Nash missed Michael Church terribly but she had come to terms. She visited the church. In the churchyard of St Nicholas Thelnetham there was a grave and an urn with flowers and a plain simple stone which read 'In Loving Memory of Michael James Church 1928–1986.'

'You don't understand,' he had told her. 'I have known him

all my working life. We are friends. He would never do anything like that to me.'

Other voices:

'To work for Lloyd's is a passion rather than a profession.'

'Lloyd's is like a great stallion that is down on its knees, and people are trying to cut off the last pieces of flesh before the whole thing collapses.'

'In a badly regulated market there is no great need for conspiracy.'

'I don't think an empire based on greed can or should survive.'

'We are seeing the end of a Great British club.'

The bell tolled in an English country churchyard, and it tolled for Lloyd's as well as Michael Church. Michael Church had to die, just as the club now had to die of which he had been a good and loyal and trusting member. Soon they would be united in death as they had been in life. But nobody was giving odds on who would be the first to be reborn.

EPILOGUE

LORD ALEXANDER saw hope of rescue from the brink of bankruptcy by the Outhwaite and Warrilow settlements. He continued
to fight off the Hardship Committee and struggle to secure redress
for the Oakeley Vaughan members. 'There are no heroes in this
story.'

BETTY ATKINS was reduced to begging the Hardship Committee
to take her house as compensation for part of her losses. She stood
to benefit from the Outhwaite settlement but still faced losses likely
to continue into the next century. She still heard nothing from her
former employers.

ENID BEMROSE did not succeed in having her late husband's deposit released to his estate. His members agency was taken over by
Murray Lawrence & Partners, and as a result of Lawrence's inter-
vention she accepted a small one-off settlement two years after her
husband's death. She has no complaint against the present agency.

TOM BENYON continued to run the Society of Names in spite
of the ingratitude of some Warrilow members.

ROGER BRADLEY continued discreetly to advise members around
the world. In the early months of 1992 he was visited by a top-level
delegation from Lloyd's who had previously dismissed his *Towards
2000* report. 'Roger,' they told him, 'we need your help.'

'BIG BILL' BROWN continued to avoid the press and run the family
broking firm.

PETER CAMERON-WEBB stopped working on the Insurance Exchange of the Americas after it was closed down due to a series of scandals. He remained at liberty in the United States of America.

JOHN CLEMENTSON the former oboist saw his losses rise towards £1 million and faced imminent bankruptcy rather than go to the Hardship Committee.

DAVID COLERIDGE announced his intention to retire and spend more time gardening – 'or rather, talking to my gardener.'

IAN HAY DAVISON continued to resist calls by external members to return to Lloyd's and finish the job.

PETER DIXON also remained at liberty in the United States of America.

PATRICK FELTRIM FAGAN retired to Surrey.

MICHAEL FREEMAN failed in his legal action to prevent Lloyd's agents drawing down the deposits of Gooda Walker members and others with massive losses on the spiral. One estimate suggested that up to 4,000 members would effectively be bankrupted as a result of the drawdowns which began after Easter 1992.

CLIVE FRANCIS the former property tycoon was forced to move to rented lodgings in the outer suburbs of London.

ANDREW GROSSMAN the 'sophisticated American' was told he was no longer required by the Foreign Service. In the face of ruin he formed The Distressed Names LMX Spiral Action Group.

SYLVIA HATTON like her friend BETTY ATKINS stood to benefit from the Outhwaite settlement. The fact that she had gone through the Hardship process made her future unclear; she too still heard nothing from her former employers.

DALE JENKINS in Tuxedo Park New York State refused to pay any more cash calls.

JACKI LEVIN and KEN LAVERY and their friends took the same view in Hamilton and Oakville, Ontario.

ROBIN KINGSLEY did not want to take any more telephone calls from distressed Lime Street Agencies members. 'I feel absolutely mortified by what has happened,' he said, 'but what can I do?'

ALAN LORD retired and it was not easy to find a successor.

CHRISTOPHER MORAN continued to run Chelsea Cloisters. From time to time he threatened to return to the insurance business.

DOMINIQUE OSBORNE continued her investigation into the collapsed Lime Street Agencies. She and her husband faced losses of over £1 million from the syndicates on the spiral.

RICHARD OUTHWAITE went on underwriting at Lloyd's for a greatly reduced syndicate.

IAN 'GOLDFINGER' POSGATE enjoyed a brief renaissance as a guest speaker at action group meetings. To some he was a 'prophet in the wilderness'; others greeted his reappearance with hollow laughter.

CHARLES ST GEORGE wound down his racing activities and was rumoured to rely heavily on his brother.

EDWARD ST GEORGE felt impelled to give a series of newspaper interviews explaining all he had done for the Bahamas.

CHRISTOPHER THOMAS-EVERARD continued to fight to keep the farm his family had occupied since the Domesday Book.

INDEX

as Chairman 70-1, 82-4, 91, 107-8, 120-1
and computer leasing risks 43, 69, 71
and Davison 105-7
inquiries and scandal 93-4, 98, 100, 156, 285
and Fisher Report 78, 81
and new building 56-7, 69-70, 178
and Oakeley Vaughan 87, 88, 97
prosecution 117
resignation 116-18, 120
and Sasse losses 76, 116, 130
Green, Terry 299
Green, Toby 14, 32, 56, 101, 118
Gresham, syndicate 321 206, 248, 299
Griffith, Dr Gavan 89, 248
Grob, Kenneth 39, 40, 64-5, 91-2, 98-100, 102, 175, 326-7
Grossman, Andrew 206, 248, 263-6, 274, 295-7, 357

Hackett, Gen. Sir John 61
Hall, Frank B. 63-4
Hallam, Robert 165-6, 185, 197-8, 207, 247, 279
Hambro, Rupert 89, 215-16
Hamilton, Archie 82
Hampshire, Susan 89, 181, 215
Har, Den 47-8, 49, 54, 66, 210
Hardship Committee, *see* Members' Hardship Committee
Harker, Elizabeth 89-90, 248-9
Harper, Howard 217
'Harrison's folly' 10, 11, 129
Hart, Michael 215
Hastings, Max 216
Hatton, Sylvia 74-5, 253
and action group 217, 218-20
and Hardship Committee 255, 292, 357
and Outhwaite 124, 144, 181-2, 194-7, 357
Hayward, Jack 52-3, 85, 125, 202-3
Heath, C.E. (brokers) 24, 29, 79, 112, 319
Heath, Cuthbert Eden 8, 9, 10-11, 13, 49, 112, 262-3
Heath, Edward 61, 215
Hewes, Bob 260-1, 273, 340
Higgins, Alec 93-4, 96
Hill, Roy 234
Hill, William 25
Hinchliffe, John 125-7, 201-3, 224-6
Hirsch, Jay D. 58, 88, 224, 255-6
Hiscox, Ralph 33, 286
Hitchings, Christopher 315-16
Hoare Govett Investment Research 315
Hogg Robinson 70
Holden, Wing-Comm. 'Gus' 60, 89, 249
Holloway, syndicate 604 231
Hook, Colin 294-5

Howden, Alexander (Underwriting) Ltd 73
'Gang of Four' 99, 122
legal action 225
and Posgate 39, 51, 65, 82, 91, 99, 208
problems 82, 98-102
sale 64-5, 91-2
Hozier, Col. Henry 8-9
Hudson, Cathleen 48
Hudson, Havelock, as Chairman 48, 53, 55
Hughesden, Charles 27
Hurricane Alicia 233
Hurricane Betsy 31, 32, 43, 59, 67, 167, 339
Hurricane Carol 15
Hurricane Hugo 233, 247, 257, 278, 310
Hussey, Marmaduke 'Duke' 61
Hussey, Maurice 142

Imperial company 101, 116-18
Indonesia, seizure of Dutch ships 22-3
information
lack of 103, 138, 189, 204, 274, 293, 302
and Oakeley Vaughan 88, 96, 97, 136
and Pulbrook 259-60
on reinsurance spirals 111
and Sasse losses 49-50, 66-7
and Warrilow 183
information, inside 7, 290
Ingham, Bernard 306
insider preference 4, 73-4, 111, 149, 179, 190-1, 327, 334-6, 339-44, 345
insurance
aviation 9-10, 12, 13, 15-16, 37, 46
'big risk' 37-9, 40, 43-4
'buzz-bomb' 14
cargo 55
innovative 15, 27, 36, 68, 107-8
marine 7, 13, 16, 48
motor 12
non-marine 8
role of Lloyd's xi
see also Errors and Omissions policies; estate protection; long-tail policies; premiums; reinsurance; stop loss insurance
Insurance Companies Act 1958 136
Insurance Companies Act 1982 127
intelligence, naval 7, 8
invisible earning, Lloyd's contribution xii, 4, 37, 40

Jacklin, Tony 61, 215
James, Fred S. 64
Janson Green 14, 32, 43, 71, 89, 117, 120, 132, 323, 339
Jenkins, Dale 90, 246-7, 274, 295-6, 322, 357
Johnson, David 317-18
Johnson Matthey affair 157